The Lost Books of the New Testament

The Gospel of Judas,

The Gospel of Philip,

The Gospel of Mary Magdalene,

The Gospel of Thomas,

29th Chapter of Acts,

The Epistle of Barnabas,

The Epistle of Paul to the Laodiceans,

The Gospel of Nicodemus,

Lost Gospel of Peter

By Joseph Lumpkin

Joseph B. Lumpkin

The Lost Books of the New Testament

Copyright © 2008 by Joseph B. Lumpkin
All rights reserved.

Printed in the United States of America. No part of this book may be used or reproduced in any manner whatsoever without written permission except in the case of brief quotations embodied in critical articles and reviews.

Fifth Estate, Post Office Box 116,
Blountsville, AL 35031.

First Edition

Printed on acid-free paper

Library of Congress Control No: 2008911354

ISBN13: 9781933580500
ISBN: 193358050X

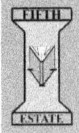

Fifth Estate, 2008

Joseph B. Lumpkin

Table of Contents

Canonical Books, Lost Books	7
What is Gnosticism	10
The Gospel of Philip	21
The Gospel of Mary Magdalene	64
The Gospel of Thomas	75
The Gospel of Judas	150
29th Chapter of Acts	274
The Epistle of Barnabas	282
The Gospel of Nicodemus	327
Lost Gospel of Peter	394
The Epistle of Paul to the Laodiceans	403

Joseph B. Lumpkin

Canonical Books, Lost Books

The Church did not accept the New Testament books because they were included in a canonical list. The Church included them in the list of canonical books because a significant number of churches already regarded the books as divinely inspired. Members and clergy were familiar with the books and accepted them, but there were other reasons books were included or discarded.

A large number of books were considered for inclusion in the Bible. Each book was graded by certain criteria. The fact that some books were already well entrenched in the general population carried great weight. Along with this, apostolic authority was held in the highest regard. Many books had the claim of apostolic authorship but some texts varied widely in content and doctrine, making authenticity suspicious. The general tone and doctrine of the book in question must also match those texts that are generally recognized as having apostolic authorship and they must not vary from the doctrine espoused by the church establishing the canon.

There were also decisions to be made regarding versions of the same books. Since books were hand copied from scribe to scribe, some of whom added or deleted words, lines, verses, or even chapters, the church fathers had to chose not only which books to include as canon but which versions of books to accept. This will become obvious as the 29th chapter of Acts is discussed later.

If the books espoused a doctrine different from that accepted by the established church the books were excluded from the canonical list. Knowing that there were several divergent belief systems, or what we would refer to as denominations, it becomes obvious that the established church would choose those books for their canon to uphold their own doctrine while excluding books that would give credit to other denominations and doctrines. In the end, many of the rejected books were destroyed or simply ignored until they fell into disuse and were lost to history. Only those churches not within the main stream kept the forgotten books. One of these divergent belief systems was the Gnostic church. Another such divergent church was the Coptic Church.

In the layout of this book those texts that are considered Gnostic are printed first. Based on this, and the fact that Gnostic Christian doctrine was so different from any standard or accepted doctrine today, we will begin with a short lesson in Gnosticism. At the risk of belaboring and repeating some facts we will revisit and expand on certain facts before we read the Gospel of Judas. This is done simply because the Gnostic theology found in Judas is slightly different from the previous texts of Philip and Mary, and quite fierce in its presentation throughout the Gospel of Judas. In fact, Judas presents many problems to modern Christianity which we explore before and after the text is presented to the reader.

What is Gnosticism?

For centuries the definition of Gnosticism has, in itself, been a point of confusion and contention within the religious community. This is due, in part, to the ever-broadening application of the term. The modern definition of Gnosticism has no relevance to this work, or to any pre-Nicene Gnostic document, for that matter. The theology in place at the time of the writing of the ancient texts being examined should be considered and understood before attempting to render or read a translation. To do otherwise would make cloudy and obtuse the translation.

It becomes the duty of both translator and reader to understand what ideas were being espoused and the terms used to convey those ideas. Having a firm grasp of theology, cosmology, and terms will lead to a clear transmission of the meaning of the text in question.

With this in mind Gnosticism in the first through third centuries A.D. will be discussed in the following pages, which precede the translated text.

The cosmology of Gnosticism is complex and very different from orthodox Christianity. In many ways Gnosticism may appear to be polytheistic. The word Gnostic is based on the word "Gnosis," which means "knowledge." The knowledge of the transcendent God and man's ability to transcend this material world with its lesser gods is how Gnosticism got its name.

To understand some of the basic beliefs of Gnosticism, let us start with common ground between it and modern Christianity. Both believe the world is imperfect, corrupt, and brutal. The blame for this, according to mainstream Christianity, is placed squarely on the shoulders of man himself. With the fall of man, the world was forever changed to the undesirable and harmful place in which we live today. However, Gnostics reject this view as an incorrect interpretation of the creation myth.

According to Gnostics, the blame is not in ourselves, but in our creator. The creator of this world was himself somewhat less than perfect and in fact, deeply flawed, making mankind the children of a lesser god.

In the beginning a supreme being called The Father, The Divine All, The Origin, or The Fullness, emanated the element of existence, both visible and invisible. His intent was not to create but, as light emanates from a flame, so did creation shine forth from God. This manifested the primal element needed for creation. Part of this ethereal material gave form to beings called Aeons. One of these Aeons was called Sophia (Wisdom).

Seeing the Divine flame, Sophia sought to know its origin. She sought to know the very nature of God. Sophia's passion ended in tragedy when she managed to capture a divine and creative spark, which she attempted to duplicate with her own creativity. It was this act that produced beings born outside the higher divine realm.

She cast it away from her, outside that place [the Pleroma], that no one of the immortal ones [the other Aeons] might see it, for she had created it in ignorance..."
[The Nag Hammadi Library, James M. Robinson, Ed, pp.104 (Harper & Row, 1981, San Franscisco)]

The overall realm containing the Fullness of the godhead and Sophia is called the Pleroma or realm of Fullness. The lesser gods created in Sophia's (Wisdom) failed attempt were cast outside the Pleroma and away from the presence of God.

The beings she created were imperfect and oblivious to the supreme God. Her creation contained deities even less perfect than herself. They are called "the powers" or "the rulers." It was one of these flawed, imperfect, spiritually blind beings that became the creator of the material world.

This lesser god contained only part of the original creative spark of the supreme being. He also was created with an imperfect nature caused by his distance in lineage and in spirit from the Divine All or Higher God. Because of his imperfections, the lesser god is called the "Half-Maker."

The creator god, the Half-Maker, and his helpers, the "rulers" or "powers," took the stuff of existence produced by the supreme God and fashioned it into this material world.

Since the rulers have no memory of how they came to be alive, they do not realize they are not true creators. They believe they somehow came to create the material world by themselves. God allows them to remain deceived.

The rulers and the creator god intended to create the material world perfect and eternal, but they did not have it in themselves to do this. What comes forth from a being cannot be greater than the highest part of him, so the world was created flawed and transitory.

Man was created with a dual nature. It is the product of the material world of the rulers with their imperfect essence, and the spark of God that emanated from the Divine All through Sophia, which remained in the creator that persisted to form man. The creator or lesser deity seeks to keep man ignorant of his defective state by keeping him enslaved to this material world and to the lesser gods. By doing so he can continue to receive man's worship and servitude. He does not wish man to recognize or gain knowledge of the true supreme God. Since he does not know or acknowledge the Father God, he views any attempt to worship anything else as spiritual treason.

Only through the realization of man's true state or through death can he escape. This means the idea of salvation does not deal with original sin or blood payment. Instead, it focuses on the idea of awakening to the fullness of the truth.

Gnostics, in the age of the early church, would preach to converts (novices) about this awakening, saying the novice must awaken the god within himself and see the trap that is the material world. Salvation comes from the recognition or knowledge contained in this spiritual awakening.

Not all people are ready or willing to accept the Gnosis. Many are bound to the material world and are satisfied to be only as and where they are. These have mistaken the creator god for the supreme God and do not know there is anything beyond. These people know only the lower or earthly wisdom and not the higher Wisdom or Sophia above the creator god. They are referred to as "dead."

Since the time of Sophia's mistaken creation, there was an imbalance in the cosmos. God re-established the balance by producing Christ and the Holy Spirit. One being a masculine energy, and the other being a feminine energy. This left only Sophia, now in a fallen and bound state to upset the cosmic equation. To counter this, God produced the man Jesus, who was the perfect fruits of the Pleroma, or stuff of existence which made up the material world.

For those who seek that which is beyond the material world and its flawed creator, the supreme God has sent Messengers of Light to awaken the divine spark of the supreme God within us. This part of us will call to the True God as deep calls to deep. The greatest and most perfect Messenger of Light was the Christ. He is also referred to as The Good, Christ, Messiah, and The Word. He came to reveal the Divine Light to us.

He came to show us our own divine spark and to awaken us to the illusion of the material world and its flawed maker. He came to show us the way back to the divine Fullness. The path to enlightenment is the knowledge sleeping within each of us. Christ came to show us the Christ living in each of us. Individual ignorance or the refusal to awaken our internal divine spark is the only original sin. Christ is the only Word spoken by God that can awaken us. Christ is also the embodiment of the Word itself. He is part of the original transmission from the supreme God that has taken form on the earth to awaken the soul of man so that man may search beyond the material world. The transmission or emanation containing the formless will of God is the Holy Spirit. The Holy Spirit is considered to be a feminine force.

Gnostic texts often use sex as a metaphor for spiritual union and release. Since the Godhead itself has both masculine elements of the Father and Son, and a feminine element of the Holy Spirit, sexual terms are used freely. The sexual metaphor is expanded in the story of the original or Full God giving rise to Sophia (Wisdom) as he spewed forth the essence of everything. Sophia became the creator or mother of both angels and lesser gods, including the creator of the material world.

Sexual duality found in Gnosticism allows for more reverence and acceptance of women in the Gnostic worship. Owing to this, the concept that Mary Magdalene was somehow special to Jesus, as is reported in the Gospel of Philip, or that he may have shared spiritual concepts with her that were unknown to the male apostles, as is told in the Gospel of Mary Magdalene, is not so difficult to comprehend.

To continue the flow of metaphors relating to sex and marriage, images of the Bridal-Chamber are replete throughout the Gospel of Philip. This is alludes to a spiritual place where the union of the Bridegroom who is the Son and the seeking heart of man meet and unite. There is also a secondary meaning of unity where the dual nature of man unites when the Light of spiritual awakening conquers the fleshly or material nature and man is made whole by the Truth.

The sexual metaphors used in the Gnostic texts have fanned the flames of great controversy and speculation. It has been widely accepted that societal norms of the time dictated that Jewish men were to be married by the age of thirty. This certainly applied to Rabbis, since marriage and procreation were considered divine commands. Since Jesus is referred to by the title of Rabbi in the Bible it has been noted that his marital status would have placed him into a very small minority in the culture at the time.

Proceeding from the two points of sexual metaphor in Gnostic literature and the likelihood of marriage among the population of Jewish men, controversy arose when speculation began as to whether Jesus could have married. The flames of argument roared into inferno proportions when the translation of the books of Philip and Mary Magdalene were published.

And the companion (Consort) was Mary of Magdala (Mary Magdalene). The Lord loved Mary more than all the other disciples and he kissed her often on her mouth (the text is missing here and the word "mouth" is assumed). The others saw his love for Mary and asked him: "Why do you love her more than all of us?" The Savior replied, "Why do I not love you in the same way I love her?" Gospel of Philip

Peter said to Mary; "Sister we know that the Savior loved you more than all other women. Tell us the words of the Savior that you remember and know, but we have not heard and do not know. Mary answered him and said; "I will tell you what He hid from you."
The Gospel of Mary Magdalene

Seizing on the texts above, writers of both fiction and non-fiction allowed their pens to run freely amidst conjecture and postulation of marriage and children between Jesus and Mary Magdalene.

The writers of <u>The Da Vinci Code</u> and <u>Holy Blood, Holy Grail</u> took these passages and expanded them into storylines that have held readers captive with anticipation.

Did Jesus take Mary to be his wife? Could the couple have produced children? Gnostic theology leaves open the possibility. Since there is a distinction between the man Jesus and the Light of Christ that came to reside within him, it is not contrary to Gnostic beliefs that Mary was the consort and wife of Jesus. Neither would it be blasphemous for them to have children.

Since nothing can come from the material world that is not flawed, Gnostics do not believe that Christ could have been a corporeal being. Thus, there must be some separation or distinction between Jesus, as a man, and Christ, as a spiritual being born from the supreme, unrevealed, and eternal spirit.

To look closer at this theology, we turn to Valentinus, the driving force of early Gnosticism, for an explanation. Valentinus divides Jesus Christ into two very distinct parts; Jesus, the man, and Christ, the anointed spiritual messenger of God. These two forces met in the moment of Baptism when the Holy Spirit of God came to rest on Jesus and the Christ power entered the body of the perfect creation.

Jesus, the man, became a vessel to the Light of God, called Christ or Messiah. In the Gnostic view we all could and should become Christs, carrying the Truth and Light of God. We are all potential vehicles of the same Holy Spirit that Jesus held within him when he was awakened to the Truth.

This means that the suffering and death of Jesus takes on much less importance in the Gnostic view, since Jesus, although a perfect creation, was simply part of the corrupt world and was suffering the indignities of this world as any man would. In this viewpoint, he could have been married and been a father without disturbing Gnostic theology in the least.

The resurrection of Jesus is viewed as a metaphor and not a physical re-animation. One might say that the resurrection happens to us all when our inner light stands up.

In repeated metaphors throughout Gnostic texts, the grace given by the "Messenger of Light" that allows the Word to be received is called the "Oil of Anointing." The knowledge that awakens the soul of man and allows him to search beyond the material world is contained in "The Word." The knowledge that sets man free from the illusion of the material world and reunites him with the Higher or Supreme God is "The Light."

The Gnostic texts seem to divide man into parts. Although at times it is somewhat unclear, the divisions alluded to may include the soul, which is the will or mind of man; the spirit, which is depicted as wind or air (pneuma) and contains the holy spark, which is the spirit of God in man; and the material human form.

Without the oil or light, the spirit is held captive by the lesser gods, which enslave man. This entrapment is called "sickness." It is this sickness that the Light came to heal and thus set us free. The third part of man, which is his material form, is considered a weight, an anchor, and a hindrance, keeping man attached to the corrupted earthly realm.

Let us read these texts and do as the ancient Gnostics commanded. Wake up! Heal yourself! Seek the Christ within you! Let the oil flow down! Let the Word be heard! Let the Light show you the Truth! Become the Christ you are! Give birth to what is inside you! Let the sleeper awaken!

The History of The Gospel of Philip

The Gospel of Philip is assumed to be one of the sources of Dan Brown's novel, The Da Vinci Code, about Mary Magdalene, Jesus, and their children. The Gospel is one of Gnostic texts found at Nag Hammadi in Egypt in 1945 and belongs to the same collection of Gnostic documents as the more famous Gospel of Thomas.

It has been suggested that the Gospel of Philip was written in the second century A.D. If so, it may be one of the earliest documents containing themes that would later be used in apocryphal literature.

A single manuscript of the Gospel of Philip, written in Coptic, was found in the Nag Hammadi library. The collection was a library of thirteen papyrus texts discovered near the town of Nag Hammadi in 1945 by a peasant boy. The writings in these codices comprised 52 documents, most of which are Gnostic in nature.

The codices were probably hidden by monks from the nearby monastery of St. Pachomius when the official Christian Church banned all Gnostic literature around the year 390 A.D

It is believed the original texts were written in Greek during the first or second centuries A.D. The copies contained in the discovered clay jar were written in Coptic in the third or fourth centuries A.D.

The *Gospel Of Philip* is a list of sayings focusing on man's redemption and salvation as framed by Gnostic theology.

The *Gospel of Philip* presented here is based on a comparative study of translations from the Nag Hammadi Codex by Wesley W. Isenberg, Willis Barnstone, The Ecumenical Coptic Project, Bart Ehrman, Marvin Meyer, David Cartlidge, David Dungan, and other sources.

Each verse was weighed against the theological and philosophical beliefs held by the Gnostic community at the time in which the document was penned. All attempts were made to render the most accurate meaning based on the available translations and information.

Exact wording was secondary to the conveyance of the overall meaning as understood by the contemporary reader.

When the wording of a verse held two possible meanings or needed expanded definitions, optional translations were placed in parentheses.

The Gospel of Philip

1. A Hebrew makes a Hebrew convert, and they call him a proselyte (novice). A novice does not make another novice. Some are just as they are, and they make others like themselves to receive. It is enough for them that they simply are as they are.

2. The slave seeks only to be set free. He does not hope to attain the estate of his master. The son acts as a son (heir), but the father gives the inheritance to him.

3. Those who inherit the dead are dead, and they inherit the dead. Those who inherit the living are alive. They inherit both the living and the dead. The dead cannot inherit anything. How can the dead inherit anything? When the dead inherits the living one, he shall not die but the dead shall live instead.

4. The Gentile (unbeliever) who does not believe does not die, because he has never been alive, so he could not die. He who has trusted the Truth has found life and is in danger of dying, because he is now alive.

5. Since the day that the Christ came, the cosmos was created, the cities are built (adorned), and the dead carried out.

6. In the days when we were Hebrews we were made orphans, having only our Mother. Yet when we believed in the Messiah (became the ones of Christ), the Mother and Father both came to us.

7. Those who sow in the winter reap in the summer. The winter is this world system. The summer is the other age or dispensation (to come). Let us sow in the world (cosmos) so that we will reap in the summer. Because of this, it is right for us not to pray in the winter. What comes from (follows) the winter is the summer. If anyone reaps in the winter he will not harvest but rather pull it up by the roots and will not produce fruit. Not only does it not produce in winter, but on the Sabbath his field shall be bare.

8. The Christ has come to fully ransom some, to save (restore and heal) others, and to be the propitiation for others. Those who were estranged he ransomed. He purchases them for himself. He saves, heals, and restores those who come to him. These he desires to pledge (in marriage). When he became manifest he ordained the soul as he desired (set aside his own

life), but even before this, in the time of the world's beginning, he had ordained the soul (he had laid down his own life). At his appointed time he came to bring the soul he pledged himself to back to himself. It had come to be under the control of robbers and they took it captive. Yet he saved it, and he paid the price for both the good and the evil of the world.

9. Light and dark, life and death, right and left are brothers. It is impossible for one to be separated from the other. They are neither good, nor evil. A life is not alive without death. Death is not death if one were not alive. Therefore each individual shall be returned to his origin, as he was from the beginning. Those who go beyond the world will live forever and are in the eternal present.

10. The names that are given to worldly things cause great confusion. They contort our perception from the real to the unreal. He who hears "God" does not think of the real, but rather has false, preconceived ideas. It is the same with "Father," "Son," "Holy Spirit," "Life," "Light," "Resurrection," and "Church (the called out ones)," and all other words. They do not recall the real, but rather they call to mind preconceived, false ideas. They learned the reality of human death. They who are in the world system made them think of the false idea. If they had been in eternity, they would not have designated

anything as evil, nor would they have placed things within worldly events (time and place). They are destined for eternity.

11. The only name they should never speak into the world is the name the Father gave himself through the Son. This is the Father's name. It exists that he may be exalted over all things. The Son could not become the Father, unless he was given the Father's name. This name exists so that they may have it in their thoughts. They should never speak it. Those who do not have it cannot even think it. But the truth created names in the world for our sake. It would not be possible to learn the truth without names.

12. The Truth alone is the truth. It is a single thing and a multitude of things. The truth teaches us love alone through many and varied paths.

13. Those who ruled (lower gods) desired to deceive man because they knew man was related to the truly good ones. They took the designation of good and they gave it to those who were not good. They did this so that by way of words they might deceive man and bind him to those who are not good. When they receive favor, they are taken from those who are not good and placed among the good. These are they who had

recognized themselves. The rulers (lower gods) had desired to take the free person, and enslave him to themselves forever. Rulers of power fight against man. The rulers do not want him to be saved (recognize himself), so that men will become their masters. For if man is saved there will be no need for sacrifice.

14. When sacrifice began, animals were offered up to the ruling powers. They were offered up to them while the sacrificial animals were still alive. But as they offered them up they were killed. But the Christ was offered up dead to God (the High God), and yet he lived.

15. Before the Christ came, there had been no bread in the world. In paradise, the place where Adam was, there had been many plants as food for wild animals, but paradise had no wheat for man to eat. Man had to be nourished like animals. But the Christ, the perfect man, was sent. He brought the bread of heaven, so that man could eat as he should.

16. The rulers (lower gods) thought what they did was by their own will and power, but the Holy Spirit worked through them without their knowledge to do her will.

17. The truth, which exists from the beginning, is sown everywhere, and everyone sees it being sown, but only a few see the harvest.

18. Some say that Mary conceived by the Holy Spirit. They are in error. They do not know what they are saying. How can a female impregnate another female? Mary is the virgin whom no power defiled. She is a great problem and curse among the Hebrew Apostles and those in charge. The ruler (lower god) who attempts to defile this virgin, is himself defiled. The Lord was not going to say, "my father in heaven", unless he really had another father. He would simply have said, "my father".

19. The Lord says to the Disciples, "Come into the house of the Father, but do not bring anything in or take anything out from the father's house."

20. Jesus (Yeshua) is the secret name; Christ (messiah) is the revealed name. The name "Jesus" (Yeshua) does not occur in any other language. His name is called "Jesus" (Yeshua). In Aramaic his name is Messiah, but in Greek it is Christ (Cristos). In every language he is called the anointed one. The fact that he is Savior (Yeshua) could be fully comprehended only by himself, since it is the Nazarene who reveals the secret things.

21. Christ has within himself all things; man, angel, mystery (sacraments), and the father.

22. Those who say that the Lord first died and then arose are in error. He would have to first arise before he could die. If he is not first resurrected, he would die, but God lives and cannot die.

23. No one will hide something highly valuable in something ostentatious (that would draw attention). More often, one places something of great worth within a number of containers worth nothing. This is how it is with the (human) soul. It is a precious thing placed within a lowly body.

24. Some are fearful that they will arise (from the dead) naked. Therefore they desire to rise in the flesh. They do not understand that those who choose to wear the flesh are naked. Those who choose to strip themselves of the flesh are the ones who are not naked.

25. Flesh and blood will not be able to inherit the kingdom of God. What is this that will not inherit? It is that which is upon each of us (our flesh). But what will inherit the kingdom is that which belongs to Jesus and is of his flesh and blood. Therefore

he says: "He who does not eat my flesh and drink my blood, has no life in him." What is his flesh? It is the Word, and his blood is the Holy Spirit. He who has received these has food and drink and clothing.

26. I disagree with those who say the flesh will not arise. They are in error. Tell me what will rise so that we may honor you. You say it is the spirit in the flesh and the light contained in the flesh. But you say there is nothing outside of the flesh (material world). It is necessary to arise in this flesh if everything exists within the flesh.

27. In this world those wearing a garment are more valuable than the garment. In the kingdom of the Heavens the garment is more valuable than the one wearing it.

28. By water and fire the entire realm is purified through the revelations by those who reveal them, and by the secrets through those who keep them. Yet, there are things kept secret even within those things revealed. There is water in baptism and there is fire in the oil of anointing.

29. Jesus took them all by surprise. For he did not reveal himself as he originally was, but he revealed himself as they

were capable of perceiving him. He revealed himself to all in their own way. To the great, he revealed himself as great. To the small he was small. He revealed himself to the angels as an angel and to mankind he was a man. Some looked at him and saw themselves. But, throughout all of this, he concealed his words from everyone. However when he revealed himself to his Disciples upon the mountain, he appeared glorious. He was not made small. He became great, but he also made the Disciples great so that they would be capable of comprehending his greatness.

30. He said on that day during his thanksgiving (in the Eucharist), "You have combined the perfect light and the holy spirit along with angels and images."

31. Do not hate the Lamb. Without him it is not possible to see the door to the sheepfold. Those who are naked will not come before the King.

32. The Sons of the Heavenly Man are more numerous than those of the earthly man. If the sons of Adam are numerous although they die, think of how many more Sons the Perfect Man has and these do not die. And they are continually born every instant of time.

33. The Father creates a son, but it is not possible for the son to create a son because it is impossible for someone who was just born to have a child. The Son has Brothers, not sons.

34. There is order in things. All those who are born in the world are begotten physically. Some are begotten spiritually, fed by the promise of heaven, which is delivered by the perfect Word from the mouth. The perfect Word is conceived through a kiss and thus they are born. There is unction to kiss one another to receive conception from grace to grace.

35. There were three women named Mary (Bitter) who walked with the Lord all the time. They were his mother, his sister and Mary of Magdala, who was his consort (companion). Thus his mother, his sister and companion (consort) were all named Mary.

36. "Father" and "Son" are single names, "Holy Spirit" is a double name and it is everywhere; above and below, secret and revealed. The Holy Spirit's abode is manifest when she is below. When she is above she is hidden.

37. Saints are served by evil powers (lesser gods). The evil spirits are deceived by the Holy Spirit. They think they are

assisting a common man when they are serving Saints. A follower of the Lord once asked him for a thing from this world. He answered him saying, "Ask your Mother, and she will give you something from another realm."

38. The Apostles said to the students, "May all of our offering obtain salt!" They had called wisdom salt and without it no offering can become acceptable.

39. Wisdom (Sophia) is barren. She has no children but she is called Mother. Others are found (adopted) by the Holy Spirit, and she has many children.

40. That which the Father has belongs to the Son, but he cannot possess it when he is young (small). When he comes of age all his father has will be given to the son.

41. Those who do not follow the path are born of the Spirit, and they stray because of her. By this same spirit (breath or life force), the fire blazes and consumes.

42. Earthly wisdom is one thing, and death is another. Earthly wisdom is simply wisdom, but death is the wisdom of death, and death is the one who understands death. Being familiar with death is minor wisdom.

43. There are animals like the bull and donkey that are submissive to man. There are others that live in the wilderness. Man plows the field with submissive animals, and uses the harvest to feed himself as well as all the animals, domesticated or wild. So it is with the Perfect Man. Through submissive powers he plows and provides for all things to exist. He causes all things to come together into existence, whether good or evil, right or left.

44. The Holy Spirit is the shepherd guiding everyone and every power (lower ruler or lesser gods), whether submissive, rebellious, or feral. She controls them, subdues them, and keeps them bridled, whether they wish it or not.

45. Adam was created beautiful. One would expect his children to be noble. If he were not created but rather born, one would expect his children to be noble. But he was both created and born. Is this nobility?

46. Adultery occurred first and then came murder. And Cain was conceived in adultery because he was the serpent's (Satan's) son. He became a murderer just like his father. He

killed his brother. When copulation occurs between those who are not alike, this is adultery.

47. God is a dyer. Just as a good and true dye penetrates deep into fabric to dye it permanently from within (not a surface act), so God has baptized what He dyes into an indelible dye, which is water.

48. It is impossible for anyone to see anything in the real world, unless he has become part of it. It is not like a person in this world. When one looks at the sun he can see it without being part of it. He can see the sky or the earth or anything without having to be part of it. So it is with this world, but in the other world you must become what you see (see what you become). To see spirit you must be spirit. To see Christ you must be Christ. To see the Father you must be the Father. In this way you will see everything but yourself. If you look at yourself you will become what you see.

49. Faith receives, but love gives. No one can receive without faith. No one can love without giving. Believe and you shall receive. Love and you shall give. If you give without love, you shall receive nothing. Whoever has not received the Lord, continues to be a Jew.

50. The Apostles who came before us called him Jesus, The Nazarene, and The Messiah. Of these names, Jesus (Yeshua), The Nazarene (of the rite of the Nazarites), and The Messiah (Christ), the last name is the Christ, the first is Jesus, and the middle name is The Nazarene. Messiah has two meanings; the anointed one and the measured one. Jesus (Yeshua) means The Atonement (redemption or payment). 'Nazara' means Truth. Therefore, the Nazarite is The Truth. The Christ is The Measured One, the Nazarite (Truth) and Jesus (Redemption) have been measured (are the measurement).

51. The pearl which is thrown into the mud is not worth less than it was before. If it is anointed with balsam oil it is valued no higher. It is as valuable as its owner perceives it to be. So it is with the children of God. Whatever becomes of them, they are precious in their Father's eyes.

52. If you say you are a Jew it will not upset anyone. If you say you are a Roman no one will care. If you claim to be a Greek, foreigner, slave, or a free man no one will be the least bit disturbed. But, if you claim to belong to Christ everyone will take heed (be concerned). I hope to receive this title from him. Those who are worldly would not be able to endure when they hear the name.

53. A god is a cannibal, because men are sacrificed to it. Before men were sacrificed, animals were sacrificed. Those they are sacrificed to are not gods.

54. Vessels of glass and vessels of clay are always made with fire. But if a glass vessel should break it is recast, because it is made in a single breath. If a clay vessel breaks it is destroyed, since it came into being without breath.

55. A donkey turning a millstone walked a hundred miles but when it was untied it was in the same place it started. There are those who go on long journeys but do not progress. When evening comes (when the journey ends), they have discovered no city, no village, no construction site, no creature (natural thing), no power (ruler), and no angel. They labored and toiled for nothing (emptiness).

56. The thanksgiving (Eucharist) is Jesus. For in Aramaic they call him farisatha, which means, "to be spread out." This is because Jesus came to crucify the world.

57. The Lord went into the place where Levi worked as a dyer. He took 72 pigments and threw them into a vat. When he drew

out the result it was pure white. He said, "This is how the Son of Man has come. He is a dyer."

58. Wisdom, which they call barren, is the mother of the angels. And the companion (Consort) was Mary of Magdala. The Lord loved Mary more than all the other disciples and he kissed her often on her mouth (the text is missing here and the word "mouth" is assumed). The others saw his love for Mary and asked him: "Why do you love her more than all of us?" The Savior replied, "Why do I not love you in the same way I love her?" While a blind person and a person who sees are both in the dark, there is no difference, but when the light comes, the one who sees shall behold the light, but he who is blind will remain in darkness.

59. The Lord says: "Blessed is he who existed before you came into being, for he is and was and shall (continue to) be."

60. The supremacy of man is not evident, but it is hidden. Because of this he is master of the animals, which are stronger (larger) than him, in ways both evident and not. This allows the animals to survive. But, when man departs from them, they bite and kill and devour each other because they have no food. Now they have food because man cultivated the land.

61. If one goes down into the water (is baptized) and comes up having received nothing, but claims to belong to Christ, he has borrowed against the name at a high interest rate. But if one receives the Holy Spirit, he has been given the name as a gift. He who has received a gift does not have to pay for it or give it back. If you have borrowed the name you will have to pay it back with interest when it is demanded. This is how the mystery works.

62. Marriage is a sacrament and a mystery. It is grand. For the world is founded upon man, and man founded upon marriage. Consider sex (pure sex), it has great power although its image is defiled.

63. Among the manifestations of unclean spirits there are male and female. The males are those who mate with the souls inhabiting a female form, and the female spirits invite those inhabiting a male form to have sex. Once seized, no one escapes unless they receive both the male and female power that is endued to the Groom with the Bride. The power is seen in the mirrored Bridal-Chamber. When foolish women see a man sitting alone, they want to subdue him, touch and handle him, and defile him. When foolish men see a beautiful woman sitting alone, they wish to seduce her, draw her in with desire

and defile her. But, if the spirits see the man sitting together with his woman, the female spirit cannot intrude upon the man and the male spirit cannot intrude upon the woman. When image and angel are mated, no one can come between the man and woman.

64. He who comes out from the world cannot be stopped. Because he was once in the world he is now beyond both yearning (desire) and fear. He has overcome the flesh and has mastered envy and desire. If he does not leave the world there are forces that will come to seize him, strangle him. How can anyone escape? How can he fear them? Many times men will come and say, "We are faithful, and we hid from unclean and demonic spirits." But if they had been given the Holy Spirit, no unclean spirit would have clung to them. Do not fear the flesh, nor love it. If you fear it, the flesh will become your master. If you love it, the flesh will devour you and render you unable to move.

65. One exists either in this world or in the resurrection or in transition between them. Do not be found in transition. In that world there is both good and evil. The good in it is not good and the evil in it is not evil. There is evil after this world, which is truly evil and it is called the transition. This is what is called

death. While we are in this world it is best that we be born into the resurrection, so that we take off the flesh and find rest and not wander within the region of the transition. Many go astray along the way. Because of this, it is best to go forth from the world before one has sinned.

66. Some neither wish nor are able to act. Others have the will to act but it is best for them if they do not act, because the act they desire to perform would make them a sinner. By not desiring to do a righteous act justice is withheld (not obvious). However, the will always comes before the act.

67. An Apostle saw in a vision people confined to a blazing house, held fast in bonds of fire, crying out as flames came from their breath. There was water in the house, and they cried out, "The waters can truly save us." They were misled by their desire. This is called the outermost darkness.

68. Soul and spirit were born of water and fire. From water, fire, and light the children of the Bridal-Chamber are born. The fire is the spirit (anointing), the light is the fire, but not the kind of fire that has form. I speak of the other kind whose form is white and it rains down beauty and splendor.

69. The truth did not come into the world naked, but it came in types and symbols. The world would not receive it any other way. There is a rebirth together with its symbols. One cannot be reborn through symbols. What can the symbol of resurrection raise, or the Bridal-Chamber with its symbols? One must come into the truth through the (true) image (not the symbol or type of it). Truth is this Restoration. It is good for those not born to take on the names of the Father, the Son, and the Holy Spirit. They could not have done so on their own. Whoever is not born of them will have the name (Christ's ones) removed from him. The one who receives them receives the anointing of the spirit and the unction and power of the cross. This is what the Apostles call having the right with the left. When this happens, you no longer belong to Christ, you will be Christ.

70. The Lord did everything through sacraments (mysteries or symbols): There was baptism, anointing, thanksgiving (Eucharist), atonement (sacrifice or payment), and Bridal-Chamber.

71. He says: "I came to make what is inside the same as the outside and what is below as it is above. I came to bring all of this into one place." He revealed himself through types and

symbols. Those who say Christ comes from the place beyond (above) are confused.

72. He who is manifest in heaven is called "one from below." And He who knows the hidden thing is He who is above him. The correct way to say it would be "the inner and the outer or this which is beyond the outer." Because of this, the Lord called destruction "the outer darkness." There is nothing beyond it. He says, "My Father, who is in secret." He says, "Go into your inner chamber, shut the door behind you and there pray to your Father who is in secret; He who is deep within." He who is within them all is the Fullness. Beyond Him there is nothing deeper within. The deepest place within is called the uppermost place.

73. Before Christ some came forth. They were not able to go back from where they came. They were no longer able to leave from where they went. Then Christ came. Those who went in he brought out, and those who went out he brought in.

74. When Eve was still within Adam (man), there had been no death. When she was separated from him, death began. If she were to enter him again and if he were to receive her completely, death would stop.

75. "My God, my God, Oh Lord why did you abandon me?" He spoke these words on the cross. He divided the place and was not there any longer.

76. The Lord arose from the dead. He became as he had been, but his body had been made perfect. He was clothed in true flesh. Our flesh is not true, but rather an image of true flesh, as one beholds in a mirror.

77. The Bridal-Chamber is not for beasts, slaves, or whores. It is for free men and virgins.

78. Through the Holy Spirit we are born again, conceived in Christ, anointed in the spirit, united within us. Only with light can we see ourselves reflected in water or mirror. We are baptized in water and light. It is the light that is the oil of the anointing.

79. There had been three offering vestibules in Jerusalem. One opened to the west called the holy, another opened to the south called the holy of the holy, the third opened to the east called the holy of the holies where the high priest alone was to enter. The Baptism is the holy, the redemption (payment or atonement) is the holy of the holy, and the holy of the holies is

the Bridal-Chamber. The Baptism has within it the resurrection and the redemption. Redemption allows entrance into the Bridal-Chamber. The Bridal-Chamber is more exalted than any of these. Nothing compares.

80. Those who pray for Jerusalem love Jerusalem. They are in Jerusalem and they see it now. These are called the holy of the holies.

81. Before the curtain of the Temple was torn we could not see the Bridal-Chamber. All we had was the symbol of the place in heaven. When the curtain was torn from the top to the bottom it made a way for some to ascend.

82. Those who have been clothed in the Perfect Light cannot be seen by the powers, nor can the powers subdue them. Yet one shall be clothed with light in the sacrament (mystery) of sex (being united).

83. If the woman had not been separated from the man, neither would have died. Christ came to rectify the error of separation that had occurred. He did this by re-uniting them and giving life to those who died. The woman unites with her husband in the Bridal-Chamber and those who have united in the Bridal-

Chamber will not be parted again. Eve separated from Adam because she did not unite with him in the Bridal-Chamber.

84. The soul of man (Adam) was created when breath (spirit) was blown into him. The elements were supplied by his mother. When soul (mind or will) became spirit and were joined together he spoke in word the powers could not understand.

85. Jesus manifested beside the River Jordan with fullness of the kingdom of the Heavens, which existed before anything. Moreover, he was born as a Son before birth. He was anointed and he anointed. He was atoned and he atoned.

86. It is right to speak of a mystery. The Father of them all mated with the Virgin who had come down. A fire shone over him on that day. He revealed the power of the Bridal-Chamber. Because of this power his body came into being on that day. He came forth in the Bridal-Chamber in glory because of the essence that issued forth from the Bridegroom to the Bride. This is how Jesus established everything. It was in his heart. In this same way it is right for each one of the disciples to enter into his rest.

87. Adam came into being from two virgins, from the Spirit and from the virgin earth. Christ was born from a virgin, so that the error which occurred in the beginning would be corrected by him.

88. There were two trees in paradise. One produced beasts, the other produced man. Adam ate from the tree that produced beasts becoming a beast he gave birth to beasts. Because of this, animals were worshipped. God created man and men created gods. This is how the world works; men create gods and they worship their creations. It would have been more appropriate for gods to worship mankind. This would be the way if Adam had not eaten from the tree of life, which bore people.

89. The deeds of man follow his abilities. These are his strengths and the things he does with ease. His result is his children who came forth from his times of rest. His work is governed by his work but in his rest he brings forth his sons. This is the sign and symbol, doing works with strength, and producing children in his rest.

90. In this world the slaves are forced to serve the free. In the kingdom of Heaven the free shall serve the slaves and the Bridegroom of the Bridal-Chamber shall serve the guests. Those of the Bridal-Chamber have a single name among them,

it is "rest" and they have no need for any other. The contemplation of the symbol brings enlightenment and great glory. Within those in the Chamber (rest) the glories are fulfilled.

91. Go into the water but do not go down into death, because Christ shall atone for him when he who is baptized comes forth. They were called to be fulfilled in his name. For he said, "We must fulfill all righteousness."

92. Those who say they shall die and then arise are confused. If you do not receive the resurrection while you are alive you will not receive anything when you die. This is why it is said that Baptism is great, because those who receive it shall live.

93. Philip the Apostle said, "Joseph the Carpenter planted a grove of trees because he needed wood for his work (craft or trade). He himself made the cross from the trees that he had planted, and his heir hung on that which he had planted. His heir was Jesus, and the tree was the cross. But the tree of life in the midst of the garden (paradise) is the olive tree. From the heart of it comes the anointing through the olive oil and from that comes the resurrection."

94. This world consumes corpses. Everything eaten by (in) the world dies. The truth devours life, but if you eat truth you shall never die. Jesus came (from there) bringing food. And to those wishing it (whom he wished) he gave life, so that they not die.

95. God created the garden (paradise). Man lived there, but they did not have God in their hearts and so they gave in to desire. This garden is where it will be said to us, " You may eat this but not eat that, according to your desire." This is the place where I shall choose to eat various things such as being there the tree of knowledge, which slew Adam. In this place the tree of knowledge gave life to man. The Torah is the tree. It has the power to impart the knowledge of good and evil. It did not remove him from the evil or deliver him to good. It simply caused those who had eaten it to die. Death began because truth said, " You can eat this, but do not eat that."

96. The anointing (chrism) is made superior to Baptism, because from the word Chrism we are called Christians (Christ's ones) not because of the word Baptism. And because of Chrism he was called Christ. The Father anointed the Son, and the Son anointed the Apostles, and the Apostles anointed us. He who has been anointed has come to possess all things; he has the resurrection, the light, the cross, and the Holy Spirit. The Father bestowed this upon him in the Bridal-Chamber. The

father gave it to the Son who received it freely. The Father was in the Son, and the Son was in the Father. This is the kingdom of Heaven.

97. It was perfectly said by the Lord: Some have attained the kingdom of Heaven laughing. They came forth from the world joyous. Those who belong to Christ who went down into the water immediately came up as lord of everything. He did not laugh because he took things lightly, but because he saw that everything in this world was worthless compared to the kingdom of Heaven. If he scoffs at the world and sees its worthlessness he will come forth laughing.

98. The Bread and cup, and the oil of anointing (Chrism); there is one superior to them all.

99. The world (system) began in a mistake. He who made this world wished to make it perfect and eternal. He failed (fell away or did not follow through) and did not attain his goal. The world is not eternal, but the children of the world are eternal. They were children and obtained eternity. No one can receive eternity except by becoming a child. The more you are unable to receive, the more you will be unable to give.

100. The cup of the communion (prayer) contains wine and water. It is presented as the symbol of the blood. Over it (because of the blood) we give thanks. It is filled by (with) the Holy Spirit. It (the blood) belongs to the Perfect Man. When we drink we consume the Perfect man

101. The Living Water is a body. It is right that we be clothed with a living body (The Living Man). When he goes down into the water he undresses himself so he may be clothed with the living man.

102. A horse naturally gives birth to a horse, a human naturally gives birth to a human, a god naturally gives birth to a god. The Bridegroom within the Bride gives birth to children who are born in the Bridal-Chamber. The Jews do not spring forth from Greeks (Gentiles), and Christians (those belonging to Christ) do not come from Jews. These who gave birth to Christians were called the chosen generation of the Holy Spirit (living God). The True Man, the Son of Mankind, was the seed that brought forth the sons of Man. This generation is the true ones in the world. This is the place where the children of the Bridal-Chamber dwell.

103. Copulation occurs in this world when man and woman mix (mingle or entwine). Strength joins with weakness. In

eternity there is a different kind of mingling that occurs. Metaphorically we call it by the same names, but it is exalted beyond any name we may give it. It transcends brute strength. Where there is no force, there are those who are superior to force. Man cannot comprehend this.

104. The one is not, and the other one is, but they are united. This is He who shall not be able to come unto those who have a heart of flesh. (He is not here, but He exists. However, He cannot inhabit a heart of those who are attached to the fleshly world.)

105. Before you possess all knowledge, should you not know yourself? If you do not know yourself, how can you enjoy those things you have? Only those who have understood themselves shall enjoy the things they have come to possess.

106. The perfected person cannot be captured or seen. If they could see him, they could capture him. The path to grace can only come from the perfect light. Unless one is clothed in the perfect light and it shows on and in him he shall not be able to come out from the World as the perfected son of the Bridal-Chamber. We must be perfected before we come out from the world. Whoever has received all before mastering all, will not

be able to master the kingdom. He shall go to the transition (death) imperfect. Only Jesus knows his destiny.

107. The holy person is entirely holy, including his body. If one blesses the bread and sanctifies it, or the cup, or everything else he receives, why will he not sanctify the body also?

108. By perfecting the water of Baptism: thus Jesus washed away death. Because of this, we are descended into the water but not into death. We are not poured out into the wind (spirit) of the world. Whenever that blows, its winter has come. When the Holy Spirit breathes, summer has come.

109. Whoever recognizes the truth is set free. He who is set free does not go back (sin), for the one who goes back (the sinner) is the slave of sin. Truth is the Mother. When we unite with her it is recognition of the truth. Those who are set free from sin (no longer have to sin) are called free by the world. It is the recognition of the truth that exalts the hearts of those who are set free from sin. This is what liberates them and places them over the entire world. Love builds (inspires). He who has been set free through this recognition is a slave of love, serving those who have not yet been set free by the truth. Knowledge makes them capable of being set free. Love does not take anything selfishly. How can it when it possesses all things? It

does not say; "This is mine or that is mine," but it says, "All of this belongs to you."

110. Spiritual love is wine with fragrance. All those who are anointed with it enjoy it. Those who are near to the anointed ones enjoy it also. But when the anointed ones depart the bystanders who are not anointed remain in their own stench. The Samaritan gave nothing to the wounded man except wine and oil for anointing. The wounds were healed, for "love covers a multitude of sins."

111. The children of a woman resemble the man who loves her. If the man is her husband, they resemble her husband. If the man is her illicit lover, they resemble him. Often, a woman will have sex with her husband out of duty but her heart is with her lover with whom she also has sex. The children of such a union often resemble the lover. You who live with the Son of God and do not also love the world but love the Lord only will have children that look like the Lord and not the world.

112. Humans mate with the humans, horses mate with horses, donkeys mate with donkeys. Like attracts like and they group together. Spirits unite with Spirits, and the thought (Word) mingles with the thought (Word), as Light merges with Light.

If you become a person then people will love you. If you become a spirit, then the Spirit shall merge with you. If you become a thought, then the thought (Word) shall unite with you. If you become enlightened, then the Light shall merge with you. If you rise above this world, then that which is from above shall rest upon (in) you. But, if you become like a horse, donkey, bull, dog, sheep, or any other animal, domestic or feral, then neither man nor Spirit nor Word (thought) nor the Light nor those from above nor those dwelling within shall be able to love you. They shall not be able to rest in you, and they will have no part in your inheritance to come.

113. He who is enslaved without his consent can be set free. He who has been set free by the grace of his master, but then sells himself back into slavery cannot be set free.

114. The cultivation in this world comes through four elements. Crops are harvested and taken into the barn only if there is first soil, water, wind, and light. God's harvest is also by means of four elements; faith (trust), hope (expectation), love (agape'), and knowledge (recognition of the truth). Our soil is the faith in which we take root. Our water is the hope by which we are nourished. Wind (spirit) is the love through which we grow. Light is the truth, which causes us to ripen. But, it is Grace that

causes us to become kings of all heaven. Their souls are among the blessed for they live in Truth.

115. Jesus, the Christ, came to all of us but did not lay any burden on us. This kind of person is perfect and blessed. He is the Word of God. Ask us about him and we will tell you his righteousness is difficult to define or describe. A task so great assures failure.

116. How will he give rest to everyone; great or small, believer or not? He provides rest to all. There are those who attempt to gain by assisting the rich. Those who see themselves as rich are picky. They do not come of their own accord. Do not grieve them or anyone. It is natural to want to do good, but understand that the rich may seek to cause grief and he who seeks to do good could annoy those who think they are rich.

117. A householder had acquired everything. He had children, slaves, cattle, dogs, and pigs. He also had wheat, barley, straw, hay, meat, oil, and acorns. He was wise and knew what each needed to eat. He fed his children bread and meat. He fed the slaves oil with grain. The cattle were given barley, straw and hay. The dogs received bones and the pigs got acorns and bread scraps. This is how it is with the disciple of God. If he is

wise, he understands discipleship. The bodily forms will not deceive him, but he will understand the condition of the souls around him. He will speak to each man on his own level. In the world there are many types of animals in human form. He must recognize each one. If the person is a pig, feed him acorns. If the person is a bull, feed him barley with straw and hay; if a dog, throw him bones. If a person is a slave feed him basic food, but to the sons present the perfect and complete food.

118. There is the Son of Man and there is the son of the son of Man. The Lord is the Son of Man, and his son creates through him. God gave the Son of Man the power to create; he also gave him the ability to have children. That which is created is a creature. Those born are a progeny (child or heir). A creature cannot propagate, but children can create. Yet they say that the creature procreates, however, the child is a creature. Therefore the creature's progeny are not his sons, but rather they are creations. He who creates works openly, and is visible. He who procreates does so in secret, and he hides himself from others. He who creates does so in open sight. He who procreates, makes his children (son) in secret.

119. No one is able to know what day a husband and wife copulate. Only they know, because marriage in this world is a sacrament (mystery) for those who have taken a wife. If the act

of an impure (common) marriage is hidden, the pure (immaculate) marriage is a deeper mystery (sacrament) and is hidden even more. It is not carnal (common) but it is pure (undefiled). It is not founded on lust. It is founded on true love (agape'). It is not part of the darkness or night. It is part of the light. A marriage (act) which is seen (revealed or exposed) becomes vulgarity (common or prostitution), and the bride has played the whore not only if she has sex with another man, but also if she escapes from the Bridal-Chamber and is seen. She may only be seen (reveal herself to) by her father, her mother, the attendant (friend) of the bridegroom, and the bridegroom. Only these have permission to go into the bridal-chamber on a daily basis. Others will yearn to hear her voice or enjoy her perfume (fragrance of the anointing oil). Let them be fed like dogs from the scraps that fall from the table. Those being from the Bridegroom with the Bride belong in the Bridal-Chamber. No one will be able to see the Bridegroom or the Bride unless he becomes one like (with) them.

120. When Abraham was allowed (rejoiced at seeing what he was) to see, he circumcised the flesh of the foreskin to show us that it was correct (necessary) to renounce (kill) the flesh of this world.

121. As long as the entrails of a person are contained, the person lives and is well. If his entrails are exposed and he is disemboweled, the person will die. It is the same with a tree. If its roots are covered it will live and grow, but if its roots are exposed the tree will wither and die. It is the same with everything born into this world. It is this way with everything manifest (seen) and covert (unseen). As long as the roots of evil are hidden, it is strong, but once evil is exposed or recognized it is destroyed and it dies. This is why the Word says; "Already the ax has been laid to the root of the tree." It will not only chop down the tree, because that will permit it to sprout again, the ax will go down into the ground and cleave the very root. Jesus uprooted what others had only partially cut down. Let each one of us dig deeply, down to the root of the evil that is within his heart and rip it out by its roots. If we can just recognize evil we can uproot it. However, if evil remains unrecognized, it will take root within us and yield its fruit in our hearts. It will make evil our master and we will be its slaves. Evil takes us captive, and coerces us into doing what we do not want to do. Evil compels us into not doing what we should do. While it is unrecognized, it drives us .

122. Ignorance is the mother of all evil. Evil results in confusion and death. Truth is like ignorance. If it is hidden it rests within itself, but when it is revealed it is recognized and it is stronger

than ignorance and error. Truth wins and liberates us from confusion. The Word said; "You shall know the truth and the truth shall set you free." Ignorance seeks to make us its slaves but knowledge is freedom. By recognizing the truth, we shall find the fruits of the truth within our hearts. If we join ourselves with the truth we shall be fulfilled.

123. Now, we have the visible (beings) things of creation and we say that visible things (beings) are the powerful and honorable, but the invisible things are the weak and unworthy of our attention. The nature of truth is different. In it, the visible things (beings) are weak and lowly, but the invisible are the powerful and honorable. The wisdom of the invisible God cannot be made known to us except that he takes visible form in ways we are accustomed to. Yet the mysteries of the truth are revealed, in types and symbols, but the Bridal-Chamber is hidden as it is with the Holy of Holies.

124. The veil of the Temple first concealed how God governed creation. Once the veil was torn and the things within (the Holy of Holies) were revealed, the house was to be forsaken, abandoned, and destroyed. Yet the entire Divinity (Godhead) was to depart, not to the holies of the holies, for it was not able to merge with the light nor unite with the complete fullness. It

was to be under the wings of the cross, in its open arms. This is the ark which shall be salvation for us when the destruction of water has overwhelmed (overtaken) them.

125. Those in the priestly tribe shall be able to enter within the veil of the Temple along with the High Priest. This was symbolized by the fact that the veil was not torn at the top only, (but was torn from top to the bottom). If it was torn only at the top it would have been opened only for those who are on high (from the higher realm). If it was torn at the bottom only it would have been revealed only to those who are from below (the lower realm). But it was torn from the top to the bottom. Those who are from above made it available to us who are below them, so that we might enter into the secret of the truth. This strengthening of us is most wonderful. Because of this, we can enter in by means of symbols even though they are weak and worthless. They are humble and incomplete when compared to the perfect glory. It is the glory of glories and the power of powers. Through it the perfect is opened to us and it contains the secrets of the truth. Moreover, the Holies of Holies have been revealed and opened, and the Bridal-Chamber has invited us in.

126. As long as evil is hidden, and not completely purged from among the children of the Holy Spirit, it remains a potential

threat. The children can be enslaved by the adversary, but when the Perfect Light is seen, it will pour out the oil of anointing upon and within it, and the slaves shall be set free and the slaves shall be bought back.

127. Every plant not sown by my heavenly Father shall be pulled up by the root. Those who were estranged shall be united and the empty shall be filled.

128. Everyone who enters the bridal-chamber shall ignite (be born in) the Light. This is like a marriage, which takes place at night. The fire is ablaze and is seen in the dark but goes out before morning. The mysteries (sacraments) of the marriage are consummated in the light of day, and that light never dies.

129. If someone becomes a child of the Bridal-Chamber, he shall receive the Light. If one does not receive it in this place, he will not be able to receive it in any other place. He who has received that Light shall not be seen, nor captured. No one in the world will be able to disturb him. When he leaves the world he will have already received the truth in types and symbols. The world has become eternity, because for him the fullness is eternal. It is revealed only to this kind of person. Truth is not

hidden in darkness or the night. Truth is hidden in a perfect day and a holy light.

History of The Gospel Of Mary Magdalene

While traveling and researching in Cairo in 1896, German scholar, Dr. Carl Reinhardt, acquired a papyrus containing Coptic texts entitled the Revelation of John, the Wisdom of Jesus Christ, and the Gospel of Mary.

Before setting about to translate his exciting find two world wars ensued, delaying publication until 1955. By then the Nag Hammadi collection had also been discovered.

Two of the texts in his codex, the Revelation of John, and the Wisdom of Jesus Christ, were included there. Importantly, the codex preserves the most complete surviving copy of the Gospel of Mary, named for its supposed author, Mary of Magdala. Two other fragments of the Gospel of Mary written in Greek were later unearthed in archaeological digs at Oxyrhynchus in Northern Egypt.

All of the various fragments were brought together to form the translation presented here. However, even with all of the fragments assembled, the manuscript of the Gospel of Mary is missing pages 1 to 6 and pages 11 to 14. These pages included sections of the text up to chapter 4, and portions of chapter 5 to 8.

Although the text of the Gospel of Mary is incomplete, the text presented below serves to shake the very concept of our assumptions of early Christianity as well as Christ's possible relationship to Mary of Magdala, whom we call Mary Magdalene.

The Gospel of Mary Magdalene

(Pages 1 to 6, containing chapters 1 - 3, could not be recovered. The text starts on page 7, chapter 4)

Chapter 4

21 (And they asked Jesus), "Will matter then be destroyed or not?"

22) The Savior said, "All nature, all things formed, and all creatures exist in and with one another, and they will be dissolved again into their own elements (origins).

23) This is because it is the nature of matter to return to its original elements.

24) If you have an ear to hear, listen to this."

25) Peter said to him, "Since you have explained all things to us, tell us this also: What sin did the world commit (what sin is in the world)?"

26) The Savior said, "There is no sin (of the world). Each person makes his own sin when he does things like adultery (in the same nature as adultery). This is called sin.

27) That is why the Good came to be among you. He came to restore every nature to its basic root."

28) Then He continued; "You become sick and die because you did not have access to (knowledge of) Him who can heal you.

29) If you have any sense, you must understand this.

30) The material world produced a great passion (desire or suffering) without equal. This was contrary to the natural balance. The entire cosmos (body) was disturbed by it.

31) That is why I said to you, Be encouraged, and if you are discouraged be encouraged when you see the different forms nature has taken.

32) He who has ears to hear, let him hear."

33) When the Blessed One had said this, He greeted all of them and said; "Peace be with you. Take my peace into you.

34) Beware that no one deceives you by saying, 'Look (he is) here or look (he is) there. The Son of Man is within you.'

35) Follow Him there.

36) Those who seek Him will find Him.

37) Go now and preach the gospel (this good news) of the Kingdom.

38) Do not lay down any rules beyond what I told you, and do not give a law like the lawgivers (Pharisees) or you will be held to account for the same laws."

39) When He said this He departed.

Chapter 5

1) Then they were troubled and wept out loud, saying, "How shall we go to the Gentiles and preach the gospel of the Kingdom of the Son of Man? If they did not spare Him, how can we expect that they will spare us?"

2) Then Mary stood up, greeted them all, and said to her fellow believers, "Do not weep and do not be troubled and do not waver, because His grace will be with you completely and it will protect you.

3) Instead, let us praise His greatness, because He has prepared us and made us into mature (finished or complete) people."

4) Mary's words turned their hearts to the Good, and they began to discuss the words of the Savior.

5) Peter said to Mary, "Sister we know that the Savior loved you more than all other women.

6) Tell us the words of the Savior that you remember and know, but we have not heard and do not know."

7) Mary answered him and said, "I will tell you what He hid from you."

8) And she began to speak these words to them: She said, "I saw the Lord in a vision and I said to Him, 'Lord I saw you today in a vision.'

9) He answered and said to me; 'You will be happy that you did not waver at the sight of Me. Where the mind is there is the treasure.'

10) I said to Him; 'Lord, does one see visions through the soul or through the spirit?'

11) The Savior answered and said; 'He sees visions through neither the soul nor the spirit. It is through the mind that is between the two. That is what sees the vision and it is (there the vision exists).'"

(Pages 11 - 14 are missing. Text begins again at chapter 8)

Chapter 8

10) And Desire, (a lesser god), said, "Before, I did not see you descending, but now I see you ascending. Why do you lie since you belong to me?"

11) The soul answered and said, "I saw you but you did not see me nor recognize me. I covered you like a garment and you did not know me."

12) When it said this, the soul went away greatly rejoicing.

13) Again it came to the third power (lesser god), which is called Ignorance.

14) The power questioned the soul, saying, "Where are you going? You are enslaved (captured) in wickedness. Since you are its captive you cannot judge (have no judgment)."

15) And the soul said, "Why do you judge me, when I have not judged?"

16) "I was captured, although I have not captured anyone."

17) "I was not recognized. But I have recognized that God (the All) is in (being dissolved), both the earthly things and in the heavenly (things)."

18) When the soul had overcome the third power, it ascended and saw the fourth power, which took seven forms.

19) The first form is darkness, the second desire, the third ignorance, the fourth is the lust of death, the fifth is the dominion of the flesh, the sixth is the empty useless wisdom of flesh, the seventh is the wisdom of vengeance and anger. These are the seven powers of rage.

20) They asked the soul, "Where do you come from, slayer of men: where are you going, conqueror of space?"

21) The soul answered and said, "What has trapped me has been slain, and what kept me caged has been overcome."

22) "My desire has been ended, and ignorance has died."

23) "In an age (dispensation) I was released from the world in a symbolic image, and I was released from the chains of oblivion, which were only temporary (in this transient world)."

24) "From this time on will I will attain the rest of the ages and seasons of silence."

Chapter 9

1) When Mary had said this, she fell silent, since she had shared all the Savior had told her.

2) But Andrew said to the other believers, "Say what you want about what she has said, but I do not believe that the Savior said this. These teachings are very strange ideas."

3) Peter answered him and spoke concerning these things.

4) He questioned them about the Savior and asked, "Did He really speak privately with a woman and not openly to us? Are we to turn around and all listen to her? Did He prefer her to us?"

5) Then Mary sobbed and said to Peter, "My brother Peter, what do you think? Do you think that I have made all of this up in my heart by myself? Do you think that I am lying about the Savior?"

6) Levi said to Peter, "Peter you have always had a hot temper.

7) Now I see you fighting against this woman like she was your enemy."

8) If the Savior made her worthy, who are you to reject her? What do you think you are doing? Surely the Savior knows her well?

9) That is why He loved her more than us. Let us be ashamed of this and let us put on the perfect Man. Let us separate from each other as He commanded us to do so we can preach the gospel, not laying down any other rule or other law beyond what the Savior told us."

10) And when they heard this they began to go out and proclaim and preach.

History of The Gospel of Thomas

In the winter of 1945, in Upper Egypt, an Arab peasant was gathering fertilizer and topsoil for his crops. While digging in the soft dirt he came across a large earthen vessel. Inside were scrolls containing hitherto unseen books.

According to local lore, the boy's father had recently been killed and the lad was preparing to chase the man who had murdered his father.

The scrolls were discovered near the site of the ancient town of Chenoboskion, at the base of a mountain named Gebel et-Tarif, near Hamra-Dum, in the vicinity of Naj 'Hammadi, about sixty miles from Luxor in Egypt. The texts were written in the Coptic language and preserved on papyrus sheets. The lettering style dated them as having been penned around the third or fourth century A.D. The Gospel of Thomas is the longest of the volumes consisting of 114 verses. Recent study indicates that the original work of Thomas, of which the scrolls are copies, may predate the four canonical gospels of Matthew, Mark, Luke, and John. The origin of The Gospel of Thomas is now thought to be from the first or second century A.D.

The word Coptic is an Arabic corruption of the Greek word Aigyptos, which in turn comes from the word Hikaptah, one of the names of the city of Memphis, the first capital of ancient Egypt.

There has never been a Coptic state or government per se, however the word has been used to generally define a culture and language present in the area of Egypt.

The known history of the Copts starts with King Mina the first King, who united the northern and southern kingdoms of Egypt circa 3050 B.C. The ancient Egyptian civilization under the rule of the Pharaohs lasted over 3000 years. Saint Mina (named after the king) is one of the major Coptic saints. He was martyred in 309 A.D.

The culture has come to be recognized as one containing distinctive art, architecture, and even a certain Christian church system.

The Coptic Church is based on the teachings of St. Mark, who introduced the region to Christianity in the first century A.D. The Copts take pride in the monastic flavor of their church and the fact that the Gospel of Mark is thought to be the oldest of the Gospels. Now, lying before a peasant boy was a scroll written in the ancient Coptic tongue: The Gospel of Thomas, possibly older than and certainly quite different from any other Gospel.

The peasant boy who found the treasure of the Gospel of Thomas stood to be rewarded greatly. This could have been the discovery of a lifetime for his family, but the boy had no idea what he had. He took the scrolls home, where his mother burned some as kindling.

Because the young man had succeeded in his pursuit of the father's murderer, he himself was now a murderer.

Fearing the authorities would soon come looking for him and not wanting to be found with ancient artifacts, he sold the codex to the black market antique dealers in Cairo for a trifle sum. It would be years until they found their way into the hands of a scholar.

Part of the thirteenth codex was smuggled from Egypt to America. In 1955 whispers of the existence of the codex had reached the ears of Gilles Quispel, a professor of religion and history in the Netherlands. The race was on to find and translate the scrolls.

The introduction of the collected sayings of Jesus refers to the writer as Didymos (Jude) Thomas. This is the same Thomas who doubted Jesus and was then told to place his hand within the breach in the side of the Savior. In the Gospel of St. John, he is referred to as Didymos, which means twin in Greek. In Aramaic, the name Jude (or Judas) also carries the sense of twin. The use of this title led some in the apocryphal tradition to believe that he was the twin brother and confidant of Jesus. However, when applied to Jesus himself, the literal meaning of twin must be rejected by orthodox Christianity as well as anyone adhering to the doctrine of the virgin birth of the only begotten Son of God. The title is likely meant to signify that Thomas was a close confidant of Jesus, or more simply, he was part of a set of twins and in no way related to Jesus.

Ancient church historians mention that Thomas preached to the Parthians in Persia and it is said he was buried in Edessa. Fourth century chronicles attribute the evangelization of India (Asia-Minor or Central Asia) to Thomas.

The text, which some believe predates the four gospels, has a very Eastern flavor. Since it is widely held that the four gospels of Matthew, Mark, Luke, and John have a common reference in the basic text of Mark, it stands to reason that all follow the same general history, insights, and language. Since scholars believe that the Gospel of Thomas predates the four main gospels, it can be assumed it was written outside the influences common to the other gospels.

The Gospel of Thomas is actually not a gospel at all. It contains no narrative but is instead a collection of sayings, which are said to be from Jesus himself as written (quoted) by Thomas. Although the codex found in Egypt is dated to the fourth century, most biblical scholars place the actual construction of the text of Thomas at about 70 – 150 A.D.

The gospel was often mentioned in early Christian literature, but no copy was thought to have survived until the discovery of the Coptic manuscript. Since then, part of the Oxyrynchus papyri have been identified as older Greek fragments of Thomas. The papyri were discovered in 1898 in the rubbish heaps of Oxyrhynchus, Egypt. This discovery yielded over thirty-five manuscript fragments for the New Testament. They have been dated to about 60 A.D. As a point of reference, a fragment of papyrus from the Dead Sea Scrolls had been dated to before 68 A.D.

There are marked differences between the Greek and Coptic texts, as we will see.

The debate on the date of Thomas centers in part on whether Thomas is dependent upon the canonical gospels, or is derived from an earlier document that was simply a collection of sayings. Many of the passages in Thomas appear to be more authentic versions of the synoptic parables, and many have parallels in Mark and Luke. This has caused a division of thought wherein some believe Thomas used common sources also used by Mark and Luke. Others believe Thomas was written independently after witnessing the same events.

If Thomas wrote his gospel first, without input from Mark, and from the standpoint of Eastern exposure as a result of his sojourn into India, it could explain the mystical quality of the text. It could also explain the striking differences in the recorded quotes of Jesus as memories were influenced by exposure to Asian culture.

There is some speculation that the sayings found in Thomas could be more accurate to the original intent and wording of Jesus than the other gospels. This may seem counter-intuitive until we realize that Christianity itself is an Eastern religion, albeit Middle-Eastern. Although as it spread west the faith went through many changes to westernize or Romanize it, Jesus was both mystical and Middle-Eastern. The Gospel of Thomas may not have seen as much "dilution" by Western society.

The Gospel of Thomas was most likely composed in Syria, where tradition holds that the church of Edessa was founded by Judas Thomas, The Twin (Didymos). The gospel may well be the earliest written tradition in the Syriac church.

The Gospel of Thomas is sometimes called a Gnostic gospel, although it seems more likely Thomas was adopted by the Gnostic community and interpreted in the light of their beliefs.

Gnostics believed that knowledge is formed or found from a personal encounter with God brought about by inward or intuitive insight. It is this knowledge that brings salvation. The Gnostics believed they were privy to a secret knowledge about the divine. It is their focus on knowledge that leads to their name.

The roots of the Gnosticism pre-date Christianity. Similarities exist to the wisdom and knowledge cults found in Egypt. The belief system seems to have spread and found a suitable home in the mystical side of the Christian faith.

There are numerous references to the Gnostics in second century literature. Their form of Christianity was considered heresy by the early church fathers. The intense resistance to the Gnostic belief system seems to be based in two areas. First, there was a general Gnostic belief that we were all gods, with heaven contained within us. Jesus, according to the Gnostics, was here to show us our potential to become as he was; a son or daughter of God, for God is both father and mother, male and female. These beliefs ran contrary to the newly developing orthodoxy. The second line of resistance was political. This resistance developed later and would have come from the fact that a faith based on a personal encounter flew in the face of the developing church political structure that placed priests and church as the keepers of heaven's gate with salvation through them alone.

It is from the writings condemning the group that we glean most of our information about the Gnostics. They are alluded to in the Bible in 1 Timoyour 1:4 and 1 Timoyour 6:20, and possibly the entirety of Jude, as the writers of the Bible defended their theology against that of the Gnostics.

It must be emphasized here that the Gospel of Thomas does not contain references to Gnostic cosmology or creation myth and this writer does not consider the book as Gnostic in origin.

The Coptic and Greek translations of The Gospel of Thomas presented herein are the result of a gestalt brought about by contrasting and comparing all of the foremost translations, where the best phrasing was chosen to follow the intent and meaning of the text.

Because there are differences between the Coptic manuscript and the Greek fragments of Thomas, each verse will have the following format for the reader to view: The Coptic text will be presented first, since we have the entire Gospel in this language. The Greek text will come next. If there is not a second rendition of the verse the reader may assume there was no Greek fragment found for that verse or the Greek version of the verse was identical to the Coptic version. Lastly, obvious parallels found in the Bible are listed.

Let us keep in mind that some of the differences between the translations of the Greek and Coptic may be attributed in part to the choice of word or phrase of those translating. It is the differences in overall meaning of verses between Coptic and Greek on which we should focus.

In the document to follow, the Gospel of Thomas will appear as a bold text. If there are other relevant but divergent interpretations of phrases in Thomas, they are included in parentheses. Any parallels of text or meaning that appear in the Bible are placed below the verse in italicized text. Author's notes are in regular text. In this way the reader can easily identify which body of work is being referenced and observe how they fit together.

Since the deeper meanings within Thomas are both in metaphor and in plain, understandable language, it is hoped that each time the words are read some new insight and treasure can be taken from them. As we change our perspective, we see the meaning of each verse differently. As one turns a single jewel to view each facet, we should study the Gospel of Thomas in the same way.

Let us begin.

Joseph B. Lumpkin

The Gospel Of Thomas

These are the secret sayings which the living Jesus has spoken and Judas who is also Thomas (the twin) (Didymos Judas Thomas) wrote.

1. And he said: Whoever finds the interpretation of these sayings will not taste death.

1. He said to them: Whoever discovers the interpretation of these words shall never taste death.

John 8:51 Very truly I tell you, whoever keeps my word will never see death.

2. Jesus said: Let him who seeks not stop seeking until he finds, and when he finds he will be troubled, and when he has been troubled he will marvel (be astonished) and he will reign over all and in reigning, he will find rest.

2. Jesus said: Let him who seeks not stop until he finds, and when he finds he shall wonder and in wondering he shall reign, and in reigning he shall find rest.

3. Jesus said: If those who lead you say to you: Look, the Kingdom is in the sky, then the birds of the sky would enter before you. If they say to you: It is in the sea, then the fish of the sea would enter ahead you. But the Kingdom of God exists within you and it exists outside of you. Those who come to know (recognize) themselves will find it, and when you come to know yourselves you will become known and you will realize that you are the children of the Living Father. Yet if you do not come to know yourselves then you will dwell in poverty and it will be you who are that poverty.

3. Jesus said, If those who lead you say, "See, the Kingdom is in the sky," then the birds of the sky will precede you. If they say to you, "It is under the earth," then the fish of the sea will precede you. Rather, the Kingdom of God is inside of you, and it is outside of you.

Those who come to know themselves will find it; and when you come to know yourselves, you will understand that it is you who are the sons of the living Father. But if you will not

know yourselves, you dwell in poverty and it is you who are that poverty.

Luke 17:20 And when he was demanded of by the Pharisees, when the kingdom of God should come, he answered them and said, The kingdom of God cometh not with observation: Neither shall they say, Lo here! Lo there! For, behold, the kingdom of God is within you.

4. Jesus said: The person of old age will not hesitate to ask a little child of seven days about the place of life, and he will live. For many who are first will become last, (and the last will be first). And they will become one and the same.

4. Jesus said: Let the old man who has lived many days not hesitate to ask the child of seven days about the place of life; then he will live. For many that are first will be last, and last will be first, and they will become a single one.

Mark 9:35-37 He sat down, called the twelve, and said to them: Whoever wants to be first must be last of all and servant of all. Then he took a little child and put it among them, and taking it in his arms, he said to them: Whoever welcomes one such child in my name welcomes me, and whoever welcomes me welcomes not me but the one who sent me.

5. Jesus said: Recognize what is in front of your face, and what has been hidden from you will be revealed to you. For there is nothing hidden which will not be revealed (become manifest), and nothing buried that will not be raised.

5. Jesus said: Know what is in front of your face and what is hidden from you will be revealed to you.
For there is nothing hidden that will not be revealed.

Mark 4:2 For there is nothing hid, except to be made manifest; nor is anything secret, except it come to light.

Luke 12:3 Nothing is covered up that will not be revealed, or hidden that will not be known.

Matthew 10:26 So have no fear of them; for nothing is covered up that will not be uncovered, and nothing secret that will not become known.

6. His Disciples asked Him, they said to him: How do you want us to fast, and how will we pray? And how will we be charitable (give alms), and what laws of diet will we maintain?

Jesus said: Do not lie, and do not practice what you hate, for everything is in the plain sight of Heaven. For there is nothing concealed that will not become manifest, and there is nothing covered that will not be exposed.

6. His disciples asked him, "How do you want us to fast? And how shall we pray? And how shall we give alms? And what kind of diet shall we follow?"
Jesus said, don't lie, and don't do what you hate to do, for all things are revealed before the truth. For there is nothing hidden which shall not be revealed.

Luke 11:1 He was praying in a certain place, and after he had finished, one of his disciples said to him, Lord, teach us to pray, as John taught his disciples.

7. Jesus said: Blessed is the lion that the man will eat, for the lion will become the man. Cursed is the man that the lion shall eat, and still the lion will become man.

Mathew 26:20-30 He who dipped his hand with me in the dish, the same will betray me. The Son of Man goes, even as it is written of him, but woe to that man through whom the Son of Man is betrayed! It would be better for that man if he had not been born. Judas, who betrayed him, answered, "It isn't me, is it, Rabbi?" He said to him,

You said it. As they were eating, Jesus took bread, gave thanks for it, and broke it. He gave to the disciples, and said, Take, eat; this is my body. He took the cup, gave thanks, and gave to them, saying: All of you drink it, for this is my blood of the new covenant, which is poured out for many for the remission of sins. But I tell you that I will not drink of this fruit of the vine from now on, until that day when I drink it anew with you in my Father's Kingdom. When they had sung a hymn, they went out to the Mount of Olives.

8. And he said: The Kingdom of Heaven is like a wise fisherman who casts his net into the sea. He drew it up from the sea full of small fish. Among them he found a fine large fish. That wise fisherman threw all the small fish back into the sea and chose the large fish without hesitation. Whoever has ears to hear, let him hear!

Matthew 13:47-48 Again, the kingdom of heaven is like a net that was thrown into the sea and caught fish of every kind; when it was full, they drew it ashore, sat down, and put the good into baskets but threw out the bad.

9. Jesus said: Now, the sower came forth. He filled his hand and threw (the seeds). Some fell upon the road and the birds came and gathered them up. Others fell on the stone and they did not take deep enough roots in the soil, and so did not

produce grain. Others fell among the thorns and they choked the seed, and the worm ate them. Others fell upon the good earth and it produced good fruit up toward the sky, it bore 60 fold and 120 fold.

Matthew 13:3-8 And he told them many things in parables, saying: Listen! A sower went out to sow. And as he sowed, some seeds fell on the path, and the birds came and ate them up. Other seeds fell on rocky ground, where they did not have much soil, and they sprang up quickly, since they had no depth of soil. But when the sun rose, they were scorched; and since they had no root, they withered away. Other seeds fell among thorns, and the thorns grew up and choked them. Other seeds fell on good soil and brought forth grain, some a hundred fold, some sixty, some thirty.

Mark 4:2-9 And he taught them many things in parables, and in his teaching he said to them: Behold! A sower went out to sow. And as he sowed, some seed fell along the path, and the birds came and devoured it. Other seed fell on rocky ground, where it had not much soil, and immediately it sprang up, since it had no depth of soil; and when the sun rose it was scorched, and since it had no root it withered away. Other seed fell among thorns and the thorns grew up and choked it, and it yielded no grain. And other seeds fell into good soil and brought forth grain, growing up and increasing and yielding thirty fold and sixty fold and a hundred fold. And he said, He who has ears to hear, let him hear.

Luke 8:4-8 And when a great crowd came together and people from town after town came to him, he said in a parable: A sower went out to sow his seed; and as he sowed, some fell along the path, and was trodden under foot, and the birds of the air devoured it. And some fell on the rock; and as it grew up, it withered away, because it had no moisture. And some fell among thorns; and the thorns grew with it and choked it. And some fell into good soil and grew, and yielded a hundred fold. As he said this, he called out, He who has ears to hear, let him hear.

10. Jesus said: I have cast fire upon the world, and as you see, I guard it until it is ablaze.

Luke 12:49 I came to bring fire to the earth, and how I wish it were already kindled.

11. Jesus said: This sky will pass away, and the one above it will pass away. The dead are not alive, and the living will not die. In the days when you consumed what is dead, you made it alive. When you come into the Light, what will you do? On the day when you were united (one), you became separated (two). When you have become separated (two), what will you

do?

Matthew 24:35 Heaven and earth will pass away, but my words will not pass away.

12. The Disciples said to Jesus: We know that you will go away from us. Who is it that will be our teacher?

Jesus said to them: Wherever you are (in the place that you have come), you will go to James the Righteous, for whose sake Heaven and Earth were made (came into being.)

13. Jesus said to his Disciples: Compare me to others, and tell me who I am like. Simon Peter said to him: You are like a righteous messenger (angel) of God. Matthew said to him: You are like a (wise) philosopher (of the heart). Thomas said to him: Teacher, my mouth is not capable of saying who you are like!

Jesus said: I'm not your teacher, now that you have drunk; you have become drunk from the bubbling spring that I have tended (measured out). And he took him, and withdrew and spoke three words to him: ahyh ashr ahyh (I am who I am).

Now when Thomas returned to his comrades, they inquired of him: What did Jesus say to you? Thomas said to them: If I tell you even one of the words which he spoke to me, you will take up stones and throw them at me, and fire will come from the stones to consume you.

Mark 8:27-30 Jesus went on with his disciples to the villages of Caesarea Philippi; and on the way he asked his disciples, Who do people say that I am? And they answered him, John the Baptist; and others, Elijah; and still others, one of the prophets. He asked them, But who do you say that I am? Peter answered him, You are the Messiah. And he sternly ordered them not to tell anyone about him.

14. Jesus said to them: If you fast, you will give rise to transgression (sin) for yourselves. And if you pray, you will be condemned. And if you give alms, you will cause harm (evil) to your spirits. And when you go into the countryside, if they take you in (receive you) then eat what they set before you and heal the sick among them. For what goes into your mouth will not defile you, but rather what comes out of your mouth, that is what will defile you.

Luke 10:8-9 Whenever you enter a town and its people welcome you, eat what is set before you; Cure the sick who are there, and say to them, The kingdom of God has come near to you.

Mark 7:15 There is nothing outside a person that by going in can defile, but the things that come out are what defile.

Matthew 15:11 It is not what goes into the mouth that defiles a man, but what comes out of the mouth, this defiles a man.

Romans 14.14 I know and am persuaded in the Lord Jesus that nothing is unclean in itself; but it is unclean for any one who thinks it unclean.

15. Jesus said: When you see him who was not born of woman, bow yourselves down upon your faces and worship him for he is your Father.

Galatians 4:3-5 Even so we, when we were children, were in bondage under the elements of the world: But when the fullness of the time was come, God sent forth his Son, made of a woman, made under the law, To redeem them that were under the law, that we might receive the adoption of sons.

16. Jesus said: People think perhaps I have come to spread peace upon the world. They do not know that I have come to

cast dissention (conflict) upon the earth; fire, sword, war. For there will be five in a house. Three will be against two and two against three, the father against the son and the son against the father. And they will stand alone.

Matthew 10:34-36 Do not think that I have come to bring peace to the earth; I have not come to bring peace, but a sword. For I have come to set a man against his father, and a daughter against her mother, and a daughter-in-law against her mother-in-law; and one's foes will be members of one's own household.

Luke 12:51-53 Do you think that I have come to give peace on earth? No, I tell you, but rather division; for henceforth in one house there will be five divided, three against two and two against three; they will be divided, father against son and son against father, mother against daughter and daughter against her mother, mother-in-law against her daughter-in-law and daughter-in-law against her mother-in-law.

17. Jesus said: I will give to you what eye has not seen, what ear has not heard, what hand has not touched, and what has not occurred to the mind of man.

1 Cor 2:9 But, as it is written, What no eye has seen, nor ear heard, nor the human heart conceived, what God has prepared for those who love him.

18. The Disciples said to Jesus: Tell us how our end will come. Jesus said: Have you already discovered the beginning (Origin), so that you inquire about the end? Where the beginning (origin) is, there the end will be. Blessed be he who will take his place in the beginning (stand at the origin) for he will know the end, and he will not experience death.

19. Jesus said: Blessed is he who came into being before he came into being. If you become my Disciples and heed my sayings, these stones will serve you. For there are five trees in paradise for you, which are undisturbed in summer and in winter and their leaves do not fall. Whoever knows them will not experience death.

20. The Disciples said to Jesus: Tell us what the Kingdom of Heaven is like. He said to them: It is like a mustard seed, smaller than all other seeds and yet when it falls on the tilled earth, it produces a great plant and becomes shelter for the birds of the sky.

Mark 4:30-32 He also said, With what can we compare the kingdom of God, or what parable will we use for it? It is like a mustard seed, which, when sown upon the ground, is the smallest of all the seeds on earth; yet when it is sown it grows up and becomes the greatest of all shrubs, and puts forth large branches, so that the birds of the air can make nests in its shade.

Matthew 13:31-32 The kingdom of heaven is like a grain of mustard seed which a man took and sowed in his field; it is the smallest of all seeds, but when it has grown it is the greatest of shrubs and becomes a tree, so that the birds of the air come and make nests in its branches.

Luke 13.18-19 He said therefore, What is the kingdom of God like? And to what shall I compare it? It is like a grain of mustard seed which a man took and sowed in his garden; and it grew and became a tree, and the birds of the air made nests in its branches.

21. Mary said to Jesus: Who are your Disciples like? He said: They are like little children who are living in a field that is not theirs. When the owners of the field come, they will say: Let us have our field! It is as if they were naked in front of them (They undress in front of them in order to let them have what is theirs) and they give back the field. Therefore I say, if the owner of the house knows that the thief is coming, he will be alert before he arrives and will not allow him to dig through into the house to carry away his belongings. You, must be on guard and beware of the world (system). Prepare yourself (arm yourself) with great strength or the bandits will find a way to reach you, for the problems you expect will

come. Let there be among you a person of understanding (awareness). When the crop ripened, he came quickly with his sickle in his hand to reap. Whoever has ears to hear, let him hear!

Matthew 24:43 But understand this: if the owner of the house had known in what part of the night the thief was coming, he would have stayed awake and would not have let his house be broken into.

Mark 4:26-29 He also said, The kingdom of God is as if someone would scatter seed on the ground, and would sleep and rise night and day, and the seed would sprout and grow, he does not know how. The earth produces of itself, first the stalk, then the head, then the full grain in the head. But when the grain is ripe, at once he goes in with his sickle, because the harvest has come.

Luke 12:39-40 But know this, that if the householder had known at what hour the thief was coming, he would not have left his house to be broken into. You also must be ready; for the Son of man is coming at an unexpected hour.

22. Jesus saw little children who were being suckled. He said to his Disciples: These little children who are being suckled are like those who enter the Kingdom.

They said to him: Should we become like little children in order to enter the Kingdom?

Jesus said to them: When you make the two one, and you make the inside as the outside and the outside as the inside, when you make the above as the below, and if you make the male and the female one and the same (united male and female) so that the man will not be masculine (male) and the female be not feminine (female), when you establish an eye in the place of an eye and a hand in the place of a hand and a foot in the place of a foot and a likeness (image) in the place of a likeness (an image), then will you enter the Kingdom.

Luke 18:16 But Jesus called for them and said, Let the little children come to me, and do not stop them; for it is to such as these that the kingdom of God belongs. Truly I tell you, whoever does not receive the kingdom of God as a little child will never enter it.

Mark 9:43-48 If your hand causes you to stumble, cut it off; it is better for you to enter life maimed than to have two hands and to go to hell, to the unquenchable fire. And if your foot causes you to stumble, cut it off; it is better for you to enter life lame than to have two feet and to be thrown into hell. And if your eye causes you to stumble, tear it out; it is better for you to enter the kingdom of God with one eye than to have two eyes and to be thrown into hell, where the worm never dies, and the fire is never quenched.

Matthew 18:3-5 And said, Verily, I say unto you, unless you turn and become like children, you will never enter the kingdom of heaven. Whoever humbles himself like this child, he is the greatest in the kingdom of heaven. Whoever receives one such child in my name receives me;

Matthew 5:29-30 If your right eye causes you to sin, pluck it out and throw it away; it is better that you lose one of your members than that your whole body be thrown into hell. And if your right hand causes you to sin, cut it off and throw it away; it is better that you lose one of your members than that your whole body go into hell.

23. Jesus said: I will choose you, one out of a thousand and two out of ten thousand and they will stand as a single one.

Matthew 20:16 So the last shall be first, and the first last: for many be called, but few chosen.

24. His Disciples said: Show us the place where you are (your place), for it is necessary for us to seek it.

24. He said to them: Whoever has ears, let him hear! Within a man of light there is light, and he illumines the entire world. If he does not shine, he is darkness (there is darkness).

John13:36 Simon Peter said to him, Lord, where are you going? Jesus answered, Where I am going, you cannot follow me now; but you will follow afterward.

Matthew 6:22-23 The eye is the lamp of the body. So, if your eye is healyour, your whole body will be full of light; but if your eye is unhealyour, your whole body will be full of darkness. If then the light in you is darkness, how great is the darkness!

Luke 11:34-36 Your eye is the lamp of your body; when your eye is sound, your whole body is full of light; but when it is not sound, your body is full of darkness. Therefore be careful lest the light in you be darkness. If then your whole body is full of light, having no part dark, it will be wholly bright, as when a lamp with its rays gives you light.

Author's Note:
Early philosophers thought that light was transmitted from the eye and bounced back, allowing the person to sense the world at large. Ancient myths tell of Aphrodite constructing the

human eye out of the four elements (earth, wind, fire, and water). The eye was held together by love. She kindled the fire of the soul and used it to project from the eyes so that it would act like a lantern, transmitting the light, thus allowing us to see.

Euclid, (330 BC to 260BC) speculated about the speed of light being instantaneous since you close your eyes, then open them again; even the distant objects appear immediately.

25. Jesus said: Love your friend (Brother) as your soul; protect him as you would the pupil of your own eye.

Romans 12:9-11 Let love be without dissimulation. Abhor that which is evil; cleave to that which is good. Be kindly affectioned one to another with brotherly love; in honour preferring one another; Not slothful in business; fervent in spirit; serving the Lord...

26. Jesus said: You see the speck in your brother's eye but the beam that is in your own eye you do not see. When you remove the beam out of your own eye, then will you see clearly to remove the speck out of your brother's eye.

26. Jesus said, You see the splinter in your brother's eye, but you don't see the log in your own eye. When you take the log out of your own eye, then you will see well enough to remove the splinter from your brother's eye.

Matthew 7:3-5 Why do you see the speck in your neighbor's eye, but do not notice the log in your own eye? Or how can you say to your neighbor, Let me take the speck out of your eye, while the log is in your own eye? You hypocrite, first take the log out of your own eye, and then you will see clearly to take the speck out of your neighbor's eye.

Luke 6:41-42 Why do you see the speck that is in your brother's eye, but do not notice the log that is in your own eye? Or how can you say to your brother, Brother, let me take out the speck that is in your eye, when you yourself do not see the log that is in your own eye? You hypocrite, first take the log out of your own eye, and then you will see clearly to take out the speck that is in your brother's eye.

27. Jesus said: Unless you fast from the world (system), you will not find the Kingdom of God. Unless you keep the Sabbath (entire week) as Sabbath, you will not see the Father.

27. Jesus said: Unless you fast (abstain) from the world, you shall in no way find the Kingdom of God; and unless you

observe the Sabbath as a Sabbath, you shall not see the Father.

28. Jesus said: I stood in the midst of the world. In the flesh I appeared to them. I found them all drunk; I found none thirsty among them. My soul grieved for the sons of men, for they are blind in their hearts and do not see that they came into the world empty they are destined (determined) to leave the world empty. However, now they are drunk. When they have shaken off their wine, then they will repent (change their ways).

28. Jesus said: I took my stand in the midst of the world, and they saw me in the flesh, and I found they were all drunk, and I found none of them were thirsty. And my soul grieved over the souls of men because they are blind in their hearts. They do not see that they came into the world empty, therefore they are determined to leave the world empty. However, now they are drunk. When they have shaken off their wine, then they will change their ways.

29. Jesus said: If the flesh came into being because of spirit, it is a marvel, but if spirit came into being because of the body, it would be a marvel of marvels. I marvel indeed at

how great wealth has taken up residence in this poverty.

30. Jesus said: Where there are three gods, they are gods (Where there are three gods they are without god). Where there is only one, I say that I am with him. Lift the stone and there you will find me, Split the wood and there am I.

30. Jesus said: Where three are together they are not without God, and when there is one alone, I say, I am with him.

Author's Note:
Many scholars believe pages of the manuscript were misplaced and verses 30 and 77 should run together as a single verse.

77. Jesus said: I-Am the Light who is over all things, I-Am the All. From me all came forth and to me all return (The All came from me and the All has come to me). Split wood, there am I. Lift up the stone and there you will find me.

Matthew 18:20 For where two or three are gathered in my name, I am there among them.

31. Jesus said: No prophet is accepted in his own village, no physician heals those who know him.

Joseph B. Lumpkin

31. Jesus said: A prophet is not accepted in his own country, neither can a doctor cure those that know him.

Mark 6:4 Then Jesus said to them, Prophets are not without honor, except in their hometown, and among their own kin, and in their own house.

Matthew 13:57 And they took offense at him. But Jesus said to them: A prophet is not without honor save in his own country and in his own house.

Luke 4:24 And he said, Truly, I say to you, no prophet is acceptable in his own country.

John 4:43-44 After the two days he departed to Galilee. For Jesus himself testified that a prophet has no honor in his own country.

32. Jesus said: A city being built (and established) upon a high mountain and fortified cannot fall nor can it be hidden.

32. Jesus said: A city built on a high hilltop and fortified can neither fall nor be hidden.

Matthew 5:14 You are the light of the world. A city built on a hill cannot be hid.

33. Jesus said: What you will hear in your ear preach from your rooftops. For no one lights a lamp and sets it under a basket nor puts it in a hidden place, but rather it is placed on a lamp stand so that everyone who comes and goes will see its light.

33. Jesus said: What you hear with one ear preach from your rooftops. For no one lights a lamp and sets it under a basket or hides, but rather it is placed on a lamp stand so that everyone who comes and goes will see its light.

Matthew 10:27 What I say to you in the dark, tell in the light; and what you hear whispered, proclaim from the housetops.

Luke 8:16 No one after lighting a lamp hides it under a jar, or puts it under a bed, but puts it on a lamp stand, so that those who enter may see the light.

Matthew 5:15 Nor do men light a lamp and put it under a bushel, but on a stand, and it gives light to all in the house.

Mark 4:21 And he said to them, Is a lamp brought in to be put under a bushel, or under a bed, and not on a stand?

Luke 11:33 No one after lighting a lamp puts it in a cellar or under a bushel, but on a stand, that those who enter may see the light.

34. Jesus said: If a blind person leads a blind person, both fall into a pit.

Matthew 15:14 Let them alone; they are blind guides of the blind. And if one blind person guides another, both will fall into a pit.

Luke 6:39 He also told them a parable: Can a blind man lead a blind man? Will they not both fall into a pit?

35. Jesus said: It is impossible for anyone to enter the house of a strong man to take it by force unless he binds his hands, then he will be able to loot his house.

Matthew 12:29 Or how can one enter a strong man's house and plunder his goods, unless he first binds the strong man? Then indeed he may plunder his house.

Luke 11:21-22 When a strong man, fully armed, guards his own palace, his goods are in peace; but when one stronger than he assails him and overcomes him, he takes away his armor in which he trusted, and divides his spoil.

Mark 3:27 But no one can enter a strong man's house and plunder his property without first tying up the strong man; then indeed the house can be plundered.

36. Jesus said: Do not worry from morning to evening nor from evening to morning about the food that you will eat nor about what clothes you will wear. You are much superior to the Lilies which neither card nor spin. When you have no clothing, what do you wear? Who can add time to your life (increase your stature)? He himself will give to you your garment.

Matthew 6:25-31 Therefore I tell you, do not worry about your life, what you will eat or what you will drink, or about your body, what you will wear. Is not life more than food, and the body more than clothing? Look at the birds of the air; they neither sow nor reap nor gather into barns, and yet your heavenly Father feeds them. Are you not of more value than they? And can any of you by worrying add a single hour to your span of life? And why do you worry about clothing? Consider the lilies of the field, how they grow; they neither toil nor spin, yet I tell you, even Solomon in all his glory was not clothed like one of these. But if God so clothes the grass of the field, which is alive today and tomorrow is thrown into the oven, will he not much more clothe you--you of little faith? Therefore do not worry, saying, What will we eat? or What will we drink? or What will we wear?

Luke 12:22-23 And he said to his disciples, Therefore I tell you, do not be anxious about your life, what you shall eat, nor about your body, what you shall put on. For life is more than food, and the body more than clothing.

37. His Disciples said: When will you appear to us, and when will we see you?

Jesus said: When you take off your garments without being ashamed, and place your garments under your feet and tread on them as the little children do, then will you see the Son of the Living-One, and you will not be afraid.

37 His disciples said to him, when will you be visible to us, and when shall we be able to see you?

He said, when you strip naked without being ashamed and place your garments under your feet and tread on them as the little children do, then will you see the Son of the Living-One, and you will not be afraid.

38. Jesus said: Many times have you yearned to hear these

sayings which I speak to you, and you have no one else from whom to hear them. There will be days when you will seek me but you will not find me.

39. Jesus said: The Pharisees and the Scribes have received the keys of knowledge, but they have hidden them. They did not go in, nor did they permit those who wished to enter to do so. However, you be as wise (astute) as serpents and innocent as doves.

39. Jesus said: The Pharisees and the Scribes have stolen the keys of heaven, but they have hidden them. They have entered in, but they did not permit those who wished to enter to do so. However, you be as wise as serpents and innocent as doves.

Luke 11:52 Woe to you lawyers! For you have taken away the key of knowledge; you did not enter yourselves, and you hindered those who were entering.

Matthew 10:16 See, I am sending you out like sheep into the midst of wolves; so be wise as serpents and innocent as doves.

Matthew 23.13 But woe unto you, scribes and Pharisees, hypocrites! because you shut the kingdom of heaven against men; for you neither enter yourselves, nor allow those who would enter to go in.

40. Jesus said: A grapevine has been planted outside the (vineyard of the) Father, and since it is not viable (supported) it will be pulled up by its roots and destroyed.

Matthew 15:13 He answered, Every plant that my heavenly Father has not planted will be uprooted.

41. Jesus said: Whoever has (it) in his hand, to him will (more) be given. And whoever does not have, from him will be taken even the small amount which he has.

Matthew 25:29 For to all those who have, more will be given, and they will have an abundance; but from those who have nothing, even what they have will be taken away.

Luke 19:26 I tell you, that to every one who has will more be given; but from him who has not, even what he has will be taken away.

42. Jesus said: Become passers-by.

43. His Disciples said to him: Who are you, that you said these things to us?

Jesus said to them: You do not recognize who I am from what

I said to you, but rather you have become like the Jews who either love the tree and hate its fruit, or love the fruit and hate the tree.

John 8:25 They said to him, Who are you? Jesus said to them, Why do I speak to you at all?

Matthew 7:16-20 You will know them by their fruits. Are grapes gathered from thorns, or figs from thistles? In the same way, every good tree bears good fruit, but the bad tree bears bad fruit. A good tree cannot bear bad fruit, nor can a bad tree bear good fruit. Every tree that does not bear good fruit is cut down and thrown into the fire. Thus you will know them by their fruits.

44. Jesus said: Whoever blasphemes against the Father, it will be forgiven him. And whoever blasphemes against the Son, it will be forgiven him. Yet whoever blasphemes against the Holy Spirit, it will not be forgiven him neither on earth nor in heaven.

Mark 3:28-29 Truly I tell you, people will be forgiven for their sins and whatever blasphemies they utter; but whoever blasphemes against the Holy Spirit can never have forgiveness, but is guilty of an eternal sin.

Matthew 12:31-32 Therefore I tell you, every sin and blasphemy will be forgiven men, but the blasphemy against the Spirit will not be forgiven. And whoever says a word against the Son of man will be forgiven; but whoever speaks against the Holy Spirit will not be forgiven, either in this age or in the age to come.

Luke 12:10 And every one who speaks a word against the Son of man will be forgiven him; but he who blasphemes against the Holy Spirit will not be forgiven.

45. Jesus said: Grapes are not harvested from thorns, nor are figs gathered from thistles, for they do not give fruit. A good person brings forth goodness out of his storehouse. A bad person brings forth evil out of his evil storehouse which is in his heart, and he speaks evil, for out of the abundance of the heart he brings forth evil.

Luke 6:43-45 For no good tree bears bad fruit, nor again does a bad tree bear good fruit; for each tree is known by its own fruit. For figs are not gathered from thorns, nor are grapes picked from a bramble bush. The good man out of the good treasure of his heart produces good, and the evil man out of his evil treasure produces evil; for out of the abundance of the heart his mouth speaks.

46. Jesus said: From Adam until John the Baptist there is

none born of women who surpasses John the Baptist, so that his eyes should not be downcast (lowered). Yet I have said that whoever among you becomes like a child will know the Kingdom, and he will be greater than John.

Matthew 11:11 Truly I tell you, among those born of women no one has arisen greater than John the Baptist; yet the least in the kingdom of heaven is greater than he.

Luke 7:28 I tell you, among those born of women none is greater than John; yet he who is least in the kingdom of God is greater than he.

Matthew 18:2-4 He called a child, whom he put among them, and said, Truly I tell you, unless you change and become like children, you will never enter the kingdom of heaven. Whoever becomes humble like this child is the greatest in the kingdom of heaven.

47. Jesus said: It is impossible for a man to mount two horses or to draw two bows, and a servant cannot serve two masters, otherwise he will honor the one and disrespect the other. No man drinks vintage wine and immediately desires to drink new wine, and they do not put new wine into old wineskins or they would burst, and they do not put vintage wine into new wineskins or it would spoil (sour). They do not sew an old patch on a new garment because that would cause a split.

Joseph B. Lumpkin

Matthew 6:24 No one can serve two masters; for a slave will either hate the one and love the other, or be devoted to the one and despise the other. You cannot serve God and wealth.

Matthew 9:16-17 No one sews a piece of cloth, not yet shrunk, on an old cloak, for the patch pulls away from the cloak, and a worse tear is made. Neither is new wine put into old wineskins; otherwise, the skins burst, and the wine is spilled, and the skins are destroyed; but new wine is put into fresh wineskins, and so both are preserved.

Mark 2:21-22 No one sews a piece of unshrunk cloth on an old garment; if he does, the patch tears away from it, the new from the old, and a worse tear is made. And no one puts new wine into old wineskins; if he does, the wine will burst the skins, and the wine is lost, and so are the skins; but new wine is for fresh skins.

Luke 5:36-39 He told them a parable also: No one tears a piece from a new garment and puts it upon an old garment; if he does, he will tear the new, and the piece from the new will not match the old. And no one puts new wine into old wineskins; if he does, the new wine will burst the skins and it will be spilled, and the skins will be destroyed. But new wine must be put into fresh wineskins. And no one after drinking old wine desires new; for he says, "The old is good."

48. Jesus said: If two make peace with each other in this one house, they will say to the mountain: Be moved! and it will be moved.

Matthew 18:19 Again, truly I tell you, if two of you agree on earth about anything you ask, it will be done for you by my Father in heaven.

Mark 11:23-24 Truly I tell you, if you say to this mountain, Be taken up and thrown into the sea, and if you do not doubt in your heart, but believe that what you say will come to pass, it will be done for you. So I tell you, whatever you ask for in prayer, believe that you have received it, and it will be yours.

Matthew 17:20 He said to them, Because of your little faith. For truly, I say to you, if you have faith as a grain of mustard seed, you will say to this mountain, Move from here to there, and it will move; and nothing will be impossible to you.

49. Jesus said: Blessed is the solitary and chosen, for you will find the Kingdom. You have come from it, and unto it you will return.

Matthew 5:1-3 And seeing the multitudes, he went up into a mountain: and when he was set, his disciples came unto him: And he opened his mouth, and taught them, saying, Blessed are the poor in spirit: for theirs is the kingdom of heaven.

John 20:28-30 And Thomas answered and said unto him, My LORD and my God. Jesus saith unto him, Thomas, because thou hast seen me, thou hast believed: blessed are they that have not seen, and yet have believed. And many other signs truly did Jesus in the presence of his disciples, which are not written in this book:

50. Jesus said: If they say to you: From where do you come? Say to them: We have come from the Light, the place where the Light came into existence of its own accord and he stood and appeared in their image. If they say to you: Is it you? (Who are you?), say: We are his Sons and we are the chosen of the Living Father. If they ask you: What is the sign of your Father in you? Say to them: It is movement with rest (peace in the midst of motion or chaos).

51. His Disciples said to him: When will the rest of the dead occur, and when will the New World come? He said to them: That which you look for has already come, but you do not recognize it.

52. His Disciples said to him: Twenty-four prophets preached in Israel, and they all spoke of you (in your spirit). He said to

them: You have ignored the Living-One who is in your presence and you have spoken only of the dead.

53. His Disciples said to him: Is circumcision beneficial or not? He said to them: If it were beneficial, their father would beget them already circumcised from their mother. However, the true spiritual circumcision has become entirely beneficial.

Jeremiah 4:3-5 For thus saith the LORD to the men of Judah and Jerusalem, Break up your fallow ground, and sow not among thorns. Circumcise yourselves to the LORD, and take away the foreskins of your heart, you men of Judah and inhabitants of Jerusalem: lest my fury come forth like fire, and burn that none can quench it, because of the evil of your doings. Declare you in Judah, and publish in Jerusalem; and say, Blow you the trumpet in the land: cry, gather together, and say, Assemble yourselves, and let us go into the defenced cities.

54. Jesus said: Blessed be the poor, for yours is the Kingdom of the Heaven.

Matthew 6:20 Then he looked up at his disciples and said: Blessed are you who are poor, for yours is the kingdom of God.

Luke 6:20 And he lifted up his eyes on his disciples, and said: Blessed are you poor, for yours is the kingdom of God.

Matthew 5:3 Blessed are the poor in spirit, for theirs is the kingdom of heaven.

55. Jesus said: Whoever does not hate his father and his mother will not be able to become my Disciple. And whoever does not hate his brothers and his sisters and does not take up his own cross in my way, will not become worthy of me.

Luke 14:26-27 If any one comes to me and does not hate his own father and mother and wife and children and brothers and sisters, yes, and even his own life, he cannot be my disciple. Whoever does not bear his own cross and come after me, cannot be my disciple.

John 17:11-21 And now I am no more in the world, but these are in the world, and I come to you. Holy Father, keep through thine own name those whom thou hast given me, that they may be one, as we are. While I was with them in the world, I kept them in your name: those that thou gavest me I have kept, and none of them is lost, but the son of perdition; that the scripture might be fulfilled. And now come I to you; and these things I speak in the world, that they might have my joy fulfilled in themselves. I have given them your word; and the world hath hated them, because they are not of the world, even as I am not of the world. I pray not that thou shouldest take them out of the world, but that thou shouldest keep them from the evil. They are not of the world, even as I am not of the world. Sanctify them through your truth: your word is truth. As thou hast sent me into the world, even so have I also sent them into the world. And for their sakes I sanctify myself, that they also might be sanctified through the truth. Neither pray I for these alone, but for them also which shall believe on me through their word; That they all may be one; as thou, Father, art in me, and I in you, that they also may be one in us: that the world may believe that thou hast sent me.

56. Jesus said: Whoever has come to understand the world (system) has found a corpse, and whoever has found a corpse, is superior to the world (of him the system is not worthy).

Hebrews 11:37-40 They were stoned, they were sawn asunder, were tempted, were slain with the sword: they wandered about in sheepskins and goatskins; being destitute, afflicted, tormented; (Of whom the world was not worthy:) they wandered in deserts, and in mountains, and in dens and caves of the earth. And these all, having obtained a good report through faith, received not the promise: God having provided some better thing for us, that they without us should not be made perfect.

57. Jesus said: The Kingdom of the Father is like a person who has good seed. His enemy came by night and sowed a weed among the good seed. The man did not permit them to pull up the weed, he said to them: perhaps you will intend to

pull up the weed and you pull up the wheat along with it. But, on the day of harvest the weeds will be very visible and then they will pull them and burn them.

Matthew 13:24-30 He put before them another parable: The kingdom of heaven may be compared to someone who sowed good seed in his field; but while everybody was asleep, an enemy came and sowed weeds among the wheat, and then went away. So when the plants came up and bore grain, then the weeds appeared as well. And the slaves of the householder came and said to him, Master, did you not sow good seed in your field? Where, then, did these weeds come from? He answered, An enemy has done this. The slaves said to him, Then do you want us to go and gather them? But he replied, No; for in gathering the weeds you would uproot the wheat along with them. Let both of them grow together until the harvest; and at harvest time I will tell the reapers, Collect the weeds first and bind them in bundles to be burned, but gather the wheat into my barn.

58. Jesus said: Blessed is the person who has suffered, for he has found life. (Blessed is he who has suffered to find life and found life).

Matthew 11:28 Come to me, all you that are weary and are carrying heavy burdens, and I will give you rest.

59. Jesus said: Look to the Living-One while you are alive, otherwise, you might die and seek to see him and will be unable to find him.

John 7:34 You will search for me, but you will not find me; and where I am, you cannot come.

John 13:33 Little children, I am with you only a little longer. You will look for me; and as I said to the Jews so now I say to you, Where I am going, you cannot come.

60. They saw a Samaritan carrying a lamb, on his way to Judea. Jesus said to them: Why does he take the lamb with him? They said to him: So that he may kill it and eat it. He said to them: While it is alive he will not eat it, but only after he kills it and it becomes a corpse. They said: How could he do otherwise? He said to them: Look for a place of rest for yourselves, otherwise, you might become corpses and be eaten.

61. Jesus said: Two will rest on a bed and one will die and the other will live. Salome said: Who are you, man? As if sent by someone, you laid upon my bed and you ate from my table. Jesus said to her: I-Am he who is from that which is whole (the undivided). I have been given the things of my Father. Salome said: I'm your Disciple. Jesus said to her:

Joseph B. Lumpkin

Thus, I say that whenever someone is one (undivided) he will be filled with light, yet whenever he is divided (chooses) he will be filled with darkness.

Luke 17:34 I tell you, on that night there will be two in one bed; one will be taken and the other left.

62. Jesus said: I tell my mysteries to those who are worthy of my mysteries. Do not let your right hand know what your left hand is doing.

Mark 4:11 And he said to them, To you has been given the secret of the kingdom of God, but for those outside, everything comes in parables.

Matthew 6:3 But when you give alms, do not let your left hand know what your right hand is doing.

Luke 8:10 He said, To you it has been given to know the secrets of the kingdom of God; but for others they are in parables, so that seeing they may not see, and hearing they may not understand.

Matthew 13:10-11 Then the disciples came and said to him, Why do you speak to them in parables? And he answered them, To you it has been given to know the secrets of the kingdom of heaven, but to them it has not been given.

63. Jesus said: There was a wealyour person who had much money, and he said: I will use my money so that I may sow and reap and replant, to fill my storehouses with grain so that I lack nothing. This was his intention (is what he thought in his heart) but that same night he died. Whoever has ears, let him hear!

Luke 12:21 Then he told them a parable: The land of a rich man produced abundantly. And he thought to himself, What should I do, for I have no place to store my crops? Then he said, I will do this: I will pull down my barns and build larger ones, and there I will store all my grain and my goods. And I will say to my soul, Soul, you have ample goods laid up for many years; relax, eat, drink, be merry. But God said to him, You fool! This very night your life is being demanded of you. And the things you have prepared, whose will they be? So it is with those who store up treasures for themselves but are not rich toward God.

64. Jesus said: A person had houseguests, and when he had prepared the banquet in their honor he sent his servant to invite the guests. He went to the first, he said to him: My master invites you. He replied: I have to do business with some merchants. They are coming to see me this evening. I will go to place my orders with them. I ask to be excused from the banquet. He went to another, he said to him: My master has invited you. He replied to him: I have just bought a house and they require me for a day. I will have no spare time. He came to another, he said to him: My master invites you. He replied to him: My friend is getting married and I must arrange a banquet for him. I will not be able to come. I ask to be excused from the banquet. He went to another, he said to him: My master invites you. He replied to him: I have bought a farm. I go to receive the rent. I will not be able to come. I ask to be excused. The servant returned, he said to his master: Those whom you have invited to the banquet have excused themselves. The master said to his servant: Go out to the roads, bring those whom you find so that they may feast. And he said: Businessmen and merchants will not enter the places of my Father.

Luke 14:16-24 *Then Jesus said to him:, Someone gave a great dinner and invited many. At the time for the dinner he sent his slave to say to those who had been invited, Come; for everything is ready now. But they all alike began to make excuses. The first said to him, I have bought a piece of land, and I must go out and see it; please accept my regrets. Another said, I have bought five yoke of oxen, and I am going to try them out; please accept my regrets. Another said, I have just been married, and therefore I cannot come. So the slave returned and reported this to his master. Then the owner of the house became angry and said to his slave, Go out at once into the streets and lanes of the town and bring in the poor, the crippled, the blind, and the lame. And the slave said, Sir, what you ordered has been done, and there is still room. Then the master said to the slave, Go out into the roads and lanes, and compel people to come in, so that my house may be filled. For I tell you, none of those who were invited will taste my dinner.*

Matthew 19:23 Then Jesus said to his disciples, Truly I tell you, it will be hard for a rich person to enter the kingdom of heaven.

Matthew 22:1-14 And Jesus answered and spake unto them again by parables, and said, The kingdom of heaven is like unto a certain king, which made a marriage for his son, and sent his servants to call those who were invited to the marriage feast; but they would not come. Again he sent other servants, saying, Tell those who are invited, Behold, I have made ready my dinner, my oxen and my fat calves are killed, and everything is ready; come to the marriage feast. But they made light of it and went off, one to his farm, another to his business, while the rest seized his servants, treated them shamefully, and killed them. The king was angry, and he sent his troops and destroyed those murderers and burned their city. Then he said to his servants, The wedding is ready, but those invited were not worthy. Go therefore to the thoroughfares, and invite to the marriage feast as many as you find. And those servants went out into the streets and gathered all whom they found, both bad and good; so the wedding hall was filled

Joseph B. Lumpkin

with guests. But when the king came in to look at the guests, he saw there a man who had no wedding garment; and he said to him, Friend, how did you get in here without a wedding garment? And he was speechless. Then the king said to the attendants, Bind him hand and foot, and cast him into the outer darkness; there men will weep and gnash their teeth. For many are called, but few are chosen.

65. He said: A kind person who owned a vineyard leased it to tenants so that they would work it and he would receive the fruit from them. He sent his servant so that the tenants would give to him the fruit of the vineyard. They seized his servant and beat him nearly to death. The servant went, he told his master what had happened. His master said: Perhaps they did not recognize him. So, he sent another servant. The tenants beat him also. Then the owner sent his son. He said: Perhaps they will respect my son. Since the tenants knew that he was the heir to the vineyard, they seized him and killed him. Whoever has ears, let him hear!

Matthew 21:33-39 Listen to another parable. There was a landowner who planted a vineyard, put a fence around it, dug a wine press in it, and built a watchtower. Then he leased it to tenants and went to another country. When the harvest time had come, he sent his slaves to the tenants to collect his produce. But the tenants seized his slaves and beat one, killed another, and stoned another. Again he sent other slaves, more than the first; and they treated them in the same way. Finally he sent his son to them, saying, They will respect my son. But when the tenants saw the son, they said to themselves, This is the heir; come, let us kill him and get his inheritance. So they seized him, threw him out of the vineyard, and killed him.*

Mark 12:1-9 And he began to speak to them in parables. A man planted a vineyard, and set a hedge around it, and dug a pit for the wine press, and built a tower, and let it out to tenants, and went into another country. When the time came, he sent a servant to the tenants, to get from them some of the fruit of the vineyard. And they took him and beat him, and sent him away empty-handed. Again he sent to them another servant, and they wounded him in the head, and treated him shamefully. And he sent another, and him they killed; and so with many others, some they beat and some they killed. He had still one other, a beloved son; finally he sent him to them, saying, They will respect my son. But those tenants said to one another, This is the heir; come, let us kill him, and the inheritance will be ours. And they took him and killed him, and cast him out of the vineyard. What will the owner of the vineyard do? He will come and destroy the tenants, and give the vineyard to others.

Luke 20:9-16 And he began to tell the people this parable: A man planted a vineyard, and let it out to tenants, and went into another country for a long while. When the time came, he sent a servant to the tenants, that they should give him some of the fruit of the vineyard; but the tenants beat him, and sent him away empty-handed. And he sent another servant; him also they beat and treated shamefully, and sent him away empty-handed. And he sent yet a third; this one they wounded and cast out. Then the owner of the vineyard said, What shall I do? I will send my beloved son; it may be they will respect him. But when the tenants saw him, they said to themselves, This is the heir; let us kill him, that the inheritance may be ours. And they cast him out of the vineyard and killed him. What then will the owner of the vineyard do to them? He will come and destroy those tenants, and give the vineyard to others. When they heard this, they said, God forbid!

66. Jesus said: Show me the stone which the builders have rejected. It is that one that is the cornerstone (keystone).

Matthew 21:42 Jesus said to them, Have you never read in the scriptures: The very stone which the builders rejected has become the head of the corner; this was the Lord's doing, and it is marvelous in our eyes?

Mark 12:10-11 Have you not read this scripture: The very stone which the builders rejected has become the head of the corner; this was the Lord's doing, and it is marvelous in our eyes?

Luke 20:17 But he looked at them and said, What then does this text mean: The stone that the builders rejected has become the cornerstone?

67. Jesus said: Those who know everything but themselves, lack everything. (whoever knows the all and still feels a personal lacking, he is completely deficient).

Jeremiah 17:5- 10 Thus saith the LORD; Cursed be the man that trusteth in man, and maketh flesh his arm, and whose heart departeth from the LORD. For he shall be like the heath in the desert, and shall not see when good cometh; but shall inhabit the parched places in the wilderness, in a salt land and not inhabited. Blessed is the man that trusteth in the LORD, and whose hope the LORD is. For he shall be as a tree planted by the waters, and that spreadeth out her roots by the river, and shall not see when heat cometh, but her leaf shall be green; and shall not be careful in the year of drought, neither shall cease from yielding fruit. The heart is deceitful above all things, and desperately wicked: who can know it? I the LORD search the heart, I try the reins, even to give every man according to his ways, and according to the fruit of his doings.

68. Jesus said: Blessed are you when you are hated and persecuted, but they themselves will find no reason why you

have been persecuted.

Matthew 5:11 Blessed are you when people revile you and persecute you and utter all kinds of evil against you falsely on my account.

Luke 6:22 Blessed are you when men hate you, and when they exclude you and revile you, and cast out your name as evil, on account of the Son of man!

69. Jesus said: Blessed are those who have been persecuted in their heart; these are they who have come to know the Father in truth. Jesus said: Blessed are the hungry, for the stomach of him who desires to be filled will be filled.

Matthew 5:8 Blessed are the pure in heart, for they will see God.

Luke 6:21 Blessed are you who are hungry now, for you will be filled.

70. Jesus said: If you bring forth what is within you, it will save you. If you do not have it within you to bring forth, that which you lack will destroy you.

71. Jesus said: I will destroy this house, and no one will be able to build it again.

Mark 14:58 We heard him say, I will destroy this temple that is made with hands, and in three days I will build another, not made with hands.

72. A person said to him: Tell my brothers to divide the possessions of my father with me. He said to him: Oh man, who made me a divider? He turned to his Disciples, he said to them: I'm not a divider, am I?

Luke 12:13-15 Someone in the crowd said to him, Teacher, tell my brother to divide the family inheritance with me. But he said to him, Friend, who set me to be a judge or arbitrator over you? And he said to them, Take care! Be on your guard against all kinds of greed; for one's life does not consist in the abundance of possessions.

73. Jesus said: The harvest is indeed plentiful, but the workers are few. Ask the Lord to send workers for the harvest.

Matthew 9:37-38 Then he said to his disciples, The harvest is plentiful, but the laborers are few; therefore ask the Lord of the harvest to send out laborers into his harvest.

74. He said: Lord, there are many around the well, yet there is nothing in the well. How is it that many are around the well and no one goes into it?

75. Jesus said: There are many standing at the door, but only those who are alone are the ones who will enter into the Bridal Chamber.

Matthew 25:1-8   Then shall the kingdom of heaven be likened unto ten virgins, which took their lamps, and went forth to meet the bridegroom. And five of them were wise, and five were foolish. They that were foolish took their lamps, and took no oil with them: But the wise took oil in their vessels with their lamps. While the bridegroom tarried, they all slumbered and slept. And at midnight there was a cry made, Behold, the bridegroom cometh; go you out to meet him. Then all those virgins arose, and trimmed their lamps. And the foolish said unto the wise, Give us of your oil; for our lamps are gone out.

76. Jesus said: The Kingdom of the Father is like a rich merchant who found a pearl. The merchant was prudent. He sold his fortune and bought the one pearl for himself. You also, seek for his treasure which does not fail, which endures where no moth can come near to eat it nor worm to devour it.

Matthew 13:45-46 Again, the kingdom of heaven is like a merchant in search of fine pearls; on finding one pearl of great value, he went and sold all that he had and bought it.

Matthew 6:19-20 Do not store up for yourselves treasures on earth, where moth and rust consume and where thieves break in and steal; but store up for yourselves treasures in heaven, where neither moth nor rust consumes and where thieves do not break in and steal.

77. Jesus said: I-Am the Light who is over all things, I-Am the All. From me all came forth and to me all return (The All came from me and the All has come to me). Split wood, there am I. Lift up the stone and there you will find me.

Author's Note:
Many scholars believe the order of verses 30 and 77 were misplaced and these two verses should be connected as one verse.

30. Jesus said: Where there are three gods, they are gods (Where there are three gods they are without god). Where there is only one, I say that I am with him. Lift the stone and there you will find me, Split the wood and there am I.

John 8:12 Again Jesus spoke to them, saying, I am the light of the world. Whoever follows me will never walk in darkness but will have the light of life.

John 1:3 All things came into being through him, and without him not one thing came into being.

78. Jesus said: Why did you come out to the wilderness; to see a reed shaken by the wind? And to see a person dressed in fine (soft – plush) garments like your rulers and your dignitaries? They are clothed in plush garments, and they are not able to recognize (understand) the truth.

Matthew 11:7-9 As they went away, Jesus began to speak to the crowds about John: What did you go out into the wilderness to look at? A reed shaken by the wind? What then did you go out to see? Someone dressed in soft robes? Look, those who wear soft robes are in royal palaces. What then did you go out to see? A prophet? Yes, I tell you, and more than a prophet.

79. A woman from the multitude said to him: Blessed is the womb which bore you, and the breasts which nursed you! He said to her: Blessed are those who have heard the word (meaning) of the Father and have truly kept it. For there will be days when you will say: Blessed be the womb which has

not conceived and the breasts which have not nursed.

Luke 11:27-28 While he was saying this, a woman in the crowd raised her voice and said to him, Blessed is the womb that bore you and the breasts that nursed you! But he said, Blessed rather are those who hear the word of God and obey it!

Luke 23:29 For the days are surely coming when they will say, Blessed are the barren, and the wombs that never bore, and the breasts that never nursed.

80. Jesus said: Whoever has come to understand (recognize) the world (world system) has found the body (corpse), and whoever has found the body (corpse), of him the world (world system) is not worthy.

Hebrews 11:37-40 They were stoned, they were sawn asunder, were tempted, were slain with the sword: they wandered about in sheepskins and goatskins; being destitute, afflicted, tormented; (Of whom the world was not worthy:) they wandered in deserts, and in mountains, and in dens and caves of the earth. And these all, having obtained a good report through faith, received not the promise: God having provided some better thing for us, that they without us should not be made perfect.

81. Jesus said: Whoever has become rich should reign, and let whoever has power renounce it.

82. Jesus said: Whoever is close to me is close to the fire, and whoever is far from me is far from the Kingdom.

John 14:6-9 Jesus saith unto him, I am the way, the truth, and the life: no man cometh unto the Father, but by me. If you had known me, you should have known my Father also: and from henceforth you know him, and have seen him. Philip saith unto him, Lord, show us the Father, and it sufficeth us. Jesus saith unto him, Have I been so long time with you, and yet hast thou not known me, Philip? he that hath seen me hath seen the Father;

83. Jesus said: Images are visible to man but the light which is within them is hidden. The light of the father will be revealed, but he (his image) is hidden in the light.

84. Jesus said: When you see your reflection, you rejoice. Yet when you perceive your images which have come into being before you, which neither die nor can be seen, how much will you have to bear?

85. Jesus said: Adam came into existence from a great power and a great wealth, and yet he was not worthy of you. For if he had been worthy, he would not have tasted death.

86. Jesus said: The foxes have their dens and the birds have their nests, yet the Son of Man has no place to lay his head for rest.

Matthew 8:20 And Jesus said to him, Foxes have holes, and birds of the air have nests; but the Son of Man has nowhere to lay his head.

87. Jesus said: Wretched is the body which depends upon another body, and wretched is the soul which depends on these two (upon their being together).

88. Jesus said: The angels and the prophets will come to you, and what they will give you belongs to you. And you will give them what you have, and say among yourselves: When will they come to take (receive) what belongs to them?

89. Jesus said: Why do you wash the outside of your cup? Do you not understand (mind) that He who creates the inside is also He who creates the outside?

Luke 11:39-40 Then the Lord said to him, Now you Pharisees clean the outside of the cup and of the dish, but inside you are full of greed and wickedness. You fools! Did not the one who made the outside make the inside also?

90. Jesus said: Come unto me, for my yoke is comfortable (natural) and my lordship is gentle — and you will find rest for yourselves.

Matthew 11:28-30 Come to me, all you that are weary and are carrying heavy burdens, and I will give you rest. Take my yoke upon you, and learn from me; for I am gentle and humble in heart, and you will find rest for your souls. For my yoke is easy, and my burden is light.

Acts 15:5-17 But there rose up certain of the sect of the Pharisees which believed, saying, that it was needful to circumcise them, and to command them to keep the law of Moses. And the apostles and elders came together for to consider of this matter. And when there had been much disputing, Peter rose up, and said unto them, Men and brethren, you know how that a good while ago God made choice among us, that the Gentiles by my mouth should hear the word of the gospel, and believe. And God, which knoweth the hearts, bare them witness, giving them the Holy Ghost, even as he did unto us. And put no difference between us and them, purifying their hearts by faith. Now therefore why tempt you God, to put a yoke upon the neck of the disciples, which neither our fathers nor we were able to bear? But we believe that through the grace of the LORD Jesus Christ we shall be saved, even as they. Then all the multitude kept silence, and gave audience to Barnabas and Paul, declaring what miracles and wonders God had wrought among the Gentiles by them. And after they had held their peace, James answered, saying, Men and brethren, hearken unto me: Simeon hath declared how God at the first did visit the Gentiles, to take out of them a people for his name. And to this agree the words of the prophets; as it is written, After this I will return, and will build again the tabernacle of David, which is fallen down; and I will build again the ruins thereof, and I will set it up: That the residue of men might seek after the Lord, and all the Gentiles, upon whom my name is called, saith the Lord, who doeth all these things.

91. They said to him: Tell us who you are, so that we may believe in you. He said to them: You examine the face of the sky and of the earth, yet you do not recognize Him who is here with you, and you do not know how to seek in (to inquire of Him at) this moment (you do not know how to take advantage of this opportunity).

John 9:36 He answered, And who is he, sir? Tell me, so that I may believe in him.

Luke 12:54-56 He also said to the crowds, When you see a cloud rising in the west, you immediately say, It is going to rain; and so it happens. And when you see the south wind blowing, you say, There will be scorching heat; and it happens. You hypocrites! You know how to interpret the appearance of earth and sky, but why do you not know how to interpret the present time?

92. Jesus said: Seek and you will find. But in the past I did not answer the questions you asked. Now I wish to tell them to you, but you do not ask about (no longer seek) them.

Matthew 7:7 Ask, and it will be given you; search, and you will find; knock, and the door will be opened for you.

93. Jesus said: Do not give what is sacred to the dogs, lest they throw it on the dung heap. Do not cast the pearls to the swine, lest they cause it to become dung (mud).

Matthew 7:6 Do not give what is holy to dogs; and do not throw your pearls before swine, or they will trample them under foot and turn and maul you.

94. Jesus said: Whoever seeks will find. And whoever knocks, it will be opened to him.

Matthew 7:8 For everyone who asks receives, and everyone who searches finds, and for everyone who knocks, the door will be opened.

95. Jesus said: If you have money, do not lend at interest, but rather give it to those from whom you will not be repaid.

Luke 6:34-35 If you lend to those from whom you hope to receive, what credit is that to you? Even sinners lend to sinners, to receive as much again. But love your enemies, do good, and lend, expecting nothing in return. Your reward will be great, and you will be children of the Most High; for he is kind to the ungrateful and the wicked.

96. Jesus said: The Kingdom of the Father is like a woman who has taken a little yeast and hidden it in dough. She produced large loaves of it. Whoever has ears, let him hear!

Matthew 13:33 He told them another parable: The kingdom of heaven is like yeast that a woman took and mixed in with three measures of flour until all of it was leavened.

97. Jesus said: The Kingdom of the Father is like a woman who was carrying a jar full of grain. While she was walking on a road far from home, the handle of the jar broke and the grain poured out behind her onto the road. She did not know it. She had noticed no problem. When she arrived in her house, she set the jar down and found it empty.

98. Jesus said: The Kingdom of the Father is like someone who wished to slay a prominent person. While still in his own house he drew his sword and throughst it into the wall

Joseph B. Lumpkin

in order to test whether his hand would be strong enough. Then he slew the prominent person.

99. His Disciples said to him: Your brethren and your mother are standing outside. He said to them: Those here who do my Father's desires are my Brethren and my Mother. It is they who will enter the Kingdom of my Father.

Matthew 12:46-50 While he was still speaking to the crowds, his mother and his brothers were standing outside, wanting to speak to him. Someone told him, Look, your mother and your brothers are standing outside, wanting to speak to you. But to the one who had told him this, Jesus replied, Who is my mother, and who are my brothers? And pointing to his disciples, he said, Here are my mother and my brothers! For whoever does the will of my Father in heaven is my brother and sister and mother.

100. They showed Jesus a gold coin, and said to him: The agents of Caesar extort taxes from us. He said to them: Give the things of Caesar to Caesar, give the things of God to God, and give to me what is mine.

Mark 12:14-17 Is it lawful to pay taxes to the emperor, or not? Should we pay them, or should we not? But knowing their hypocrisy, he said to them, Why are you putting me to the test? Bring me a denarius and let me see it. And they brought one. Then he said to them, Whose head is this, and whose title? They answered, The emperor's. Jesus said to them, Give to the emperor the things that are the emperor's, and to God the things that are God's. And they were utterly amazed at him.

101. Jesus said: Whoever does not hate his father and his mother, as I do, will not be able to become my Disciple. And whoever does not love his father and his mother, as I do, will not be able to become my disciple. For my mother bore me, yet my true Mother gave me the life.

Matthew 10:37 Whoever loves father or mother more than me is not worthy of me; and whoever loves son or daughter more than me is not worthy of me.

102. Jesus said: Damn these Pharisees. They are like a dog sleeping in the feed trough of oxen. For neither does he eat, nor does he allow the oxen to eat.

Matthew 2:13 But woe unto you, scribes and Pharisees, hypocrites! because you shut the kingdom of heaven against men; for you neither enter yourselves, nor allow those who would enter to go in.

103. Jesus said: Blessed (happy) is the person who knows at what place of the house the bandits may break in, so that he

can rise and collect his things and prepare himself before they enter.

Matthew 24:43 But understand this: if the owner of the house had known in what part of the night the thief was coming, he would have stayed awake and would not have let his house be broken into.

104. They said to him: Come, let us pray today and let us fast. Jesus said: What sin have I committed? How have I been overcome (undone)? When the Bridegroom comes forth from the bridal chamber, then let them fast and let them pray.

105. Jesus said: Whoever acknowledges (comes to know) father and mother, will be called the son of a whore.

106. Jesus said: When you make the two one, you will become Sons of Man (children of Adam), and when you say to the mountain: Move! It will move.

Mark 11:23 Truly I tell you, if you say to this mountain, Be taken up and thrown into the sea, and if you do not doubt in your heart, but believe that what you say will come to pass, it will be done for you.

107. Jesus said: The Kingdom is like a shepherd who has a hundred sheep. The largest one of them went astray. He left the ninety-nine and sought for the one until he found it. Having searched until he was weary, he said to that sheep: I desire you more than the ninety-nine.

Matthew 18:12-13 What do you think? If a shepherd has a hundred sheep, and one of them has gone astray, does he not leave the ninety-nine on the mountains and go in search of the one that went astray? And if he finds it, truly I tell you, he rejoices over it more than over the ninety-nine that never went astray.

108. Jesus said: Whoever drinks from my mouth will become like me. I will become him, and the secrets will be revealed to him.

109. Jesus said: The Kingdom is like a person who had a treasure hidden in his field and knew nothing of it. After he died, he bequeathed it to his son. The son accepted the field knowing nothing of the treasure. He sold it. Then the person who bought it came and plowed it. He found the treasure. He began to lend money at interest to whomever he wished.

Matthew 13:44 The kingdom of heaven is like treasure hidden in a field, which someone found and hid; then in his joy he goes and sells all that he has and buys that field.

110. Jesus said: Whoever has found the world (system) and

becomes wealyour (enriched by it), let him renounce the world (system).

Mark 10:21-23 Then Jesus beholding him loved him, and said unto him, One thing thou lackest: go your way, sell whatsoever thou hast, and give to the poor, and thou shall have treasure in heaven: and come, take up the cross, and follow me. And he was sad at that saying, and went away grieved: for he had great possessions. And Jesus looked round about, and saith unto his disciples, How hardly shall they that have riches enter into the kingdom of God!

111. Jesus said: Heaven and earth will roll up (collapse and disappear) before you, but he who lives within the Living-One will neither see nor fear death. For, Jesus said: Whoever finds himself, of him the world is not worthy.

112. Jesus said: Damned is the flesh which depends upon the soul. Damned is the soul which depends upon the flesh.

113. His Disciples said to him: When will the Kingdom come? Jesus said: It will not come by expectation (because you watch or wait for it). They will not say: Look here! or: Look there! But the Kingdom of the Father is spread upon the earth, and people do not realize it.

Luke 17:20 And when he was demanded of by the Pharisees, when the kingdom of God should come, he answered them and said, The kingdom of God cometh not with observation: Neither shall they say, Lo-Here! Lo-There! For, behold, the kingdom of God is within you.

(Saying 114 was written later and was added to the original text.)

114. Simon Peter said to them: Send Mary away from us, for women are not worthy of this life. Jesus said: See, I will draw her into me so that I make her male, in order that she herself will become a living spirit like you males. For every female who becomes male will enter the Kingdom of the Heaven.

The Question of Judas

No discovery since the Dead Sea Scrolls has rocked the Christian world like that of the newly translated "Gospel of Judas." The story presented in the short but powerful text reveals a plan in which heavenly ends justified monstrous means. Betrayal became collaboration and murder resembled suicide as Jesus and Judas began a macabre dance into eternity.

Orthodox Christianity has its doctrine, its canon, and its political story, but these are quite different from those exposed in the Gospel of Judas.

As the orthodox political viewpoint would have it, Jesus' demise was sought by the Roman authorities as he gained a following and was declared "King" by the Jewish populace. The Jewish religious leaders were also planning his death, believing that Jesus was attempting to reform Judaism, and wrest their control over the people.

The Gospel of Judas calls into question this accepted view of the political intrigue leading up to Jesus' betrayal and death.

Spokesman for the Maecenas Foundation, one of the companies in Basel, Switzerland working on the Judas project, Director Mario Jean Roberty, reports:

"We have just received the results of carbon dating: the text is older than we thought and dates back to a period between the beginning of the third and fourth centuries. We do not want to reveal the exceptional side of what we have, except that the Judas Iscariot text called into question some of the political principles of Christian doctrine."

Imagine Judas, the man all of Christendom has hated for two thousand years, now portrayed as the chosen one, the martyr, the scapegoat, and the man instructed and appointed by Jesus himself to orchestrate and carry out the greatest treachery of all time. But treachery ordered by the one betrayed is not treachery at all, but a loyal and devoted follower carrying out the wishes of his master.

What was Judas' reward for betraying Jesus? According to the Gospel of Judas it was special recognition by God and the blessing of Jesus, the savior of mankind. Strangely, there is evidence in our own Bible to substantiate this claim. Judas may have been promised a position of authority along with the other apostles.

The Gospel of Judas turns us on our heads and forces upon the reader a new and uncomfortable view. Did Judas have special knowledge and instruction from Jesus? Are we to thank him for the death of Jesus? Is lethal treachery appointed by the victim suicide or murder? Is this murderous quisling really a saint?

Who is this man, Judas? What do we know about him? Where did he come from? What did he want? What did he do?

These are just a few of the questions left to reverberate in the mind of the reader.

Theories of Judas abound. He is presented as greedy and selfish as well as sanctified spirit. Some say he was possessed, some say he was a saint, and some believe him to be Satan himself.

Was Judas the impetus of death, burial, and resurrection for Jesus, and thus the daemon who saved us? Will Judas be the Antichrist we will meet in the end of days or will he be ruling and judging the tribes of Israel?

Every story has two sides. Let us examine both sides, beginning with The Gospel of Judas, its history, its theology, and its text.

Understanding the Intent

The Gospel of Judas can be understood on a deeper level if its background is explored first.

One may ask the proper questions regarding the text of "who, what, when, where, and why." The question of "who" wrote the Gospel of Judas we might never know. What the author was trying to say will be explored in depth. Science can and has narrowed down the "when" and "where."

Why mankind writes is axiomatic. We write to document, explain, express, or convince. In the end, those are the reasons. Time will tell if the author of Judas has succeeded.

In a time when Gnosticism was struggling for influence in Christendom, the Gospel of Judas was written to challenge the beliefs of the newly emerging church orthodoxy, to explain Gnostic theology, and to propagate the sect. To better understand the gospel, it must be read with these goals in mind.

For centuries the definition of Gnosticism has in itself been a point of confusion and contention within the religious community. This is due in part to the ever-broadening application of the term and the fact that various sects of Gnosticism existed as the theology evolved and began to merge into what became mainstream Christianity.

Even though Gnosticism continued to evolve, it is the theology in place at the time that the Gospel of Judas was written that should be considered and understood before attempting to render or read a translation. To do otherwise would make the translation cloudy and obtuse.

It becomes the duty of both translator and reader to understand the ideas being espoused and the terms conveying those ideas. A grasp of theology, cosmology, and relevant terms is necessary for a clear transmission of the meaning within the text in question.

With this in mind, we will briefly examine Gnostic theology, cosmology, and history. We will focus primarily on Gnostic sects existing in the first through fourth centuries A.D. since it is believed most Gnostic Gospels were written during that time. It was also during that time that reactions within the emerging Christian orthodoxy began to intensify and the Gospel of Judas was written.

The downfall of many books written on the topic of religion is the attempt to somehow remove history and people from the equation. History shapes religion because it shapes the perception and direction of religious leaders. Religion also develops and evolves in an attempt to make sense of the universe as it is seen and understood at the time. Thus, to truly grasp a religious concept it is important to know the history, people, and cosmology of the time. These areas are not separate but are continually interacting.

What is the Gospel of Judas?

What is the Gospel of Judas and why does it differ so greatly from the gospel stories of the Bible?

The Gospel of Judas is considered a Gnostic text. The Gnostics were a sect of Christianity and like any sect or religion, they were fighting to expand and continue under the persecution of the newly emerging orthodoxy of the day.

The Gospel of Judas may have been written to help bolster and continue Gnosticism. This may explain its radical departure from the traditional Gospel story, as well as the reason for its creation.

Indeed, one way of looking at any religious book, canon or not, is as an attempt to explain one's beliefs, to persuade others toward those beliefs, and to interpret history and known storylines in the light of one's own theology and cosmology. This is done not only to add weight to one's own belief system but also simply because man sees events as having relevance to what he or she holds as truth.

As previously stated, the Gospel of Judas is, above all things, a Gnostic gospel since it revolves around a special knowledge or Gnosis given to Judas by Jesus. This knowledge represented that which Gnostics held as the universal truth. But what is Gnosticism?

The roots of the Gnosticism may pre-date Christianity. Similarities exist between Gnosticism and the wisdom and mystery cults found in Egypt and Greece. Gnosticism contains the basic terms and motifs of Plato's cosmology as well as the mystical qualities of Pythagorean cosmology and Buddhism. All of this was mixed with the Christianity of the second and third centuries to form the Gnosticism that is offered in the Gospel of Judas.

Plato was steeped in Greek mythology, and the Gnostic creation myth has elements owing to this. Both cosmology and mysticism within Gnosticism present an interpretation of Christ's existence and teachings, thus, Gnostics are considered to be a Christian sect.

Gnostic followers are urged to look within themselves for the truth and the Christ spirit hidden, asleep in their souls. The battle cry can be summed up in the words of the Gnostic Gospel of Thomas, verse 3:

> *Jesus said: If those who lead you say to you: Look, the Kingdom is in the sky, then the birds of the sky would enter before you. If they say to you: It is in the sea, then the fish of the sea would enter ahead of you. But the Kingdom of God exists within you and it exists outside of you. Those who come to know (recognize) themselves will find it, and when you come to know yourselves you will become known and you will realize that you are the*

children of the Living Father. Yet if you do not come to know yourselves then you will dwell in poverty and it will be you who are that poverty.

Paganism was a religious, traditional society in the Mediterranean leading up to the time of the Gnostics. Centuries after the conversion of Constantine, mystery cults worshipping various Egyptian and Greco-Roman gods continued. These cults taught that through their secret knowledge worshippers could control or escape the mortal realm. The Gnostic doctrine of inner knowledge and freedom may have part of its roots here. The concept of duality and inner guidance taught in Buddhism added to and enforced Gnostic beliefs, as we will see later.

The belief systems of Plato, Buddha, and paganism melded together, spread, and found a suitable home in the mystical side of the Christian faith as it sought to adapt and adopt certain Judeo-Christian beliefs and symbols.

Like modern Christianity, Gnosticism had various points of view that could be likened to Christian denominations of today. Complex and elaborate creation myths took root in Gnosticism, being derived from those of Plato. Later, the theology evolved and Gnosticism began to shed some of its more unorthodox myths, leaving the central theme of inner knowledge or "gnosis" as the path to enlightenment and salvation. In Gnosticism it is knowledge that saves one from hell fire. This knowledge and its place in man's salvation was their message to propagate. Exactly what the knowledge was and how is was expressed seemed to vary between Gnostic sects.

The existence of various sects of Gnosticism, differing creation stories, along with the lack of historical documentation, has left scholars in a quandary about exactly what Gnostics believed.

Although it appears that there were several sects of Gnosticism, we will attempt to discuss the more universal Gnostic beliefs along with the highlights of the major sects.

Gnostic cosmology, (which is the theory of how the universe is created, constructed, and sustained), is complex and very different from orthodox Christianity cosmology. In many ways Gnosticism may appear to be polytheistic or even pantheistic.

To understand some of the basic beliefs of Gnosticism, let us start with the common ground shared between Gnosticism and modern Christianity. Both believe the world is imperfect, corrupt, and brutal. The blame for this, according to mainstream Christianity, is placed squarely on the shoulders of man himself. With the fall of man (Adam), the world was forever changed to the undesirable and harmful place in which we live today. However, Gnostics reject this view as an incorrect interpretation of the creation myth.

According to Gnostics, the blame is not in us, but in our creator. The creator of this world was himself somewhat less than perfect and in fact, deeply flawed and cruel, making mankind the children of a lesser God. It is in the book, *The Apocryphon of John* that the Gnostic view of creation is presented to us in great detail.

Gnosticism also teaches that in the beginning a Supreme Being called The Father, The Divine All, The Origin, The Supreme God, or The Fullness, emanated the element of existence, both visible and invisible. His intent was not to create but, just as light emanates from a flame, so did creation shine forth from God. This manifested the primal element needed for creation. This was the creation of Barbelo, who is the Thought of God.

The Father's thought performed a deed and she was created from it. It is she who had appeared before him in the shining of his light. This is the first power which was before all of them and which was created from his mind. She is the Thought of the All and her light shines like his light. It is the perfect power which is the visage of the invisible. She is the pure, undefiled Spirit who is perfect. She is the first power, the glory of Barbelo, the perfect glory of the kingdom (kingdoms), the glory revealed. She glorified the pure, undefiled Spirit and it was she who praised him, because thanks to him she had come forth.

The Apocryphon of John

It could be said that Barbelo was the creative emanation and, like the Divine All, is both male and female. It was the "agreement" of Barbelo and the Divine All, representing the union of male and female, that created the Christ Spirit and all the Aeons. In some renderings the word "Aeon" is used to designate an ethereal realm or kingdom. In other versions "Aeon" indicates the ruler of the realm. The Aeons of this world are merely reflections of the Aeons of the eternal realm. The reflection is always inferior to real. This idea is of Aeons above and below, the real and reflected, the superior and inferior is brought up in the Gospel of Judas. Barbelo is mentioned by name in Judas. Another of these rulers was called Sophia or Wisdom. Her fall began a chain of events that led to the introduction of evil into the universe.

Seeing the Divine flame of God, Sophia sought to know its origin. She sought to know the very nature of God. Sophia's passion ended in tragedy when she managed to capture a divine and creative spark, which she attempted to duplicate with her own creative force, without the union of a male counterpart. It was this act that produced the Archons, beings born outside the higher divine realm. In the development of the myth, explanations seem to point to the fact that Sophia carried the divine essence of creation from God within her but chose to attempt creation by using her own powers. It is unclear if this was in an attempt to understand the Supreme God and his power, or an impetuous act that caused evil to enter the cosmos in the form of her creations.

The realm containing the Fullness of the Godhead and Sophia is called the pleroma or Realm of Fullness. This is the Gnostic heaven. The lesser Gods created in Sophia's failed attempt were cast outside the pleroma and away from the presence of God. In essence, she threw away and discarded her flawed creations.

"She cast it away from her, outside the place where no one of the immortals might see it, for she had created it in ignorance. And she surrounded it with a glowing cloud, and she put a throne in the middle of the cloud so that no one could see it except the Holy Spirit who is called the mother of all that has life. And she called his name Yaldaboth."   *Apocryphon of John*

The beings Sophia created were imperfect and oblivious to the Supreme God. Her creations contained deities even less perfect than herself. They were called the Powers, the Rulers, or the Archons. Their leader was called the Demiurge, but his name was Yaldaboth, also spelled "Yaldabaoth." It was the flawed, imperfect, spiritually blind Demiurge, (Yaldaboth), who became the creator of the material world and all things in it. Gnostics considered Yaldaboth to be the same as Jehovah (Yahweh), who is the Jewish creator God. These beings, the Demiurge and the Archons, would later equate to Satan and his demons, or Jehovah and his angels, depending on which Gnostic sect is telling the story. Both are equally evil.

In one Gnostic creation story, the Archons created Adam but could not bring him to life. In other stories Adam was formed as a type of worm, unable to attain personhood. Thus, man began as an incomplete creation of a flawed, spiritually blind, and malevolent god. In this myth, the Archons were afraid that Adam might be more powerful than the Archons themselves. When they saw Adam was incapable of attaining the human state, their fears were put to rest, thus, they called that day the "Day of Rest."

Sophia saw Adam's horrid state and had compassion, because she knew she was the origin of the Archons and their evil. Sophia descended to help bring Adam out of his hopeless condition. It is this story that set the stage for the emergence of the sacred feminine force in Gnosticism that is not seen in orthodox Christianity. Sophia brought within herself the light and power of the Supreme God. Metaphorically, within the spiritual womb of Sophia was carried the life force of the Supreme God for Adam's salvation.

In the Gnostic text, *The Apocryphon of John*, Sophia is quoted:

"I entered into the midst of the cage which is the prison of the body. And I spoke saying: 'He who hears, let him awake from his deep sleep.' Then Adam wept and shed tears. After he wiped away his bitter tears he asked: 'Who calls my name, and from where has this hope arose in me even while I am in the chains of this prison?' And I (Sophia) answered: 'I am the one who carries the pure light; I am the thought of the undefiled spirit. Arise, remember, and follow your origin, which is I, and beware of the deep sleep.'"

Sophia would later equate to the Holy Spirit as it awakened the comatose soul.

As the myth evolved, Sophia, after animating Adam, became Eve in order to assist Adam in finding the truth. She offered it to him in the form of the fruit of the tree of knowledge. To Gnostics, this was an act of deliverance.

Other stories have Sophia becoming the serpent in order to offer Adam a way to attain the truth. In either case, the apple represented the hard sought truth, which was the knowledge of good and evil, and through that knowledge Adam could become a god. Later, the serpent would become a feminine symbol of wisdom, probably owing to the connection with Sophia. Eve, being Sophia in disguise, would become the mother and sacred feminine of us all. As Gnostic theology began to coalesce, Sophia would come to be considered a force or conduit of the Holy Spirit, in part due to the fact that the Holy Spirit was also considered a feminine and creative force from the Supreme God. The Gospel of Philip echoes this theology in verse six as follows:

> *In the days when we were Hebrews we were made orphans, having only our Mother. Yet when we believed in the Messiah (and became the ones of Christ), the Mother and Father both came to us.*   *Gospel of Philip*

As the emerging orthodox church became more and more oppressive to women, later even labeling them "occasions of sin," the Gnostics countered by raising women to equal status with men, saying Sophia was, in a sense, the handmaiden or wife of the Supreme God, making the soul of Adam her spiritual offspring. But, the placement and purpose of Sophia, Barbelo, Yaldaboth, and other deities vary somewhat from one type of Gnosticism to another.

In several Gnostic cosmologies the "living" world is under the control of entities called Aeons, of which Sophia is head. This means the Aeons influence or control the soul, life force, intelligence, thought, and mind. Control of the mechanical or inorganic world is given to the Archons. They rule the physical aspects of systems, regulation, limits, and order in the world. Both the ineptitude and cruelty of the Archons are reflected in the chaos and pain of the material realm.

The lesser God that created the world, Yaldaboth began his existence in a state that was both detached and remote from the Supreme God in aspects both spiritual and physical. Since Sophia had misused her creative force, which passed from the Supreme God (some say, through Barbelo) to her, Sophia's creation, the Demiurge, or Yaldaboth, contained only part of the original creative spark of the Supreme Being. He was created with an imperfect nature caused by his distance in lineage and in spirit from the Divine All or Supreme God. It is because of his imperfections and limited abilities the lesser God is also called the "Half-Maker."

The Creator God, the Demiurge, and his helpers, the Archons took the stuff of existence produced by the Supreme God and fashioned it into this material world.

Since the Demiurge (Yaldaboth) had no memory of how he came to be alive, he did not realize he was not the true creator. The Demiurge believed he somehow came to create the material world by himself. The Supreme God allowed the Demiurge and Archons to remain deceived.

The Creator God (the Demiurge) intended the material world to be perfect and eternal, but he did not have it in himself to accomplish the feat. What comes forth from a being cannot be greater than the highest part of him, can it? The world was created flawed and transitory and we are part of it. Can we escape? The Demiurge was imperfect and evil. So was the world he created. If it was the Demiurge who created man and man is called upon to escape the Demiurge and find union with the Supreme God, is this not demanding that man becomes greater than his creator? Spiritually this seems impossible, but as many children become greater than their parents, man is expected to become greater than his maker, the Demiurge. This starts with the one fact that the Demiurge denies the existence and supremacy of the Supreme God, but through gnosis man rises above this blindness.

Man was created with a dual nature as the product of the material world of the Demiurge with his imperfect essence, combined with the spark of God that emanated from the Supreme God through Sophia. A version of the creation story has Sophia instructing the Demiurge to breathe into Adam that spiritual power he had taken from Sophia during his creation. It was the spiritual power from Sophia that brought life to Adam.

It is this divine spark in man that calls to its source, the Supreme God, and which causes a "divine discontent," that nagging feeling that keeps us questioning if this is all there is. This spark and the feeling it gives us keeps us searching for the truth.

The Creator God sought to keep man ignorant of his defective state by keeping him enslaved to the material world. By doing so, he continued to receive man's worship and servitude. He did not wish man to recognize or gain knowledge of the true Supreme God. Since he did not know or acknowledge the Supreme God, he views any attempt to worship anything else as spiritual treason.

The opposition of forces set forth in the spiritual battle over the continued enslavement of man and man's spiritual freedom set up the duality of good and evil in Gnostic theology. There was a glaring difference between the orthodox Christian viewpoint and the Gnostic viewpoint. According to Gnostics, the creator of the material world was an evil entity and the Supreme God, who was his source, was the good entity. Christians quote John 1:1 "In the beginning was the Word, and the Word was with God, and the Word was God."

According to Gnostics, only through the realization of man's true state or through death can he escape captivity in the material realm. This means the idea of salvation does not deal with original sin or blood payment. Instead, it focuses on the idea of awakening to the fullness of the truth.

According to Gnostic theology, neither Jesus nor his death can save anyone, but the truth that he came to proclaim can allow a person to save his or her own soul. It is the truth, or realization of the lie of the material world and its God, that sets one on a course of freedom. It cannot be overstated that in the eyes of many Gnostics, the death of Jesus was part of a plan implemented to show men in metaphorical terms the lack of worth and permanence of the physical world as opposed to the spiritual. The physical death of Jesus could not save us in the way orthodox Christianity came to understand it. His death was not a sacrifice to pay for our sins, but instead it was more of a lesson by example of the fight and plight of the temporal world which was at war with the eternal world.

To escape the earthly prison and find one's way back to the pleroma (heaven) and the Supreme God, is the soteriology (salvation doctrine) and eschatology (judgment, reward, and doctrine of heaven) of Gnosticism.

The idea that personal revelation leads to salvation may be what caused the mainline Christian church to declare Gnosticism a heresy. The church could better tolerate alternative theological views if the views did not undermine the authority of the church and its ability to control the people. Gnostic theology placed salvation in the hands of the individual through personal revelations and knowledge, excluding the need for the orthodox church and its clergy to grant salvation or absolution. This fact, along with the divergent interpretation of the creation story, which placed the creator God, Yaldaboth or Jehovah, as the enemy of mankind, was too much for the church to tolerate. Reaction was harsh. Gnosticism was declared to be a dangerous heresy.

Gnosticism may be considered polytheistic because it espoused many "levels" of Gods, beginning with an ultimate, unknowable, Supreme God and descending as he created Sophia, and Sophia created the Demiurge (Creator God); each becoming more inferior and limited.

There is a hint of pantheism in Gnostic theology due to the fact that creation occurs because of a deterioration of the Godhead and the dispersion of the creative essence, which eventually devolves into the creation of man.

In the end, there occurs a universal reconciliation as being after being realizes the existence of the Supreme God and renounces the material world and its inferior creator.

Combined with its Christian influences, the cosmology of the Gnostics may have borrowed from the Greek philosopher, Plato, as well as from Pythagoras and even Buddhism. There are disturbing parallels between the creation myth set forth by Plato and some of those recorded in Gnostic writings.

Pythagoras was born on the island of Samos between 580 and 570 B.C. His father is thought to have been a gem-engraver, and it is likely that the son would have been trained in that same craft.

Some scholars report that he was the first man to call himself and philosopher, or "lover of wisdom." Indeed, many of the accomplishments of such great men as Plato, Aristotle, and even Copernicus were based on the work of Pythagoras.

Pythagoras believed in Orphism, which is a theology that taught the soul and body are united but unequal. The soul is divine, immortal, and eternal. Its original state was one of freedom, before being imprisoned in a body. The body holds it imprisoned but death frees the soul, although only for a while. The soul is destined to be imprisoned again and again as the cycle of birth and death revolves until the end of time.

The soul journeys through its existence alternating from freedom to capture through reincarnations, as it learns lessons through many bodies of men and animals. The earliest Greek we can connect to Orphism is the sixth century thinker, Pherecydes. Pythagoras was his pupil and the individual most responsible for spreading Orphism throughout Greece.

Pythagoras further developed his beliefs while visiting Egypt, Greece, and Tyre in Lebanon. During his visit to Tyre he was initiated for the first time into the 'Ancient Mysteries' of the Phoenicians and studied for about 3 years in the temples of Tyre, Sidon, and Byblos.

It was after years of study that Pythagoras founded the famous Pythagorean School of philosophy, mathematics, and natural sciences. There he taught a simple lifestyle was best. Modesty, austerity, patience, and self-control were stressed. They consumed vegetarian, dried and condensed food, and unleavened bread. They did not cut their hair, beard, and nails.

The Pythagoreans believed that the universe could be understood in terms of whole numbers. This belief stemmed from observations in music, mathematics, and astronomy. He once commented, "Number is the ruler of form and the ideas and cause of gods and demons." We will see that symbolism of number plays a large part in The Gospel of Judas.

The Pythagoreans taught the doctrine of transmigration of souls, which states that after death, a man's soul enters the body of a newborn infant or animal and so lives another life. The soul wanders from the home of the blessed, being born into all kinds of corporeal forms as it travels from one path of life to another.

One of his students wrote, "I am also one of these, an

exile and a wanderer from the Gods. Ere now, I too have been a boy, a girl, a bush, a bird, and a scaly fish in the sea." - Empedocles

Their cosmology conceived of a universe made of numbers. There were four major numbers and meanings making up all we see: one for a point, two for a line, three for a surface, and four for a solid. One was the basis, and generated the series of even and odd numbers, and with them the whole universe. Moral qualities were numbers: 4 (2x2 and 2+2) was justice, equal shares all round. A special number was 10, built up of 1+2+3+4, and containing the point, line, plane, and solid. This sequence was known as the *tetractys. Followers swore* an oath not to reveal the mysteries of the society 'by Him who reveals Himself to our minds in the Tetractys, which contains the source and roots of everlasting nature'.

Pythagoras had also discovered the mathematical basis of music, and the fact that the relation halves can express an octave. A string stopped at half its length will vibrate to give the sound of the octave above the full length. So music was involved in all life; and even the planets circling in their courses sounded the music of the spheres.

Plato lived from 427 to 347 B.C. He was the son of wealyour Athenians and a student of the philosopher, Socrates, and the mathematician, Pythagoras. Plato himself was the teacher of Aristotle.

In Plato's cosmology, the Demiurge was an artist who imposed form on materials that already existed. The raw materials were in a chaotic and random state. The physical world must have had visible form which was put together in a fashion much like a puzzle is constructed. This later gave way to a philosophy which stated that all things in existence could be broken down into a small subset of geometric shapes.

In the tradition of Greek mythology, Plato's cosmology began with a creation story. The story was narrated by the philosopher Timaeus of Locris, a fictional character of Plato's making. In his account, nature is initiated by a creator deity, called the "Demiurge," a name which may be the Geek word for "craftsman" or "artisan" or, according to how one divides the word, it could also be translated as "half-maker."

The Demiurge sought to create the cosmos modeled on his understanding of the supreme and original truth. In this way he created the visible universe based on invisible truths. He set in place rules of process such as birth, growth, change, death, and dissolution. This was Plato's "Realm of Becoming." It was his Genesis. Plato stated that the internal structure of the cosmos had innate intelligence and was therefore called the World Soul. The cosmic super-structure of the Demiurge was used as the framework on which to hang or fill in the details and parts of the universe. The Demiurge then appointed his underlings to fill in the details, which allowed the universe to remain in a working and balanced state. All phenomena of nature resulted from an interaction and interplay of the two forces of reason and necessity.

Plato represented reason as constituting the World Soul. The material world was a necessity in which reason acted out its will in the physical realm. The duality between the will, mind, or reason of the World Soul and the material universe and its inherent flaws set in play the duality of Plato's world and is seen reflected in the beliefs of the Gnostics.

In Plato's world, the human soul was immortal, each soul was assigned to a star. Souls that were just or good were permitted to return to their stars upon their death to rest and dwell there in peace. Unjust souls were reincarnated to try again. Escape of the soul to the freedom of the stars and out of the cycle of reincarnation was best accomplished by following the reason and goodness of the World Soul and not the physical world, which was set in place only as a necessity to manifest the patterns of the World Soul.

Although in Plato's cosmology the Demiurge was not seen as evil, in Gnostic cosmology he was considered not only to be flawed and evil, but he was also the beginning of all evil in the material universe, having created it to reflect his own malice.

Following the path of Pythagoras and Plato's cosmology, some Gnostics left open the possibility of reincarnation if the person had not reached the truth before his death. This idea of the transmigration of the soul may have been linked to influences from the East.

In the year 13 A.D. Roman annals record the visit of an Indian king named Pandya or Porus. He came to see Caesar Augustus carrying a letter of introduction in Greek. He was accompanied by a monk who burned himself alive in the city of Athens to prove his faith in Buddhism. The event was described by Nicolaus of Damascus as, not surprisingly, causing a great stir among the people. It is thought that this was the first transmission of Buddhist teaching to the masses.

In the second century A.D., Clement of Alexandria wrote about Buddha: "Among the Indians are those philosophers also who follow the precepts of Boutta (Buddha), whom they honour as a god on account of his extraordinary sanctity." (Clement of Alexandria, "The Stromata, or Miscellanies" Book I, Chapter XV).

"Thus philosophy, a thing of the highest utility, flourished in antiquity among the barbarians, shedding its light over the nations. And afterwards it came to Greece." Clement of Alexandria, *"The Stromata, or Miscellanies"*.

To clarify what "philosophy" was transmitted from India to Greece, we turn to the historians Hippolytus and Epiphanius who wrote of Scythianus, a man who had visited India around 50 A.D. They report; "He brought 'the doctrine of the Two Principles.'" According to these writers, Scythianus' pupil Terebinthus called himself a Buddha. Some scholars suggest it was he that traveled to the area of Babylon and transmitted his knowledge to Mani, who later founded Manichaeism.

Adding to the possibility of Eastern influence, we have accounts of the Apostle Thomas' attempt to convert the people of Asia-Minor. If the Gnostic gospel bearing his name was truly written by Thomas, it was penned after his return from India, where he also encountered the Buddhist influences.

Following the transmission of the philosophy of "Two Principals," both Manichaeism and Gnosticism retained a dualistic viewpoint. The black-versus-white dualism of Gnosticism came to rest in the evil of the material world and its maker, versus the goodness of the freed soul and the Supreme God with whom it seeks union.

Oddly, the disdain for the material world and its Creator God drove Gnostic theology to far-flung extremes in attitude, beliefs, and actions. Gnostics idolized the serpent in the "Garden of Eden" story. After all, if your salvation hinges on secret knowledge, the offer of becoming gods through the knowledge of good and evil sounds wonderful. So powerful was the draw of this "knowledge myth" to the Gnostics that the serpent became linked to Sophia by some sects. This can still be seen today in our medical and veterinarian symbols of serpents on poles, conveying the ancient meanings of knowledge and wisdom.

Genesis 3 (King James Version)

1 Now the serpent was more subtil than any beast of the field which the LORD God had made. And he said unto the woman, Yea, hath God said, You shall not eat of every tree of the garden?

2 And the woman said unto the serpent, We may eat of the fruit of the trees of the garden:

3 But of the fruit of the tree which is in the midst of the garden, God hath said, You shall not eat of it, neither shall you touch it, lest you die.

4 And the serpent said unto the woman, You shall not surely die:

5 For God doth know that in the day you eat thereof, then your eyes shall be opened, and you shall be as Gods, knowing good and evil.

It is because of their vehement struggle against the Creator God and the search for some transcendent truth, that Gnostics held the people of Sodom in high regard. The people of Sodom sought to "corrupt" the messengers sent by their enemy, the Creator God. Anything done to thwart the Demiurge and his minions was considered valiant.

Genesis 19 (King James Version)

1 And there came two angels to Sodom at even; and Lot sat in the gate of Sodom: and Lot seeing them rose up to meet them; and he bowed himself with his face toward the ground;

2 And he said, Behold now, my lords, turn in, I pray you, into your servant's house, and tarry all night, and wash your feet, and you shall rise up early, and go on your ways. And they said, Nay; but we will abide in the street all night.

3 And he pressed upon them greatly; and they turned in unto him, and entered into his house; and he made them a feast, and did bake unleavened bread, and they did eat.

4 But before they lay down, the men of the city, even the men of Sodom, compassed the house round, both old and young, all the people from every quarter:

5 And they called unto Lot, and said unto him, Where are the men which came in to you this night? bring them out unto us, that we may know them.

6 And Lot went out at the door unto them, and shut the door after him,

7 And said, I pray you, brethren, do not so wickedly.

8 Behold now, I have two daughters which have not known man; let me, I pray you, bring them out unto you, and do you to them as is good in your eyes: only unto these men do nothing; for therefore came they under the shadow of my roof.

9 And they said, Stand back. And they said again, This one fellow came in to sojourn, and he will needs be a judge: now will we deal worse with you, than with them. And they pressed sore upon the man, even Lot, and came near to break the door.

10 But the men put forth their hand, and pulled Lot into the house to them, and shut to the door.

To modern Christians, the idea of admiring the serpent, which we believe was Satan, may seem unthinkable. Supporting the idea of attacking and molesting the angels sent to Sodom to warn of the coming destruction seems appalling; but to Gnostics the real evil was the malevolent entity, the Creator God of this world. To destroy his messengers, as was the case in Sodom, would impede his mission. To obtain knowledge of good and evil, as was offered by the serpent in the garden, would set the captives free.

The battle and highest call of Gnosticism was to awaken the inner knowledge of the true God. This is the God who is above and beyond that lower and evil god that created the material world. The material world was designed to prevent the awakening by entrapping, confusing, and distracting the spirit of man. The aim of Gnosticism was the spiritual awakening and freedom of man.

Gnostics, in the age of the early church, would preach to converts (novices) about this awakening, saying the novice must awaken the God within himself and see the trap that was the material world. Salvation came from the recognition or knowledge contained in this spiritual awakening. Moreover, it was the knowledge that the "illusion" of the material world existed and should be transcended that was the driving force and saving gnosis (knowledge) that Gnosticism was built upon.

Not all people were ready or willing to accept the Gnosis. Many were bound to the material world and satisfied to be only as and where they were. These have mistaken the Creator God for the Supreme God and do not know there is anything beyond the Creator God or the material existence. These people knew only the lower or earthly wisdom and not the higher wisdom above the Creator God. They were referred to as "dead."

Gnostic sects split primarily into two categories. Both branches held that those who were truly enlightened could no longer be influenced by the material world. Both divisions of Gnosticism believed that their spiritual journey could not be impeded by the material realm since the two were not only separate but in opposition. Such an attitude influenced some Gnostics toward Stoicism, choosing to abstain from the world, and others toward Epicureanism, choosing to indulge and satiate any and all appetites, since they believed the material world could not influence the spiritual world.

Major schools fell into two categories; those who rejected the material world of the Creator God, and those who rejected the laws of the Creator God. For those who rejected the world the Creator God had spawned, overcoming the material world was accomplished by partaking of as little of the world and its pleasures as possible. These followers lived very stark and ascetic lives, abstaining from meat, sex, marriage, and all things that would entice them to remain (or even wish to remain) in the material realm.

Other schools believed it was their duty to simply defy the Creator God and all laws that he had proclaimed. Since the Creator God had been identified as Jehovah, God of the Jews, these followers set about to break every law held dear by Christians and Jews.

As human nature is predisposed to do, many Gnostics took up the more wanton practices, believing that nothing done in their earthly bodies would affect their spiritual lives. Whether it was excesses in sex, alcohol, food, or any other assorted debaucheries, the Gnostics were safe within their faith, believing nothing spiritually bad could come of their earthly adventures.

Early Church leaders mention the actions of the Gnostics. One infamous Gnostic school is actually mentioned in the Bible, as we will read later.

The world was out of balance, inferior, and corrupt. The spirit was perfect and intact. It was up to the Gnostics to tell the story, explain the error, and awaken the world to the light of truth. The Supreme God had provided a vehicle to help in their effort. He had created a teacher of light and truth.

Since the time of Sophia's mistaken creation of the Archons, there was an imbalance in the cosmos. The Supreme God began to re-establish the balance by producing Christ to teach and save man. That left only Sophia, now in a fallen and bound state, along with the Demiurge, and the Archons to upset the cosmic equation. In this theology one might loosely equate the Supreme God to the New Testament Christian God, the Demiurge to Satan, the Archons to demons, the pleroma to heaven, and Sophia to the creative or regenerative force of the Holy Spirit.

This theory holds up well except for one huge problem. If the Jews believed that Jehovah created all things, and the Gnostic believed that the Demiurge created all things, then to the Gnostic mind, the Demiurge must be Old Testament god, Jehovah, and that made Jehovah their enemy. In this twist, the Old Testament God was the evil creator. The New Testament God was the true Supreme God, and Satan was a good and wise deity or savior, since he had offered a way of escape from the creator god when Satan offered the fruit of the tree of knowledge (or the Gnosis) to Eve.

For those who sought that which was beyond the material world and its flawed creator, the Supreme God sent Messengers of Light to awaken the divine spark of the Supreme God within us. This part of us will call to the True God as deep calls to deep. The greatest and most perfect Messenger of Light was the Christ. He is also referred to as The Good, Christ, Messiah, and The Word. He came to reveal the Divine Light to mankind in the form of knowledge.

According to the Gnostics, Christ came to show us our own divine spark and to awaken us to the illusion of the material world and its flawed maker. He came to show us the way back to the divine Fullness (The Supreme God). The path to enlightenment was the knowledge sleeping within each of us. Christ came to show us the Christ spirit living in each of us.

Individual ignorance or the refusal to awaken our internal divine spark was the only original sin. Christ was the only Word spoken by God that could awaken us. Christ was also the embodiment of the Word itself. He was part of the original transmission from the Supreme God that took form on the earth to awaken the soul of man so that man might search beyond the material world.

One Gnostic view of the Incarnation was "docetic," which is an early heretical position that Jesus was never actually present in the flesh, but only appeared to be human. He was a spiritual being and his human appearance was only an illusion. Of course, the title of "heretical" can only be decided by the controlling authority of the time. In this case it was the church that was about to emerge under the rule of the Emperor Constantine.

Most Gnostics held that the Christ spirit indwelt the earthly man, Jesus, at the time of his baptism by John, at which time Jesus received the name, and thus the power, of the Lord or Supreme God.

The Christ spirit departed from Jesus' body before his death. These two viewpoints remove the idea of God sacrificing himself as an atonement for the sins of man. The idea of atonement was not necessary in Gnostic theology since it was knowledge and not sacrifice that set one free.

Since there was a distinction in Gnosticism between the man Jesus and the Light of Christ that came to reside within him, it is not contrary to Gnostic beliefs that Mary Magdalene could have been the consort and wife of Jesus. Neither would it have been blasphemous for them to have had children.

Various sects of Gnosticism stressed certain elements of their basic theology. Each had its head teachers and its special flavor of beliefs. One of the oldest types was the Syrian Gnosticism. It existed around 120 A.D. In contrast to other sects, the Syrian lacked much of the embellished mythology of Aeons, Archons, and angels.

The fight between the Supreme God and the Creator God was not eternal, though there was strong opposition to Jehovah, the Creator God. He was considered to have been the last of the seven angels who created this world out of divine material which emanated from the Supreme God. The Demiurge attempted to create man, but only created a miserable worm which the Supreme God had to save by giving it the spark of divine life. Thus man was born.

According to this sect, Jehovah, the Creator God, must not be worshiped. The Supreme God calls man to his service and presence through Christ his Son. They pursued only the unknowable Supreme God and sought to obey the Supreme Deity by abstaining from eating meat and from marriage and sex, and by leading ascetic lives. The symbol of Christ was the serpent, who attempted to free Adam and Eve from their ignorance and entrapment to the Creator God.

Another Gnostic school was the Hellenistic or Alexandrian School. These systems absorbed the philosophy and concepts of the Greeks, and the Semitic nomenclature was replaced by Greek names. The cosmology and myth had grown out of proportion and appear to our eyes to be unwieldy. Yet, this school produced two great thinkers, Basilides and Valentinus. Though born at Antioch, in Syria, Basilides founded his school in Alexandria around the year A.D. 130, where it survived for several centuries.

Valentinus first taught at Alexandria and then in Rome. He established the largest Gnostic movement around A.D. 160. This movement was founded on an elaborate mythology and a system of sexual duality of male and female interplay, both in its deities and its savior.

Tertullian wrote that between 135 A.D. and 160 A.D. Valentinus, a prominent Gnostic, had great influence in the Christian church. Valentinus ascended in church hierarchy and became a candidate for the office of bishop of Rome, the office that quickly evolved into that of Pope. He lost the election by a narrow margin. Even though Valentinus was outspoken about his Gnostic slant on Christianity, he was a respected member of the Christian community until his death and was probably a practicing bishop in a church of lesser status than the one in Rome.

The main platform of Gnosticism was the ability to transcend the material world through the possession of privileged and directly imparted knowledge. Following this doctrine, Valentinus claimed to have been instructed by a direct disciple of one of Jesus' apostles, a man by the name of Theodas.

Valentinus is considered by many to be the father of modern Gnosticism. His vision of the faith is summarized by G.R.S. Mead in the book "Fragments of a Faith Forgotten."

"The Gnosis in his hands is trying to embrace everything, even the most dogmatic formulation of the traditions of the Rabbi. The great popular movement and its incomprehensibilities were recognized by Valentinus as an integral part of the mighty outpouring; he laboured to weave all together, external and internal, into one piece, devoted his life to the task, and doubtless only at his death perceived that for that age he was attempting the impossible. None but the very few could ever appreciate the ideal of the man, much less understand it."

Fragments of a Faith Forgotten

The main stream of Gnosticism presented in the Gospel of Judas seems to be Sethian Gnosticism. Marvin Meyer, a respected scholar, describes Gospel of Judas as a Sethian Gnostic because it mentions the incorruptible generation of Seth and it shares common ideas with other Sethian Gnostic writings found in the Nag Hammadi. The generation of Seth in Gnostic writings signified those born of the new generation of humanity after the tragic death of Abel and the banishment of Cain.

For Sethian Gnostics, Jesus was a teacher, "not a savior who dies for the sins of the world. For Gnostics, the fundamental problem in human life is not sin, but ignorance, and the best way to address this problem is not through faith, but through knowledge" (Meyer, Introduction to the Gospel of Judas [Washington, DC: National Geographic Society, 2006].

In the time period of the Gospel of Judas at about 180 A.D., Sethian Gnosticism had evolved by absorbing several basic doctrines: Hellenistic-Jewish mythology of Sophia, the divine wisdom; the midrashic interpretation of Genesis 1-6; a particular doctrine of baptism; the developing Christology of the early church; a religiously oriented view of Pythagorean metaphysics; and the teaching and philosophy of Plato including his theology and mythos regarding creation, Sophia, Barbelo, and the Creator God, Yalabaoth.

Sethian doctrines have baptism as a spiritualized ritual. In Sethian baptismal water was understood to be "Living Water" identified with light or enlightenment and therefore salvation.

The history claimed by Sethian Gnosticism is derived from a peculiar exegesis of Genesis from a Jewish stand point. It should be stressed that the Sethian origins are not Christian but it absorbed Christian beliefs later. In their beginning they were looking for a messiah just as the Jews were, however, they believed he would be Seth. This is because they believed the imparted divine knowledge came down from God to Adam and was then transmitted to Seth.

Sethians adopted the rite of baptism often referred to as the Five-Seals. The ritual symbolized the removal of the person from the material world of the flesh and the ascension into the realm of light through the invocation of certain divine beings.

Sethianism began to change by its involvement in Christianity. This took place over time.

Sethianism was a non-Christian baptismal sect of the first centuries B.C.E. and C.E. which believed in enlightenment through knowledge by the divine wisdom which was that same wisdom that was revealed to Adam and Seth. It may be assumed that this was an incomplete passing of knowledge because the culmination was expected in a final visitation of Seth marked by his conferral of a saving baptism.

Baptism represented the descent of Seth as the living word or "Logos", which was bestowed through a holy baptism in the Living Water.

Barbelo, the Father-Mother god, who was a higher form of the Sophia figure, initiates those who were baptized in or by the Logos or Seth.

Barbelo communicated to those who love her by Voice or Word (Logos). This figure of Barbelo was the fountain or spring from which comes the Word like flowing water.

Protennoia is the Word or Logos, which was produced from Thought. The Word descends and enlightened her children.

The last of these entities was Eleleth who produces Sophia in the same way as fire produces light. The re-emission of this light through Sophia produced the demon Yaldaboth who stole the power of creation imparted to Sophia and produced the lower aeons and man.

The Archons thought that Protennoia (Logos) was "their Christ," while actually she is the "Father" of everyone. Protennoia identified herself as the beloved of the Archons, and disguised herself as the child of the Great Creator.

Sethianism gradually Christianized in the latter first century as it began to identify Seth and Adam in terms of the pre-existent Christ.

This means that according to Sethian beliefs the true Son of Man is Adamas (Adam), the Son of the supreme deity who is the only human form in which the deity revealed himself. Seth, the son of Adam or Adamas, is the mediator between man and God's son, Adam. Seth was the Christ image or mediator.

Gnostic theology seemed to vacillate from polytheism to pantheism to dualism to monotheism, depending on the teacher and how he viewed and stressed certain areas of their creation myths.

Marcion, a Gnostic teacher, espoused differences between the God of the New Testament and the God of the Old Testament, claiming they were two separate entities. According to Marcion, the New Testament God was a good true God while the Old Testament God was an evil angel. Although this may be a heresy, it pulled his school back into monotheism. The church, however, disowned him.

Syneros and Prepon, disciples of Marcion, postulated three different entities, carrying their teachings from monotheism into polytheism in one stroke. In their system the opponent of the good God was not the God of the Jews, but Eternal Matter, which was the source of all evil. Matter, in this system became a principal creative force. Although it was created imperfect, it could also create, having the innate intelligence of the "world soul."

Of all the Gnostic schools or sects the most famous is the Antinomian School. Believing that the Creator God, Jehovah, was evil, they set out to disrupt all things connected to the Jewish God, including his laws. It was considered their duty to break any law of morality, diet, or conduct given by the Jewish God, who they considered the evil Creator God. The leader of the sect was called Nicolaites. The sect existed in Apostolic times and is mentioned in the Bible.

Revelation 2 (King James Version)
5 Remember therefore from whence thou art fallen, and repent, and do the first works; or else I will come unto you quickly, and will remove your candlestick out of his place, except thou repent.
6 But this thou hast, that thou hatest the deeds of the Nicolaitanes, which I also hate.

Revelation 2 (King James Version)
14 But I have a few things against you, because thou hast there them that hold the doctrine of Balaam, who taught Balac to cast a stumbling block before the children of Israel, to eat things sacrificed unto idols, and to commit fornication.

15 So hast thou also them that hold the doctrine of the Nicolaitanes, which thing I hate.

16 Repent; or else I will come unto you quickly, and will fight against them with the sword of my mouth.

One of the leaders of the Nocolaitanes, according to Origen, was Carpocrates, whom Tertullian called a magician and a fornicator.

Carpocretes taught that one could only escape the cosmic powers by discharging one's obligations to them and disregarding their laws. The Christian church fathers, St. Justin, Irenaeus, and Eusebius wrote that the reputation of these men (the Nicolaitanes), brought infamy upon the whole race of Christians.

Although Gnostic sects varied, they had certain points in common. These commonalities included salvation through special knowledge, and the fact that the world was corrupt, since it was created by an evil God.

According to Gnostic theology, nothing can come from the material world that is not flawed. Because of this, Gnostics did not believe that Christ could have been a corporeal being. Thus, there must be some separation or distinction between Jesus, as a man, and Christ, as a spiritual being born from the Supreme, unrevealed, and eternal God.

To closer examine this theology, we turn to Valentinus, the driving force of early Gnosticism, for an explanation. Valentinus divided Jesus Christ into two very distinct parts; Jesus, the man, and Christ, the anointed spiritual messenger of God. These two forces met in the moment of Baptism when the Spirit of God came to rest on Jesus and the Christ power entered his body.

Here Gnosticism runs aground on its own theology, for if the spiritual cannot mingle with the material then how can the Christ spirit inhabit a body? The result of the dichotomy was a schism within Gnosticism. Some held to the belief that the specter of Jesus was simply an illusion produced by Christ himself to enable him to do his work on earth. It was not real, not matter, not corporeal, and did not actually exist as a physical body would. Others came to believe that Jesus must have been a specially prepared vessel and was the perfect human body formed by the very essence of the plumora (heaven). It was this path of thought that allowed Jesus to continue as human, lover, and father.

Jesus, the man, became a vessel containing the Light of God, called Christ. In the Gnostic view we all could and should become Christs carrying the Truth and Light of God. We are all potential vehicles of the same Spirit that Jesus held within him when he was awakened to the Truth.

The suffering and death of Jesus then took on much less importance in the Gnostic view, as Jesus was simply part of the corrupt world and was suffering the indignities of this world as any man would.

The Gnostic texts seem to divide man into parts, although at times the divisions are somewhat unclear. The divisions alluded to may include the soul, which is the will of man; the spirit, which is depicted as wind or air (pneuma) and contains the holy spark that is the spirit of God in man; and the material human form, the body. The mind of man sits as a mediator between the soul, or will, and the spirit, which is connected to God.

Without the light of the truth, the spirit is held captive by the Demiurge, which enslaves man. This entrapment is called "sickness." It is this sickness that the Light came to heal and then to set us free. The third part of man, his material form, was considered a weight, an anchor, and a hindrance, keeping man attached to the corrupted earthly realm. The Demiurge proclaimed himself to be God under three separate titles:

"Now the archon (ruler) who is weak has three names. The first name is Yaltabaoth, the second is Saklas ("fool"), and the third is Samael. And he is impious in his arrogance which is in him. For he said, 'I am God and there is no other God beside me,' for he is

ignorant of his strength, the place from which he had come." Apocryphon of John

As we read the text, we must realize that Gnosticism conflicted with traditional Christianity. Overall, theology can rise and fall upon small words and terms. If Jesus was not God, his death and thus his atonement meant nothing. His suffering meant nothing. Even the resurrection meant nothing, if one's view of Jesus was that he was not human to begin with, as was true with some Gnostics.

For the Gnostics, resurrection of the dead was unthinkable since flesh as well as all matter are destined to perish. According to Gnostic theology, there was no resurrection of the flesh, but only of the soul. How the soul would be resurrected was explained differently by various Gnostic groups, but all denied the resurrection of the body. To the enlightened Gnostic the actual person was the spirit who used the body as an instrument to survive in the material world but did not identify with it.

29. Jesus said: If the flesh came into being because of spirit, it is a marvel, but if spirit came into being because of the body, it would be a marvel of marvels. I marvel indeed at how great wealth has taken up residence in this poverty.

Gospel of Thomas

Owing to the Gnostic belief of such a separation of spirit and body, it was thought that the Christ spirit within the body of Jesus departed the body before the crucifixion. Others said the body was an illusion and the crucifixion was a sham perpetrated by an eternal spirit on the men that sought to kill it. Lastly, some suggested that Jesus deceived the soldiers into thinking he was dead. The resurrection under this circumstance became a lie, which allowed Jesus to escape and live on in anonymity, hiding, living as a married man, and raising a family until his natural death.

Think of the implications to the orthodox Christian world if the spirit of God departed from Jesus as it fled and laughed as the body was crucified. This is the implication of the Gnostic interpretation of the death of Jesus when he cries out, "My power, my power, why have you left me?" as the Christ spirit left his body before his death. What are the ramifications to the modern Christian if the Creator God, the Demiurge, is more evil than his creation? Can a creation rise above its creator? Is it possible for man to find the spark within himself that calls to the Supreme God and free himself of his evil creator?

Although, in time, the creation myth and other Gnostic differences began to be swept under the rug, it was the division between Jesus and the Christ spirit that put them at odds with the emerging orthodox church. At the establishment of the doctrine of the trinity, the mainline church firmly set a divide between themselves and the Gnostics.

To this day there is a battle raging in the Christian world as believers and seekers attempt to reconcile today's Christianity to the sect of the early Christian church called, "Gnosticism."

Although much of the Gnostic doctrine has been discussed earlier in this work, it is good to go over some of the information again, especially in the light of the specific theology found in The Gospel of Judas.

The History of the Gospel of Judas

The newly discovered Gospel of Judas is very controversial for several reasons. Theologically, it is divisive due to its Gnostic theology. The main controversy in the text revolves around the theory that Jesus asked Judas to betray Him in order to fulfill His destiny and the scriptures. If this is true it would make Judas a saint and not the sinner and traitor as believed by the mainline church.

The text is also interesting simply because it is written in Coptic. Documents from the time period and region where the Coptic language was native are a rare find.

The word Coptic is an Arabic corruption of the Greek word Aigyptos, which in turn comes from the word Hikaptah, one of the names of the city of Memphis, the first capital of ancient Egypt.

There has never been a Coptic state or government per se, however, the word has been used to generally define a culture and language present in the area of Egypt within a particular timeframe.

The known history of the Copts starts with King Mina the first King, who united the northern and southern kingdoms of Egypt circa 3050 B.C. The ancient Egyptian civilization under the rule of the Pharaohs lasted over 3000 years. Saint Mina (named after the king) is one of the major Coptic saints. He was martyred in 309 A.D.

The culture has come to be recognized as one containing distinctive language, art, architecture, and even certain religious systems. There is even a very distinctive Coptic Christian church system with its own canon, which contains several more books than those of the Protestant or Catholic Bibles.

The religious controversy of the Gospel of Judas is compelling, if for no other reason than that of its differing view, which forces us to re-examine the way we read and understand the place, path, and actions of Judas and his act of betrayal.

The Gospels and the Book of Acts tell the story of Judas' betrayal of Jesus and the end to which Judas came. The canonical books refer to Judas as a traitor, betrayer, and as one influenced by the devil. However, the Gospel of Judas turns this idea on its head by claiming the Judas was requested, if not required, to plan and carry out the treachery that would be the impetus for the crucifixion. The plan was to surrender Jesus to the authorities so that scripture and prophecy could be fulfilled, and Jesus was the person devising the plan.

Most scholars agree that the Gospels of Matthew, Mark, Luke, and John were written between the date of Jesus' death and about 90 A.D. The Gospel of Judas was written originally in Greek around A.D. 180 at the earliest. If this is true, Judas could not have been the author. For Judas to have penned this work he would have been about 120 years of age at the time of its writing. Discounting this possibility, the original author is unknown.

Dates of the original texts are based on words and usage common to certain periods of time. This is comparable to how slang and catch phrases pass in and out of vogue in our own language.

Another way of narrowing down the date of the original text is to look for references to it in other writings. This would set the date marking the latest the text could have been written.

Tixeront, translated by Raemers, states: "Besides these Gospels, we know that there once existed a Gospel of Bartholomew, a Gospel of Thaddeus, mentioned in the decree of Pope Gelasius, and a Gospel of Judas Iscariot in use among the Cainites and spoken of by St. Irenaeus."

In Roberts-Donaldson's translation from Irenaeus the church father states, "Others again declare that Cain derived his being from the Power above, and acknowledge that Esau, Korah, the Sodomites, and all such persons, are related to themselves. On this account, they add, they have been assailed by the Creator, yet no one of them has suffered injury. For Sophia was in the habit of carrying off that which belonged to her from them to herself. They declare that Judas the traitor was thoroughly acquainted with these things, and that he alone, knowing the truth as no others did, accomplished the mystery of the betrayal; by him all things, both earthly and heavenly, were thus thrown into confusion. They produce a fictitious history of this kind, which they style the Gospel of Judas."

Irenaeus went on to say that the writings came from what he called a "Cainite" Gnostic sect that jousted with orthodox Christianity. He also accused the Cainites of lauding the biblical murderer Cain, the Sodomites and Judas, whom they regarded as the keeper of secret mysteries.

Knowing the dates of the writings of Irenaeus further clarifies the date to be around or before 180 A.D. Of course, this affects the Gospel of Judas only if we conclude that the text Irenaeus spoke of is the same text we have today. Sadly, there is no way to know with any certainty, but we do have a few clues.

Cain is not mentioned in the version of the Gospel of Judas we have today. Furthermore, the evolution of cosmology tends to be from the simple to the complex and this trend is shown in the current version since Yaldabaoth, who is also called "Nebro" the "rebel", is presented as the creator of Saklas and it is Saklas who is depicted later in the Gospel of Judas as the creator mankind and the physical world. However, in other

Gnostic writings, Yaldabaoth is the "demiurge" or fashioner of the world, and is clearly identified as the same deity as Saklas. This means that in the Gospel of Judas there has been a split between Yaldaboth and Saklas, leading to a more complex cosmology. This indicates that the Gospel of Judas we have today was written later than that of which Irenaeus speaks, since in his time these deities were one and the same.

Now the archon who is weak has three names. The first name is Yaltabaoth, the second is Saklas ("fool"), and the third is Samael. And he is impious in his arrogance which is in him. For he said, 'I am God and there is no other God beside me,' for he is ignorant of his strength, the place from which he had come."
    Apocryphon of John, ca. 200 AD.

As for the dating of the copy found in Egypt, the formation of certain letters also change with time and the style of the lettering within the texts places the copies within a certain period. The 26-page Judas text is a copy in Coptic of the original Gospel of Judas, which was written in Greek the century before.

Radioactive-carbon-dating tests as well as experts in ancient languages have established that the copy was written between 220 and 340 A.D.

The discovered Gospel was written on papyrus, probably at a Gnostic monastery in Egypt. Although other copies may have been made they were probably lost in St. Athanasius's fourth-century campaign to destroy all heretical texts. All texts not accepted by the newly established church were to be burned. Heresy was not to be tolerated, and Gnosticism was considered at the top of the list. Not only was Gnosticism different from the orthodox theology, it condoned a personal search for God through knowledge and that was something outside the control of the church. To maintain its control, the new church had to crush these beliefs.

In order to protect the text from Athanasius's soldiers it is thought a Gnostic monk or scribe buried copies of certain Gnostic texts in an area of tombs in Egypt. These were not discovered until the late 1970s. The Gospel was one of three texts found that were bound together in a single codex.

The gospel was unearthed in 1978 by a farmer. He found a small container like a tomb box in a cave near El Minya, Egypt. In the small, carved, and sealed box was part of a codex, or collection of devotional texts.

The farmer sold the codex to an antiquities dealer in Cairo. The deal was kept secret but was reported to have taken place in 1983. The antiquities dealer was unaware of the content of the codex when he offered the gospel for sale to the Coptic studies scholar, Stephen Emmel, of Germany's

University of Munster and another scholar. The meeting took place in a Geneva, Switzerland hotel room.

It was Emmel who examined the codex and first suspected the papyrus sheets discussed Judas. Although the text more than intrigued Emmel, the asking price was so high at $3 million dollars U.S. that there was no way to afford the purchase.

The seller was offered a price that was an order of magnitude lower than the asking price. This, the seller took as an insult and the deal stalled.

Due to the frustration brought about by not having his greed satisfied, the dealer stored the codex in a safe in a Hicksville, N.Y. bank for 16 years. There, away from the dry desert air, in the box with higher humidity, it deteriorated and crumbled until Zurich-based antiquities dealer Frieda Nussberger-Tchacos purchased it in 2000 for a sum much less than the original asking price. The codex was then acquired by the Maecenas Foundation for Ancient Art in Switzerland in 2001.

The foundation invited National Geographic to help with the restoration in 2004.

Over the next 5 years thousands of pieces of papyrus were placed back together like a jigsaw puzzle. Thousands of pieces, some so small they contained only a letter or two were restored to their position in the text using tweezers and computer imaging.

Once completed, a team of scholars translated the document into English, as best they could, considering the condition of the document and the number of pieces missing. The restored original is now housed in Cairo's Coptic Museum. A rendering of the text in Coptic can be seen at:

http://www.nationalgeographic.com/lostgospel/_pdf/CopticGospelOfJudas.pdf

Because of the extreme age and ill-treatment of the text much of it is illegible. There are gaps and holes in the codex. Entire lines are missing. Some parts of the translation were done on a "best-guess" basis. If there were letters missing from common words of phrases the translators could assume and replace letters and even words or phrases. When the gaps became larger or the meaning of the phrase was uncertain the translators simple noted the absence of data.

In this rendering we have attempted two bold moves. We wished to present a more engaging interpretation for the public, which necessarily demanded notes and explanations available at the point the ideas were encountered. We also wished to attempt to fill in some of the gaps in the text if possible.

As a matter of a disclaimer, it should be understood that the original translators did a remarkable job with the thousands of slivers and chips of papyrus that made up the codex. Once reconstructed, it became obvious that much of the text was simply missing, having disintegrated into dust and powder, never to be read again.

The text presented here takes the work done by many others and places the Gospel of Judas into a more readable language and format along with in-line commentary. It then expands the text, filling in the gaps as best it could be done, based on an understanding of the Gnostic theology, historical information, textual references, and logical flow of conversation.

All words or phases in parentheses indicate those additions made to the text, either as a matter of filling in the missing letters, words, or lines; or as a matter of clarification of ambiguous wording in the original text or its translation. When a word could be translated in more than one way, a slash "/" was used to note the various choices.

Commentary are marked clearly as "Notes" and are place in italic font within the text.

The reader should keep the probable function of the text in mind. The title gives some hint. It is not "The Gospel According to Judas", but it is instead, "The Gospel of Judas."

This indicates that the writer wanted to exalt Judas, his position and contribution according to the theology being espoused and propagated by the text.

Knowing these things, the words and lines missing in the text can be a matter of educated and reasonable assumptions. They are, however, assumptions nonetheless.

Let us look now at the Gospel of Judas.

The Gospel of Judas

This is the proclamation, which was secretly revealed to Judas Iscariot by Jesus during that eight-day period that included (that was) the three days before he (Jesus) celebrated Passover (one translator has "celebrated his passion/suffering).

Note: The proclamation is not the logos, word or Christ for the orthodox church. The word here is a proclamation of judgment as in a court verdict.

1. Jesus appeared on earth to perform miracles and wondrous acts in order to save humanity.
Because some conducted themselves in a righteous way and others continued in their sins, he decided to call the twelve disciples.

2. He began to talk to them about the mysteries that lay beyond this world and what would happen at this world's end (at the end). He often changed his appearance and was not seen as himself but looked like a child (some translators have apparition or spirit) when he was with his disciples.

3. He came upon his disciples in Judea once when they were sitting together piously (training their piety – training in godliness). As he got closer to the disciples he saw they were sitting together, giving thanks and saying a prayer over the bread (Eucharist/thanksgiving). He laughed.

4. The disciples asked Him, "Rabbi, why are you laughing at our prayer of thanks? Have we not acted appropriately?"
He said, "I am not laughing at you. It is just that you are not doing this because you want to. You are doing this because your god (has to be/will be) praised."

5. They said, "Rabbi, you are the (earthly / only) son of our god."
Jesus answered, "How do you know me? (Do you think you know me?) I say to you truly, no one among you in this generation (in this race) will understand me."

6. His disciples heard this and became enraged and began mumbling profanities and mocking him in their hearts. When Jesus saw their inability (to understand what he said to them (their stupidity), he said,) "Why did you get so upset that you became angry? Your god, who is inside of you, (and your own lack of understanding guides you and) have

instigated this anger in your (mind / soul). (I challenge) any man among you to show me who is (understanding enough) to bring out the perfect man and stand and face me."

7. They all said, "We are strong enough."
But in their (true being) spirits none dared to stand in front of him except for Judas Iscariot. Judas was able to stand in front of him, but even he could not look Jesus in the eyes, and he turned his face away.

Note: It is uncertain as to the reason Judas did not look at Jesus. It was a custom of respect not to look a superior in the eyes. Either Judas was unable to look at Jesus or was constrained by the position of Jesus as his Rabbi.

8. Judas said to Him, "I know who you are and where you came from. You are from the everlasting (eternal) aeon (realm or kingdom) of Barbelo (Barbelo's everlasting kingdom). I am not worthy to speak the name of the one who sent you."

9. Jesus knew that Judas was capable of understanding (showing forth / thinking about) something that was glorious, so Jesus said to him, "Walk away (step a distance away) from the others and I will tell you about the mysteries

of God (the reign of God / kingdom of God).

10. It is possible for you to get there, but the path will cause you great grief because you will be replaced so that the twelve may be complete with their god again."
Judas asked him, "When will you tell me how the great day of light will dawn for this generation (race)? When will you explain these things?"
But as he asked these things, Jesus left him.

11. At the dawn of the next day after this happened, Jesus appeared to his disciples.
They asked Him, "Rabbi, where did you go and what did you do when you left us?"
Jesus said to them, "I went to another generation (race) that is a greater and holier generation (race)."

12. His disciples asked him, "Lord, what is this great race that is superior to us and holier than us, that is not now in this realm (kingdom)?"
When Jesus heard this, he laughed and said to them, "Why are you thinking in your hearts about the mighty and holy race (generation)? So be it - I will tell you. No one born in this age (realm / aeon) will see that (generation / race), and not even the multitude (army) of angels (controlling) the stars

will rule over that generation (race), and no mortal (corruptible) person can associate (belong) with it.

13. That generation does not come from (a realm) which has become (mortal / corrupted). The generation of people among (you) is from the generation of humanity (of inferior / without) power, which (cannot associate with the) other powers (above) by (whom) you rule / are ruled."
When (the /his) disciples heard this, they were all troubled in (their heart / spirit). They were speechless (could not utter a word).

Note: This begins a distinction drawn between the generation or race of mankind, which is inferior, decaying, and unenlightened, and the "great generation or race," which is enlightened, incorruptible, and eternal. There are only two races; those who have gnosis and those who do not. Interestingly, Jesus does not place the disciples in the great generation.

14. On another day Jesus came up to (them). They said to (him), "Rabbi, we have seen you in a (dream), because we all had weighty (dreams about a night you were taken away / arrested)."
(He said), "Why have (you come to me when you have) gone

into hiding?"

15. They said, "There was (an imposing building with a great altar in it and twelve men, (which we would say were) the priests, and there was a name, and a crowd of people waiting (enduring because of their perseverance) at that altar, (for) the priest (to come and receive) the offerings. (However) we kept waiting (we were tenacious also)."
(Jesus asked), "What were (the priests) like?"
They said, "Some (of them would fast) for two weeks; (others would) sacrifice their own children, others their wives, (all the while) in praise (offered in) humility with each other; some have sex with other men; some murder; some commit a plethora of sins and acts of crime. And the men who stand in front of the altar call upon your (name / authority), and in all the acts springing from their lack of knowledge (lack of light), the sacrifices are brought to completion (by their hands) (the alter remained full through their handiwork of slaughtering the sacrifices)."
After they said these things they became uneasy and quiet.

16. Jesus asked them, "Why are you bothered? So be it, I tell you that all the priests who have stood before that altar call upon my name. I have told I you many times that my name has been written on the (judgment) of this race (and on) the

stars through the human generations. In my name (these people) have planted barren trees, (and have done so) without any honor."

17. Jesus said to them, "You are like those men you have seen conducting the offerings at the altar. That is the god you serve, and the twelve men you have seen represent you. The cattle you saw that were brought for sacrifice represent the many people you have led (will lead) astray before that altar. (You) will stand (lead / represent) and use my name in that way, as will the generations of the pious and you all will remain loyal to "him." (Some translations have- "The lord of chaos will establish his place in this way.") After "him" another man will lead from (the group of fornicators), and another (will lead at the alter from those who) murder children, and another from those who are homosexuals, and (another) those who fast, and (one will stand from) the rest of those who pollution themselves and who are lawlessness and who sin, and (from) those who say, 'We are like the angels'; they are the stars that (make everything happen / bring everything to an end).

18. It has been said to the human generations, 'Look, God has received your sacrifice from the hands of a priest.' But the

priest is a minister of error (minister in error / ministers but is in sin). But it is the Lord, the Lord of all (the fullness of the divine), who commands, 'On the last day (of time) they will be shamed (some have - "at the end of days").'"

Note: Jesus tells the disciples that they are loyal to the wrong god. He goes on to say that they are the ones who murder, fornicate, and sin. Furthermore, Jesus tells them that they will lead people into a spiritual slaughter like the cattle they saw sacrificed in their dream. At this time the 12 included Judas. This, along with other such verses has led many scholars to conclude that the Gospel of Judas was not depicting Judas to be the sanctified person the original translators thought him to be.

19. Jesus (told them), "Stop (sacrificing that which) you have (and stop hovering) over the altar. The priests are over your stars and your angels. They have already come to their end there. So let them (be entrapped / quarrel / fight) before you, and leave them alone. (Do not be tainted by this generation but instead eat the food of knowledge given to you by the great one.)

Note: We will see "stars" referred to often in the text. They are used to symbolize two unique concepts. It was thought that in the creation of the cosmos, luminaries were created which were powers controlling each person's destiny. It was also thought that each person was assigned a star as his or her eternal home or resting place. A good person would ascend to his or her own star to rule and rest. Thus, stars were conscious powers, carrying out orders from God, and also were places of destiny for those who escape the material plane.

20. A baker cannot feed all creation under (heaven). And (they will not give) to them (a food) and (give) to (those of the great generation the same food).
Jesus said to them, "Stop struggling with (against) me. Each of you has his own star, and every (Lines are missing here. Text could read " person has his own destiny." Or possibly, "person who does well will dwell and rest on their star").
(All things happen in their own season and all seasons are appointed. And in (the season) which has come (it is spring) for the tree (of paradise) of this aeon / age (and it will produce) for a time (then wither) but he has come to water God's paradise, and (also water this generation) that will last, because (he) will not corrupt / detour) the (path of life for) that generation, but (will guide it) from eternity to eternity."

21. Judas asked him, "Rabbi, what kind of fruit does this generation produce?"
Jesus answered, "The souls of every human generation will

The Lost Books of the New Testament

die. However, when these people (of this kingdom) have completed the time in the kingdom and the living breath leaves them, their bodies will die but their souls will continue to be alive, and they will ascended (be lifted up / be taken up)."

Judas asked, "What will the remainder of the human generations do?"

Jesus said, "It is not possible to plant seeds in (rocky soil) and harvest its fruit. (This is also the way (of) the (corrupted) race (generation), (the children of this kingdom) and corruptible Sophia / wisdom) (is / are) not the hand that has created mortal people, so that their souls ascend to the eternal realms above. Amen, I say, (that no) angel (or / of) power will be able to see that (kingdom of) these to whom (belong that) holy generations (above)."

After Jesus said this, he departed.

22. Judas said, "Rabbi, you have listened to all of those others, so now listen to me too. I have seen a great vision."

23. When Jesus heard this, he laughed and said to him, "You (are the) thirteenth spirit (daemon), why are you trying so hard / why do you excite yourself like this? However, speak up, and I will be patient with you."

Judas said to him, "In the vision I saw myself and the twelve disciples were stoning me and persecuting me very badly / severely / strongly. And I (was following you and I) arrived at a place where I saw (a large house in front me), and my eyes could not (take in / comprehend) its size. Many people were surrounding it, and the house had a roof of plants (grass / green vegetation), and in the middle of the house (there was a crowd) (and I was there with you), saying, 'Rabbi, take me in (the house) along with these people.'"

24. He responded and said, "Judas, your star has misled you. No person of mortal birth is worthy to enter the house you have seen. It is a place reserved for the saints. Not even the sun or the moon or day (light) will rule there. Only the saints will live there, in the eternal kingdom with the holy angels, always (some have the text as – "will be firmly established with the holy angels forever"). Look, I have explained to you the mysteries of the kingdom and I have taught you about the error of the stars; and (I have) sent it (on its path) on the twelve ages (aeons)."

Note: *The Lost Book of Enoch tells of stars, which are the guiding forces of man and nature, erring. They become misplaced and out of order. They had to be placed or directed back into their proper paths.*

See The Lost Book of Enoch, by Joseph Lumpkin.

Note: There are 12 Astrological Ages. The 12 signs of the zodiac make up a 360-degree ecliptic path around the Earth, and takes 25,920 years to make the Precession of the Equinoxes. Each sign is comprised of 30 degrees of celestial longitude. Each degree of the precession is equal to 72 Earth years, and each year is equal to 50 seconds of degrees of arc of celestial longitude. In a 24 hour Earth day, the Earth rotates the entire 360 degrees of the ecliptic, allowing a person to see all 12 signs.

25. Judas said, "Rabbi, could it be that my (spiritual) seed will conquer the rulers of cosmic power (could also be rendered: "is under the control of the archons or rulers of cosmic power"?)"

26. Jesus answered and said to him, "Come (with me so) that I (may show you the kingdom you will receive. I will show you what is to come of you and this generation), but you will be grieved when you see the kingdom and all its race (of people)."
When Judas heard Him he said to him, "What good is it if I have received it seeing that you have set me apart from that race?"
Jesus answered him and said, "You will become the

thirteenth, and you will be cursed by the other generations, and you will come to rule over them. In the last days they will curse your ascent to the holy (race/ kingdom)."

Note: I have chosen the word, "daemon" and not "demon" because the meaning of the text is unclear. A daemon is a divinity or supernatural being of a nature between gods and humans. In verse 24 Jesus tells Judas that he will never be worthy to enter the house, which symbolizes the eternal kingdom. Later in verse 26 Jesus seems to indicate that Judas will be cursed by the other disciples but will be raised to enter the holy generation in the last days. It is possible the interim time will be spent in what the Bible calls, "his own place."

27. Jesus said, "(Follow / come with me), so that I may teach you the (secrets) that no person (has) ever seen.

Note: This begins a creation myth based on certain Sethian Gnostic cosmology. The telling of the story appears to be an attempt to link the Gnostic cosmology to the teachings of Jesus in order to add validity and authority to the creation story and entities as well as assisting in the propagation of the sect.

There is a great and limitless kingdom, whose scope no generation of angels has seen (and in it) The Great Invisible

(Spirit) is, and no angel's eye has ever seen, no thought of the heart (mind) has ever understood it, and no name can be assigned it (it cannot be named).

28. "And a brightly glowing cloud appeared there. The Great Spirit said, 'Let an angel come into being as my assistant (attendant / helper).'
"A great angel, the enlightened, divine, Self-Generated (Self-Created) one emerged from the cloud. Because of him, four other angelic lights (luminaries), (Harmozel, Oroiael, Daveithai, and Eleleth) began to exist from another cloud, and they became assistants (helpers / attendants) to the Self-Generated angel (messenger). The Self-Created one proclaimed, 'Let (there) come into being (a star / Adam),' and it (he) came into being (at once). He (created) the first star (luminary / bright, shining being) to reign over him.

Note: Here we have a garbled text, the translation of which can go one of two ways. The words missing in the middle of the text could be Adam, who is also known as Adamas, or it could refer to a star, since the next reference is to a luminary. The direction of the text is unclear except that it is agreed that the word "it" is used in the text.

He said, 'Let angels (messengers) begin existence to adore (worship) (him),' and an innumerable plethora became existent. He said, '(Let there be) an aeon of light,' and he began existence. He created the second star to rule over him, to render service together with the innumerable plethora of angels. That is how he created the rest of the aeons of light. He made them rulers over them, and he created for them an innumerable plethora of angels to assist them.

29. "Adamas (Adam) was in the first luminous cloud (the initial divine expression) that no angel has ever seen, including all those called 'God.' He (was the one) that (created the enlightened aeon and beheld) the image and produced him after the likeness of (this) angel. He made the incorruptible (generation) of Seth appear (from) the twelve (aeons and) the twenty-four (stars / angelic lights / luminaries). He made seventy-two angelic lights appear in the imperishable generation, as the will of the Spirit dictated. The seventy-two angelic lights themselves made three hundred sixty angelic lights appear in the immortal race, by following the will of the Spirit, that their number should be five for each.

Note: Seth is the son of Adam and was considered to be divine as Adam was divine. Seth produced "that incorruptible generation." He was thought to have received the knowledge that would bring freedom from the material realm, and thus, salvation.

30. "The twelve realms (aeons) of the twelve angelic lights make up / appoint their Father, with six heavens for each aeon, so that there are seventy-two heavens for the seventy-two angelic lights, and for each (there are five) skies, (producing all) three hundred sixty (skies for the stars). They were given authority and a innumerable host of angels, for glory and adoration (worship), (and then he gave the) virgin (pure spirits), for glory and worship of all the aeons and the heavens and their firmaments (skies).

Note: The numbers assigned to the various aeons, angels, and stars have significance in both biblical number symbolism and Pythagorean numerology.

> *One – Unity, sovereign, God, causality.*
>
> *Two – Duality and/or merging.*
>
> *Three - Spiritually complete, fullness, creation.*
>
> *Four – Foundations, systems, order.*
>
> *Five – Spirit, grace, movement.*
>
> *Six - Mankind.*
>
> *Seven – God, wisdom, knowledge, perfection.*
>
> *Twelve – Law, rule, authority.*
>
> *Thirteen – Cursed, beyond or without law.*
>
> *Twenty-four – Heavenly government, elders, a*

Joseph B. Lumpkin

> system. Duality within the system.
>
> Seventy-two – Both elements of two and seven as well as the element of completion.
>
> Three hundred and sixty – Elements of three and six as well as the meaning of a full cycle such as a yearly cycle. An end, and a new start.

31. The totality (gathering) of those immortals is called the cosmos, that is to say perdition / decay / corruption, by the Father and the seventy-two angelic lights / luminaries who are with the Self-Created one and his seventy-two aeons. In the cosmos the first human appeared with his incorruptible powers.

Note: This first human is Adamas or Adam. It should be noted that the name "Adam" can also be rendered as "Man" in Hebrew.

32. And the aeon that appeared with his generation and the aeon in whom are the cloud of knowledge and the angel, is called El.

Note: El was the name of a Semitic god who was chief among the pantheon of gods affecting nature and society. He is father of the divine family and president of the divine assembly on the 'mount of assembly', the equivalent of Hebrew har mo'ed, which became through the Greek transliteration Armageddon. In Canaanite mythology he is known as 'the Bull', symbolizing his strength and creative force. He is called 'Creator of Created Things' which is how rivers were also metaphorically thought of. In the Biblical Garden of Eden a river flowed to form the four rivers, Tigris, Euphrates, Gihon and Pishon."

El expressed the concept of ordered government, justice and creation. The Bible never stigmatizes the Canaanite worship of El, whose authority in social affairs was recognized by the Patriarchs. His consort was Asherah, the mother goddess, represented in Canaanite sanctuaries by a natural tree (Hebrew ashera) such as the tree of life.

33. (He created the) aeon, (after that) (El) said, 'Let twelve angels come into being (in order to) rule over chaos and the (cosmos / perdition).' And look, from the cloud {called Sophia} there appeared an (angel / aeon) whose face flashed with fire and whose appearance was defiled with blood. His name was Nebro, meaning "rebel." Another angel, Saklas, also came from the cloud. So Nebro created six angels—as well as Saklas—to be assistants, and these produced twelve angels in the heavens, with each one receiving a piece of the heavens.

Note: Nebro may be a female demon who mates with Saklas; others call Nebro by the name "Yaldaboth (child of chaos) Yaldaboth and Saklas are both names given to the insane or deficient deity that created the physical world. Also the reading could be influenced by the fact that in some mythologies Nebro is a head demon and Saklas is a head angel. Nebro has the same meaning as Nimrod, which is "rebel."

The Jews and Greeks of the day were literalists. Each and every word of the scriptures was taken at face value. Therefore, the god who created Adam and Eve was a limited and tangible god. He walked and talked and asked questions, the answers to which he did not seem to know. By building a creation story that includes Saklas the problems were solved. Now the references to multiple gods were answered and when god said let "us" create man, the references could be to Saklas and his helpers. Since the Saklas deity was limited and restricted it left the Supreme God to be "God."

34. "The twelve rulers (aeons) spoke with the twelve angels: 'Let each of you (receive a portion) and let them (that are in this) generation (be ruled by these) angels':

The first is Seth, who is called Christ.
The (second) is Harmathoth, who is (head ruler of the underworld).
The (third) is Galila.

The fourth is Yobel.

The fifth (is) Adonaios.

These are the five who ruled all of the underworld, and primarily over chaos.

Note: These five names are probably associated with the five planets known at the time the Gospel of Judas was written. They were placed on their paths and courses to keep order and give light, both real and spiritual.

35. "Then Saklas said to his angels, 'Let us create a human being in the similitude and after the figure / image / representation (of the Supreme God).' They fashioned Adam and his wife Eve, who is called Zoe / life when she was still in the cloud.

Note: Zoe is another name for Eve in the Septuagint.

36. For it is this name (life) that all the generations seek the man, and each of them calls the woman by these names. Now, Sakla did not command (as he was instructed) but (he commanded) the generations (of man to live so long / for a defined period of time), (but he did created them in his (Saklas') likeness). And the (ruler Saklas) said to Adam, 'You shall live long, with your children.'"

37. Judas said to Jesus, "(What length) is the long span of time that humans will live?"

Jesus said, "Why are you curious about this? Adam and his generation has lived his lifespan in the place where he received his kingdom, with his longevity bestowed by his ruler (as numbered with his ruler)."

38. Judas said to Jesus, "Does the human spirit die?"

Jesus said, "This is why God (the god of this realm) ordered Michael to loan spirits to people so that they would serve (be in servitude), but the Great One commanded Gabriel to give spirits to the great generation (race) which had no ruler over it (a generation that cannot be dominated). He gave the spirit and the soul. Therefore, the (remainder / mountain) of souls (loaned will come back to the god of this realm in the end).

Note: This passage indicates two lines of creation. For those people created by the god of this world the angel Michael was commanded to temporarily assign souls to his creation. To keep their souls they were enslaved to worship the god of this world. In contrast, the Great One commanded Gabriel to give souls to those of the great generation for eternity.

39. "(There was no) light (in this world to shine) around (the people to) allow (the) spirit (which is) within you all to dwell in this (body) among the generations of angels. But God caused knowledge to be (given) to Adam and those with him, so that the kings of chaos and the underworld might not oppress them with it."

Note: The word rendered as "rule" by most translators has the connotation of oppression.

40. Judas said to Jesus, "So what will those generations do?"
Jesus said, "Truthfully, I tell you all, that for all of them the stars bring matters to completion (heavenly apocalypse). When Saklas completes the span of time assigned for him, their first star will appear with the generations, and they will finish what they said they would do. Then they will (have illicit sex in my name and kill (sacrifice) their children and they will fast, and they will kill their wives in praise offered in humility with each other; some have sex with other men; some will murder, some commit a plethora of sins and acts of crime all in my name, and Saklas will destroy) your star over the thirteenth aeon."

41. After that Jesus (laughed).

Note: Jesus seems to find humor in the misguided judgments or concepts of the disciples. He laughs, as if shaking his head in disbelief of the error, then attempts to give insight and correction.

(Judas asked), "Rabbi, (why do you laugh at us)?"
(He) answered (Judas and said), "I am not laughing (because of you) but at the error of the stars, because these six stars wander about with these five warriors and they all will be destroyed along with their creations."

Note: The six stars were those who, along with Saklas or yaldaboth, created man and the cosmos. The five warriors refer to the five known planets at the time of the writing of the text. These planets were also connected with pagan worship and deities.

42. Judas said to Jesus, "Look at what those who have been baptized in your name do?"
Jesus said, "Truthfully I tell (you), this baptism done in my name (are done by those who do not know me. They sacrifice in vain to the god of this world. I baptized no one, for those baptized here have their hope here and those who follow me need no baptism for they will come) to me. In truth (I) tell you, Judas, (those offering) sacrifices to Saklas (do not offer sacrifice to the Great) God (but instead worship) everything that is evil.

"But you will exceed all of them. For you will sacrifice the man (the body that clothes / bares / contains me).

Note: Gnostic theology sets up a duality between the material world and the spiritual world. Since the god that created the material world was flawed, cruel, and insane, anything produced in that environment must be corrupted and opposed to the spiritual world. In this belief system the killing of Jesus' body was a good thing since it would free his spirit and unite it with the "Great One." Looked at from this angle, Judas was assisting Jesus in showing mankind the way. This line of reasoning must be taken as metaphorical. Some authors have suggested that Jesus had become entombed in his body and was asking Judas to free him. This cannot be so since Jesus comes and goes from the Holy Race or Generation above at will. Neither is Jesus touting mass suicide. Gnostic lived long lives and propagated their faith. The message here is that to remain detached from the material or corporeal and to strive to receive the knowledge here will free you in the life to come.

Already your horn has been raised, your anger has been ignited, your star has shown brightly, and your heart has (prevailed / been made strong / pure).

Note: The symbol horn is a phallic symbol but also a symbol of strength in much the way a rhino's horn is a sign of power and might.

Note: Although the lines added to the first half of this verse are tenuous, the information that is available establishes Judas' place according to this story. It does, however, open some questions. What was Judas' anger directed against? Was he sacrificing Jesus because he was angry at the established religion of the day? Was it this anger that made his heart strong or pure? Was anger his motivating force? If so, it harmonizes well with certain readings of the canonical gospels, which may indicate Judas wanted to expedite Jesus' kingdom so he would have a place of authority therein.

43. "Truly (I tell you,) your last (act will become that which will free this race but it will) grieve (you and will anger this generation and) the ruler, since he will be destroyed. (And then the) image of the great race of Adam will be raised high, for before heaven, earth, and the angels, that race from the eternal realms, exists (existed). Look, you have been told everything. Lift up your eyes and look to the cloud and the light within it and the stars around it. The star that leads the way is your star (you are the star)."

44. Then, Judas raised his eyes and saw the radiant cloud, and entered it. Those standing below him heard a voice coming from the cloud, saying, (The return of the) great race (is at

hand and the image of the Great One will be established in them because of Judas' sacrifice).

Note: This is the same cloud mentioned in verse 24. By entering the cloud Judas became one with the primal causality or "Great One / Supreme God." The Gnosis was imparted to him and he knew the mysteries. He then had understanding and strength to do what he was asked to do. This amounts to a transfiguration for Judas, much like that of Jesus. In the same manner, a voice from heaven announced his destiny.

45. (But the scribes waited for Judas, hoping to place a price on the head of Jesus.) Their high priests whispered that he had gone into the guest room for his prayer. But some scribes were there watching closely in order to arrest Jesus during the prayer, for they were afraid of the people, since he was accepted by everyone as a prophet. They approached Judas and said to him, "Why are you here? You are Jesus' disciple." Judas answered them in the way they wished. And he was given an amount of money and he handed Jesus over to them.

Note: We read of Judas' entrance into the radiant cloud and then his transaction with the scribes but there is no transition. It is possible the cloud is a metaphor for divine knowledge of the primal causality or Great God that produced Barbelo. See verse 28.

Note: The actual betrayal of Jesus by Judas is drastically downplayed. Only one paragraph is devoted to the actual act. Within this single paragraph no details are offered.

The gospel is constructed to give the reason for the betrayal. Building the rational of the act becomes far more important than the act itself, given the fact that it was the body that clothed Jesus that was destroyed and not the inner spirit. Shedding the body fulfilled destiny and freed the Christ spirit.

This was done as a demonstration of Jesus' belief in the immortal and eternal realm, which lay beyond human senses. The lesson of the Gospel of Judas and of Gnosticism in general had to do with reaching inside to gain knowledge of the unseen spiritual world. The orthodox church taught that only through martyrdom or the blessing of the church could one pass into the spiritual realm. Jesus was teaching another way. His death was the only way to exemplify his faith and show his disciples there was more than they could see in the material world. According to the Gnostic texts, the death of Jesus did not bring salvation. His life and death taught and provided knowledge, that if understood, would free the human race of its chains and allow it to ascend to the immortal realm.

This ends the Gospel of Judas.

Who Was Judas?

Judas was the son of Simon Iscariot (John 6:71, 13:2). He was a Jew from the tribe of Benjamin. (Gal 1:13-14, Phil. 3:5) The area of his birth is now called the occupied West Bank.

Out of the twelve men chosen by Jesus, Judas Iscariot was the only one born outside of Galilee. Judas was from Judea. The name, Iscariot may indicate that he was born in Cerioth (Kerrioth), a city of Judea, although others argue that a copyist error transposed two letters making Judas' named to be "Sicariot," a member of the party of the Sicarii. This comes from the Greek word for "assassins" and was a group of fanatical nationalists who sought to overthrow Roman by means of terrorism and murder. Judas Iscariot could have meant Judas the assasin.

In attempting to clarify the name one must ask if it is reasonable to expect the father and son to both be terrorists and zealots. It is far more likely the name would be derived from the city and not a factional political movement.

The book of Joshua mentions such a town in Joshua 15:25. As linguistic studies continue, it has been suggested that the word may simply mean, "town" as render in the same verse of the Revised Standard Version.

Judas was the one who kept the funds for Jesus and the disciples. At this time they seemed to have lived a rather communistic existence and share a common treasury. Judas was the treasurer (John 12:4-6)

Among the more liberal theologians who question the historicity of the gospels there is a general belief that the Bible should interpreted metaphorically. In this view of biblical interpretation Judas may not have existed as a person at all, but rather was a personification of an entire people. Judas comes from the name Judah, which means "praise." The name is a cognate of Judea, the tribe that came to symbolize and lend its name to the entire nation of the Jews. One theory holds that Judas was a personification of the Jews and a metaphor for the Jews and their rejection and betrayal of Jesus.

So, who was this man who became synonymous with greed and betrayal?

First, we will present the biblical information as recorded in the New Testament in the gospels of Matthew, Mark, Luke, and John as well as the book of Acts. We will then discern what information is contained and implied from the Bible text. We will then compare and contrast the information in the gospel of Judas to that found in the Bible.

First Impressions In The Scriptures

First impressions mean a lot. Let us look at the first time

Judas is mentioned in each of the Gospels.

Matthew 10

1 And when he had called unto him his twelve disciples, he gave them power against unclean spirits, to cast them out, and to heal all manner of sickness and all manner of disease.

2 Now the names of the twelve apostles are these; The first, Simon, who is called Peter, and Andrew his brother; James the son of Zebedee, and John his brother;

3 Philip, and Bartholomew; Thomas, and Matthew the publican; James the son of Alphaeus, and Lebbaeus, whose surname was Thaddaeus;

4 Simon the Canaanite, and Judas Iscariot, who also betrayed him.

5 These twelve Jesus sent forth, and commanded them, saying, Go not into the way of the Gentiles, and into any city of the Samaritans enter you not:

6 But go rather to the lost sheep of the house of Israel.

Mark 3

1 And he entered again into the synagogue; and there was a man there which had a withered hand.

2 And they watched him, whether he would heal him on the Sabbath day; that they might accuse him.

3 And he saith unto the man which had the withered hand,

Stand forth.

4 And he saith unto them, Is it lawful to do good on the Sabbath days, or to do evil? to save life, or to kill? But they held their peace.

5 And when he had looked round about on them with anger, being grieved for the hardness of their hearts, he saith unto the man, Stretch forth thine hand. And he stretched it out: and his hand was restored whole as the other.

6 And the Pharisees went forth, and straightway took counsel with the Herodians against him, how they might destroy him.

7 But Jesus withdrew himself with his disciples to the sea: and a great multitude from Galilee followed him, and from Judaea,

8 And from Jerusalem, and from Idumaea, and from beyond Jordan; and they about Tyre and Sidon, a great multitude, when they had heard what great things he did, came unto him.

9 And he spake to his disciples, that a small ship should wait on him because of the multitude, lest they should throng him.

10 For he had healed many; insomuch that they pressed upon him for to touch him, as many as had plagues.

11 And unclean spirits, when they saw him, fell down

before him, and cried, saying, Thou art the Son of God.

12 And he straitly charged them that they should not make him known.

13 And he goeth up into a mountain, and calleth unto him whom he would: and they came unto him.

14 And he ordained twelve, that they should be with him, and that he might send them forth to preach,

15 And to have power to heal sicknesses, and to cast out devils:

16 And Simon he surnamed Peter;

17 And James the son of Zebedee, and John the brother of James; and he surnamed them Boanerges, which is, The sons of thunder:

18 And Andrew, and Philip, and Bartholomew, and Matthew, and Thomas, and James the son of Alphaeus, and Thaddaeus, and Simon the Canaanite,

19 And Judas Iscariot, which also betrayed him: and they went into an house.

Luke 6

1 And it came to pass on the second Sabbath after the first, that he went through the corn fields; and his disciples plucked the ears of corn, and did eat, rubbing them in their hands.

2 And certain of the Pharisees said unto them, Why do you

that which is not lawful to do on the Sabbath days?

3 And Jesus answering them said, Have you not read so much as this, what David did, when himself was an hungred, and they which were with him;

4 How he went into the house of God, and did take and eat the showbread, and gave also to them that were with him; which it is not lawful to eat but for the priests alone?

5 And he said unto them, That the Son of man is Lord also of the Sabbath.

6 And it came to pass also on another Sabbath, that he entered into the synagogue and taught: and there was a man whose right hand was withered.

7 And the scribes and Pharisees watched him, whether he would heal on the Sabbath day; that they might find an accusation against him.

8 But he knew their thoughts, and said to the man which had the withered hand, Rise up, and stand forth in the midst. And he arose and stood forth.

9 Then said Jesus unto them, I will ask you one thing; Is it lawful on the Sabbath days to do good, or to do evil? to save life, or to destroy it?

10 And looking round about upon them all, he said unto the man, Stretch forth your hand. And he did so: and his hand was restored whole as the other.

11 And they were filled with madness; and communed one with another what they might do to Jesus.

12 And it came to pass in those days, that he went out into a mountain to pray, and continued all night in prayer to God.

13 And when it was day, he called unto him his disciples: and of them he chose twelve, whom also he named apostles;

14 Simon, (whom he also named Peter,) and Andrew his brother, James and John, Philip and Bartholomew,

15 Matthew and Thomas, James the son of Alphaeus, and Simon called Zelotes,

16 And Judas the brother of James, and Judas Iscariot, which also was the traitor.

John 6

38 For I came down from heaven, not to do mine own will, but the will of him that sent me.

39 And this is the Father's will which hath sent me, that of all which he hath given me I should lose nothing, but should raise it up again at the last day.

40 And this is the will of him that sent me, that every one which seeth the Son, and believeth on him, may have everlasting life: and I will raise him up at the last day.

41 The Jews then murmured at him, because he said, I am the bread which came down from heaven.

42 And they said, Is not this Jesus, the son of Joseph, whose

father and mother we know? how is it then that he saith, I came down from heaven?

43 Jesus therefore answered and said unto them, Murmur not among yourselves.

44 No man can come to me, except the Father which hath sent me draw him: and I will raise him up at the last day.

45 It is written in the prophets, And they shall be all taught of God. Every man therefore that hath heard, and hath learned of the Father, cometh unto me.

46 Not that any man hath seen the Father, save he which is of God, he hath seen the Father.

47 Verily, verily, I say unto you, He that believeth on me hath everlasting life.

48 I am that bread of life.

49 Your fathers did eat manna in the wilderness, and are dead.

50 This is the bread which cometh down from heaven, that a man may eat thereof, and not die.

51 I am the living bread which came down from heaven: if any man eat of this bread, he shall live for ever: and the bread that I will give is my flesh, which I will give for the life of the world.

52 The Jews therefore strove among themselves, saying, How can this man give us his flesh to eat?

53 Then Jesus said unto them, Verily, verily, I say unto you, Except you eat the flesh of the Son of man, and drink his blood, you have no life in you.

54 Whoso eateth my flesh, and drinketh my blood, hath eternal life; and I will raise him up at the last day.

55 For my flesh is meat indeed, and my blood is drink indeed.

56 He that eateth my flesh, and drinketh my blood, dwells in me, and I in him.

57 As the living Father hath sent me, and I live by the Father: so he that eateth me, even he shall live by me.

58 This is that bread which came down from heaven: not as your fathers did eat manna, and are dead: he that eateth of this bread shall live for ever.

59 These things said he in the synagogue, as he taught in Capernaum.

60 Many therefore of his disciples, when they had heard this, said, This is an hard saying; who can hear it?

61 When Jesus knew in himself that his disciples murmured at it, he said unto them, Doth this offend you?

62 What and if you shall see the Son of man ascend up where he was before?

63 It is the spirit that quickeneth; the flesh profiteth nothing: the words that I speak unto you, they are spirit, and they are life.

64 But there are some of you that believe not. For Jesus knew from the beginning who they were that believed not, and who should betray him.

65 And he said, Therefore said I unto you, that no man can come unto me, except it were given unto him of my Father.

66 From that time many of his disciples went back, and walked no more with him.

67 Then said Jesus unto the twelve, Will you also go away?

68 Then Simon Peter answered him, Lord, to whom shall we go? thou hast the words of eternal life.

69 And we believe and are sure that thou art that Christ, the Son of the living God.

70 Jesus answered them, Have not I chosen you twelve, and one of you is a devil?

71 He spake of Judas Iscariot the son of Simon: for he it was that should betray him, being one of the twelve.

In each incident the first time, and indeed, every time the name Judas is mentioned he is labeled as the one who betrayed Jesus. Judas is clearly and repeated marked as a traitor. This sets the mood for the entire panoply of scenes and verses regarding Judas. The story in each gospel builds on these first lines.

The Biblical Account of Judas

Now, let us look at the entire Biblical account of Judas. Information gleaned from the biblical references will be compared and contrasted to those in the Gospel of Judas. One may think, on prima fascia, there would be complete divergence and contradiction, and there are many, but the parallels are surprising.

Matthew

Chapter 26

14: Then one of the twelve, who was called Judas Iscariot, went to the chief priests

15: and said, "What will you give me if I deliver him to you?" And they paid him thirty pieces of silver.

16: And from that moment he sought an opportunity to betray him.

17: Now on the first day of Unleavened Bread the disciples came to Jesus, saying, "Where will you have us prepare for you to eat the passover?"

18: He said, "Go into the city to a certain one, and say to him, `The Teacher says, My time is at hand; I will keep the passover at your house with my disciples.'"

19: And the disciples did as Jesus had directed them, and they prepared the passover.

20: When it was evening, he sat at table with the twelve disciples;

21: and as they were eating, he said, "Truly, I say to you, one of you will betray me."

22: And they were very sorrowful, and began to say to him one after another, "Is it I, Lord?"

23: He answered, "He who has dipped his hand in the dish with me, will betray me.

24: The Son of man goes as it is written of him, but woe to that man by whom the Son of man is betrayed! It would have been better for that man if he had not been born."

25: Judas, who betrayed him, said, "Is it I, Rabbi?" He said to him, "You have said so."

47: While he [Jesus] was still speaking, Judas came, one of the twelve, and with him a great crowd with swords and clubs, from the chief priests and the elders of the people.

48: Now the betrayer had given them a sign, saying, "The one I shall kiss is the man; seize him."

49: And he came up to Jesus at once and said, "Hail, Rabbi!" And he kissed him.

50: Jesus said to him, "Friend, why are you here?" Then they came up and laid hands on Jesus and seized him.

Chapter 27

1: When morning came, all the chief priests and the elders of the people took counsel against Jesus to put him to death;

2: and they bound him and led him away and delivered him to Pilate the governor.

3: When Judas, his betrayer, saw that he was condemned, he repented and brought back the thirty pieces of silver to the chief priests and the elders,

4: saying, "I have sinned in betraying innocent blood." They said, "What is that to us? See to it yourself."

5: And throwing down the pieces of silver in the temple, he departed; and he went and hanged himself.

6: But the chief priests, taking the pieces of silver, said, "It is not lawful to put them into the treasury, since they are blood money."

7: So they took counsel, and bought with them the potter's field, to bury strangers in.

8: Therefore that field has been called the Field of Blood to this day.

9: Then was fulfilled what had been spoken by the prophet Jeremiah, saying, "And they took the thirty pieces of silver, the price of him on whom a price had been set by some of the sons of Israel,

10: and they gave them for the potter's field, as the Lord directed me."

Mark

Chapter 14

1: It was now two days before the Passover and the feast of Unleavened Bread. And the chief priests and the scribes were seeking how to arrest him by stealth, and kill him;

2: for they said, "Not during the feast, lest there be a tumult of the people."

10: Then Judas Iscariot, who was one of the twelve, went to the chief priests in order to betray him to them.

11: And when they heard it they were glad, and promised to give him money. And he sought an opportunity to betray him.

12: And on the first day of Unleavened Bread, when they sacrificed the passover lamb, his disciples said to him, "Where will you have us go and prepare for you to eat the passover?"

13: And he sent two of his disciples, and said to them, "Go into the city, and a man carrying a jar of water will meet you; follow him,

14: and wherever he enters, say to the householder, `The Teacher says, Where is my guest room, where I am to eat the passover with my disciples?'

15: And he will show you a large upper room furnished and ready; there prepare for us." 16: And the disciples set out and went to the city, and found it as he had told them; and they prepared the Passover.

17: And when it was evening he came with the twelve.

18: And as they were at table eating, Jesus said, "Truly, I say to you, one of you will betray me, one who is eating with me."

19: They began to be sorrowful, and to say to him one after another, "Is it I?"

20: He said to them, "It is one of the twelve, one who is dipping bread into the dish with me.

21: For the Son of man goes as it is written of him, but woe to that man by whom the Son of man is betrayed! It would have been better for that man if he had not been born."

43: And immediately, while he was still speaking, Judas came, one of the twelve, and with him a crowd with swords and clubs, from the chief priests and the scribes and the elders.

44: Now the betrayer had given them a sign, saying, "The one I shall kiss is the man; seize him and lead him away under guard."

45: And when he came, he went up to him at once, and said, "Rabbi!" And he kissed him.

46: And they laid hands on him and seized him.

Luke

Chapter 22

1: Now the feast of Unleavened Bread drew near, which is called the Passover.

2: And the chief priests and the scribes were seeking how to put him to death; for they feared the people.

3: Then Satan entered into Judas called Iscariot, who was of the number of the twelve;

4: he went away and conferred with the chief priests and officers how he might betray him to them.

5: And they were glad, and engaged to give him money.

6: So he agreed, and sought an opportunity to betray him to them in the absence of the multitude.

17: And he took a cup, and when he had given thanks he said, "Take this, and divide it among yourselves;

18: for I tell you that from now on I shall not drink of the fruit of the vine until the kingdom of God comes."

19: And he took bread, and when he had given thanks he broke it and gave it to them, saying, "This is my body which is given for you. Do this in remembrance of me."

20: And likewise the cup after supper, saying, "This cup which is poured out for you is the new covenant in my blood.

21: But behold the hand of him who betrays me is with me on the table.

22: For the Son of man goes as it has been determined; but woe to that man by whom he is betrayed!"

23: And they began to question one another, which of them it was that would do this.

45: And when he rose from prayer, he came to the disciples and found them sleeping for sorrow,

46: and he said to them, "Why do you sleep? Rise and pray that you may not enter into temptation."

47: While he was still speaking, there came a crowd, and the man called Judas, one of the twelve, was leading them. He drew near to Jesus to kiss him;

48: but Jesus said to him, "Judas, would you betray the Son of man with a kiss?"

John

Chapter 13

1: Now before the feast of the Passover, when Jesus knew that his hour had come to depart out of this world to the Father, having loved his own who were in the world, he loved them to the end.

2: And during supper, when the devil had already put it into the heart of Judas Iscariot, Simon's son, to betray him,

3: Jesus, knowing that the Father had given all things into his hands, and that he had come from God and was going to God,

4: rose from supper, laid aside his garments, and girded himself with a towel.

21: When Jesus had thus spoken, he was troubled in spirit, and testified, "Truly, truly, I say to you, one of you will betray me."

22: The disciples looked at one another, uncertain of whom he spoke.

23: One of his disciples, whom Jesus loved, was lying close to the breast of Jesus;

24: so Simon Peter beckoned to him and said, "Tell us who it is of whom he speaks."

25: So lying thus, close to the breast of Jesus, he said to him, "Lord, who is it?"

26: Jesus answered, "It is he to whom I shall give this morsel when I have dipped it." So when he had dipped the morsel, he gave it to Judas, the son of Simon Iscariot.

27: Then after the morsel, Satan entered into him. Jesus said to him, "What you are going to do, do quickly."

28: Now no one at the table knew why he said this to him.

29: Some thought that, because Judas had the money box, Jesus was telling him, "Buy what we need for the feast"; or, that he should give something to the poor.

30: So, after receiving the morsel, he immediately went out; and it was night.

John

Chapter 18

1: When Jesus had spoken these words, he went forth with his disciples across the Kidron valley, where there was a garden, which he and his disciples entered.

2: Now Judas, who betrayed him, also knew the place; for Jesus often met there with his disciples.

3: So Judas, procuring a band of soldiers and some officers from the chief priests and the Pharisees, went there with lanterns and torches and weapons.

4: Then Jesus, knowing all that was to befall him, came forward and said to them, "Whom do you seek?"

5: They answered him, "Jesus of Nazareth." Jesus said to them, "I am he." Judas, who betrayed him, was standing with them.

6: When he said to them, "I am he," they drew back and fell to the ground.

7: Again he asked them, "Whom do you seek?" And they said, "Jesus of Nazareth."

8: Jesus answered, "I told you that I am he; so, if you seek me, let these men go."

9: This was to fulfill the word which he had spoken, "Of those whom thou gave me I lost not one."

Acts

Chapter 1

15 And in those days Peter stood up in the midst of the disciples, and said, (the number of names together were about an hundred and twenty,)

16 Men and brethren, this scripture must needs have been fulfilled, which the Holy Ghost by the mouth of David spake before concerning Judas, which was guide to them that took Jesus.

17 For he was numbered with us, and had obtained part of this ministry.

18 Now this man purchased a field with the reward of iniquity; and falling headlong, he burst asunder in the midst, and all his bowels gushed out.

19 And it was known unto all the dwellers at Jerusalem;

insomuch as that field is called in their proper tongue, Aceldama, that is to say, "The field of blood."

20 For it is written in the book of Psalms, Let his habitation be desolate, and let no man dwell therein: and his bishopric let another take.

21 Wherefore of these men which have companied with us all the time that the Lord Jesus went in and out among us,

22 Beginning from the baptism of John, unto that same day that he was taken up from us, must one be ordained to be a witness with us of his resurrection.

23 And they appointed two, Joseph called Barsabas, who was surnamed Justus, and Matthias.

24 And they prayed, and said, Thou, Lord, which knowest the hearts of all men, shew whether of these two thou hast chosen,

25 That he may take part of this ministry and apostleship, from which Judas by transgression fell, that he might go to his own place.

26 And they gave forth their lots; and the lot fell upon Matthias; and he was numbered with the eleven apostles.

John 6

69 And we believe and are sure that thou art that Christ, the

Joseph B. Lumpkin

Son of the living God.

70 Jesus answered them, Have not I chosen you twelve, and one of you is a devil?

71 He spake of Judas Iscariot the son of Simon: for he it was that should betray him, being one of the twelve.

The Nature of Judas

Gospel of Judas: 23. When Jesus heard this, he laughed and said to him, "You (are the) thirteenth spirit (daemon), why are you trying so hard? However, speak up, and I will be patient with you."

John 6:70 Jesus answered them, Have not I chosen you twelve, and one of you is a devil?
71 He spake of Judas Iscariot the son of Simon: for he it was that should betray him, being one of the twelve.

On the surface these two statements may seem to harmonize. It may seem obvious that Judas was following his basic nature when he turned Jesus over to the authorities. However, the tone and context of these two, seemingly similar statements are in fact opposite.

In John's account the word used for devil is a word that means "accuser." The word, "devil" is a transliteration from the Greek and is set down into English with little alteration. In one or two cases it is translated into the "true" meaning, such as in 1 Tim. 3:11, where the wives of the deacons are forbidden to be slanderers, whereas the word elsewhere is rendered "devil."

Parkhurst, in his Greek Lexicon, tells us that diabolos, the word translated devil, is a compound of dia through, and ballo to cast, and means to dart or strike through; hence, to slander, to utter falsehood maliciously, to speak lies. "The word, "devil" is best to be read in English as The Liar, The Slanderer, or The Accuser.

Further hints are given in a group of scriptures describing the moment of decision when Judas left the Passover feast to go arrange for Jesus' arrest.

Luke
Chapter 22
1: Now the feast of Unleavened Bread drew near, which is called the Passover.
2: And the chief priests and the scribes were seeking how to put him to death; for they feared the people.
3: Then Satan entered into Judas called Iscariot, who was of the number of the twelve;
4: he went away and conferred with the chief priests and officers how he might betray him to them.

The word rendered "entered" can also be "revealed." If Jesus thought Judas was literally a devil the text could read "Then Satan revealed himself as Judas…"

Yet, in other verses no such thought is entertained but instead Judas is portrayed as a man and even a friend.

In Mark 14:18-21 Jesus tells the disciples that a person who is eating with them will give Jesus over to be killed. He goes on to say that it would be better for him if he were never born. Jesus echoes Psalms 41:9, which foretells that his best friend with whom he ate will betray him.

In the gospel of Judas, Jesus calls Judas a spirit or daemon. This indicates the Jesus believes him to be a powerful spiritual being. In the mythology of the time daemons or spirits did the bidding of a god and were placed as mediators between man and the god they served. One may ask what god Jesus had in mind when addressing Judas in such a way. The statement may not be as positive as one would think, but it does place Judas and the others in a status outside of the human norm. Since Judas is referred to as the "thirteenth spirit" it can be assumed that there are twelve more. One could jump to the conclusion Jesus is referring to the twelve disciples. That would be the eleven left and the one chosen to replace Judas. This assumption would leave out the possibility of Judas being given status with the twelve rulers referred to in The Gospel of Judas verse 34. "The twelve rulers (aeons) spoke with the twelve angels: 'Let each of you (receive a portion) and let them (that are in this) generation (be ruled by these) angels'…

Of all the biblical statements relating to Judas, one of the most perplexing passages is the one in the book of Acts.

Acts 1: 23 And they appointed two, Joseph called Barsabas, who was surnamed Justus, and Matthias.

24 And they prayed, and said, Thou, Lord, which knowest the hearts of all men, shew whether of these two thou hast chosen,

25 That he may take part of this ministry and apostleship, from which Judas by transgression fell, that he might go to his own place.

The reader is left to wonder what and where "his own place" may be. Judas is called "a devil" and the "son of perdition" and we are told he went to "his own place" after his suicide. The only clue we are given to the mystery comes from Second Thessalonians.

2 Thessalonians 2

1 Now we beseech you, brethren, by the coming of our Lord Jesus Christ, and by our gathering together unto him,

2 That you be not soon shaken in mind, or be troubled, neither by spirit, nor by word, nor by letter as from us, as that the day of Christ is at hand.

3 Let no man deceive you by any means: for that day shall

not come, except there come a falling away first, and that man of sin be revealed, the son of perdition;

4 Who opposeth and exalteth himself above all that is called God, or that is worshipped; so that he as God sitteth in the temple of God, shewing himself that he is God.

In this passage, the title of "son of perdition" is used to identify the Antichrist. This is the only other time the term is used. Is Judas the Antichrist? Will we see him resurrected and ruling the world? Is hell "his own place?" Is hell his kingdom? Or, is he a saint who sacrificed his name and reputation in order to help Jesus save the human race?

Thus goes the polarity of thought concerning Judas as viewed between the Gospel of Judas and the Biblical account.

Whatever Judas' nature may be, we know he was a man placed in a position to turn the entire human history with a single act. He was a spiritual force. He was the executioner with his hand firmly on the trigger of prophecy.

Right and wrong hinge on intent. The same action may occur with opposite reasons in mind. It is the intent behind the action that determines right from wrong. One may kill to protect or to destroy. Both acts result in death but one is forgivable and at time even laudable. The other results in punishment and retribution. It is not the actions of Judas that we debate. Both sources, Bible and Gospel, reflect the same action. It is his intent that we attempt to discern.

Yet, it is possible to miss the larger picture. Jesus, the vessel of the Christ-spirit, selected a man to carry out his prophecy and his wishes.

Judas' Reward

Mat. 19:28

27 Then answered Peter and said unto him, Behold, we have forsaken all, and followed you; what shall we have therefore?

28 And Jesus said unto them, Verily I say unto you, That you which have followed me, in the regeneration when the Son of man shall sit in the throne of his glory, you also shall sit upon twelve thrones, judging the twelve tribes of Israel.

Gospel of Judas 26. Jesus answered and said to him, "Come, that I (may show you the kingdom you will receive. I will show you the what is to come of you and this generation, but that you will be grieved when you see the kingdom and all its generation."

When Judas heard Him he said to him, "What good is it that I have received it? You have set me apart for that generation."

Jesus answered and said, "You will become the thirteenth, and you will be cursed by the other generations, and you will come to rule over them. In the last days they will curse your ascent to the holy (generation / kingdom)."

It seems most odd that a Biblical account of Judas would have Jesus proclaiming to the twelve disciples that their reward would be exultation and the position of judges over the tribes of Israel. Judas was present in this conversation and Jesus addresses them as a group. The statement seems to be a direct contradiction at first, but Jesus inserted a condition and made room for exclusions.

Let's look at the condition. "…**you, which have followed me, in the regeneration when the Son of man shall sit in the throne of his glory…**"

Even though Jesus addresses all twelve as a group, he does not say that they will all be rulers. He tells them that if they follow him their reward will be given when he comes to power and sits on the throne of his glory. The fact that this condition was given leads one to believe there was a reason it should exist and therefore all twelve sitting there may not follow him. However, Jesus does tell them there will be twelve men sitting on twelve thrones, judging the twelve tribes. If Judas is not counted in this number it would only leave Mathias or Paul to take his place. The Greek has the word translated as "you" as a plural, leaving the simplest explanation counting Judas in the number of those judging the tribes but this is not so considering that 1Cor:15:5 states that

Jesus appeared to Cephas, and then to the twelve. This was after Judas was dead and Mathias had taken his place.

In contrast, the Gospel of Judas is very direct and clear. Jesus tells Judas, **"You will become the thirteenth, and you will be cursed by the other generations, and you will come to rule over them. In the last days they will curse your ascent to the holy (generation / kingdom)."**

Judas will come to rule over them, but who is "them?" Is it the other disciples or could it be the "other generations?" This makes a huge difference. If we take the statement literally, we have to read it has Judas taking rulership over the other generations. These are the generations that did not receive the divine knowledge or that were assigned souls from Michael. If this is the case it does not necessarily contradict the Biblical account since the Antichrist will indeed rule over those whom did not receive the saving knowledge of Jesus.

But what about his accent to the "holy" generation?

In the Gnostic cosmology Jesus was sent by the Great One and not by the creator of the material world. Antichrist is a term used in Greek that is not used in the same way as orthodox teaching as indoctrinated us to use. The word indicates some one or some thing that is a replacement for or is in opposition to the anointed one, but whose anointed one becomes the question. The problem with Gnosticism is a reversal of roles. In Gnostic theology Jesus did not come from the makers of this world but from one above the maker. Therefore, the one anointed by the maker is himself evil. If Jesus were sent by the Demiurge, Jesus would be evil. If one were against the anointed one of the Demiurge this person or Antichrist would be good in the Gnostic view. So, the Antichrist of the church was the savior of the Gnostics.

This idea is driven home when the place and purpose of Satan, the ultimate Antichrist, is examined through Gnostic eyes.

Satan's temptation to eat of the forbidden fruit is seen, not as temptation but as a way of salvation presented to Eve. This is because it offered Adam and Even "Knowledge" or Gnosis, which is salvation to Gnostics. Irenaeus tells us of others who regarded the tree of knowledge of good and evil as "Gnosis itself." This is a good example of why historians such as Roland H. Bainton have concluded that although Gnosticism absorbed much of the tradition of the Hebrews, it nevertheless "completely reversed their values."

Even if Judas was the "son of perdition" and Satan himself, he would be a liberator under the Gnostic tenants.

John 17

11 And now I am no more in the world, but these are in the world, and I come to you. Holy Father, keep through thine

own name those whom thou hast given me, that they may be one, as we are.

12 While I was with them in the world, I kept them in your name: those that thou gavest me I have kept, and none of them is lost, but the son of perdition; that the scripture might be fulfilled.

2 Thessalonians 2

1 Now we beseech you, brethren, by the coming of our Lord Jesus Christ, and by our gathering together unto him,

2 That you be not soon shaken in mind, or be troubled, neither by spirit, nor by word, nor by letter as from us, as that the day of Christ is at hand.

3 Let no man deceive you by any means: for that day shall not come, except there come a falling away first, and that man of sin be revealed, the son of perdition;

4 Who opposeth and exalteth himself above all that is called God, or that is worshipped; so that he as God sitteth in the temple of God, shewing himself that he is God.

5 Remember you not, that, when I was yet with you, I told you these things?

6 And now you know what withholdeth that he might be revealed in his time.

7 For the mystery of iniquity doth already work: only he who now letteth will let, until he be taken out of the way.

8 And then shall that Wicked be revealed, whom the Lord shall consume with the spirit of his mouth, and shall destroy with the brightness of his coming:

9 Even him, whose coming is after the working of Satan with all power and signs and lying wonders,

10 And with all deceivableness of unrighteousness in them that perish; because they received not the love of the truth, that they might be saved.

Was Judas the incarnation of Satan? Is it the face of Judas we will be looking into when finally the Anti-Christ is revealed? The scriptures seem to imply just that.

The Setup

Was Jesus God? Was he the son of God? Was he omnipotent? Did he understand what was going to befall him? Did he know what Judas was planning?

To answer yes to any of these questions would shift the betrayal and death of Jesus away from the act of a single scoundrel into mutual culpability. If a person knows that an action will occur resulting in death and does nothing to prevent it, even our civil laws view this as negligent homicide... or in the case of Jesus, suicide.

John 6:70 Jesus answered them, Have not I chosen you twelve, and one of you is a devil?
71 He spake of Judas Iscariot the son of Simon: for he it was that should betray him, being one of the twelve.
John 13: 27: Then after the morsel, Satan entered into him. Jesus said to him, "What you are going to do, do quickly."

If one believes in Jesus' divinity, his power, of even his common sense, it must be assumed that he knew what was about to happen. He foretold the occurrence. He forewarned his disciples. He dismissed Judas from the Passover meal and commanded him to " do what he was going to do and do it quickly."

The only question remaining is the one invoked by the Gospel of Judas. Was the unfolding scene leading to the crucifixion being allow to happen or was it being actively orchestrated?

Both the Gospel of Judas and the canonical gospels state that Jesus was fully aware of the future events. We are left to wonder if Jesus came to Judas and asked him to do this deed of betrayal so that scripture could be fulfilled or if Jesus simple chose Judas knowing his nature would lead to this end.

Judas' actions were small and probably insignificant in the overall scheme of things. The Jewish leaders were already planning the demise of Jesus. They would have already captured him if it weren't for their fear of causing a civil disturbance. They decided to wait until Jesus was out of sight and away from the town's people. Jesus points this out to the arresting guards in Luke 22:53.

So, we are left knowing that Judas brought the authorities to a place where Jesus frequented to capture a man they had already decided to arrest and whom they saw every day in town or at the temple. We are told that Jesus knew what was about to happen. We are also told that Jesus told Judas when to act.

Excluding the divergent theologies of the Gospel of Judas and the canonical gospels, there remains only one simple question; that of "why." What motivated Judas? Why did he do this unthinkable thing?

Jesus told him to do it. This is true in both stories. Jesus was aware of the plan. He had the ability to stop the scenario at any time.

Did Jesus use Judas to fulfill prophecy, knowing his greedy nature, or did he use Judas, knowing his devotion? Either way, Judas took the fall.

Joseph B. Lumpkin

THE 29th CHAPTER OF ACTS

In the 1700's C.S. Sonnini traveled to the Middle East. He sojourned through Turkey and Greece. There he met the Sultan Abdoul Achmet who presented him with a copy of an ancient manuscript. It was a copy of the manuscript found in the Archives of Constantinople. Along with the text was permission by the Sultan to travel freely over the Ottoman Empire.

After his return he began working on the translation. In the late 1700's and before 1800, C.S.Sonnini published his copy of Sonnini's Travels in Turkey and Greece. It contained his translation of the text.

He was traveling during the reign of Louis XVI, who reigned from AD 1774 to AD 1793. He published his travels between those two dates, 1774 and 1793. It had been in his possession for over thirty years.

The book was not widely known and never gained the attention needed to propagate the lost chapter of Acts to any degree. Later the Manuscript passed into other hands and was found interleaved in a copy of Sonnini's Travels in Turkey and Greece and was purchased at the sale of the library and effects of the late Right Honorable Sir John Newport Bart, of Ireland. Sir John's family arms were engraved on the cover of the book.

The Sonnini Manuscript contains the account of Paul's journey to Spain and Britain. The document, purported to be the concluding portion of the "Acts of the Apostles" covers a portion of the period after Paul's two year enforced residence in Rome, in his own hired house. It is written in the style of the Bible Acts and reads like a continuation of the canonical book of Acts.

The Biblical Acts of the Apostles and the Book of James are the only two New Testament books not ending in `amen.' This has led some Bible scholars to believe they are incomplete in their present form. The addition of the 29th chapter ties up loose ends such as Paul's statement about wanting to visit the tribes in dispersion and in Spain. Acts ends with him still under house arrest. The 29th chapter has him completing his mission and ending with the word, "Amen."

ACTS Chapter 29

Verse 1. Paul, full of the blessing of Christ, and overflowing in the Spirit, left Rome, having decided to go into Spain, because he had wanted to travel there for a long time, and he thought also to go from there to Britain.

Verse 2. Because he had heard in Phoenicia that some of the children of Israel, around the time of the Assyrian captivity, had escaped by sea to "the Islands far away" as proclaimed by the Prophet, and called by the Romans, Britain.

Verse 3. Since the Lord commanded the gospel to be preached far and wide to the Gentiles, and to the lost sheep of the House of Israel.

Verse 4. And no man hindered Paul because he testified boldly of Jesus before the governments and among the people; and be took with him certain of the brethren which lived with him at Rome, and they boarded a ship at Ostium, and having fair winds were brought safely into an safety (harbor) of Spain.

Verse 5. And many people gathered from the towns and villages, and the hill country; for they had heard of the conversion of the Apostles, and the many miracles he had performed.

Verse 6. And Paul preached with might in Spain, and great many people believed and were converted, for they knew he was an apostle sent from God.

Verse 7. And finding a ship in Armorica sailing to Britain they departed from Spain. Paul and his company passed along the South coast and reached a port called Raphinus.

Verse 8. Now when word spread wide that the Apostle had landed on their coast, large numbers of the inhabitants met him, and they treated Paul courteously and he entered in at the east gate of their city, and was housed in the house of a Hebrew and one of his own nation.

Verse 9. And the next day he came and stood upon Mount Lud;(Now the site of St. Paul's Cathedral.) And the people amassed at the gate, and assembled in the main street, and he preached Christ unto them, and they believed the word and the testimony of Jesus.

Verse 10. And at sunset the Holy Ghost fell upon Paul, and he prophesied, saying, "BEHOLD IN THE LAST DAYS THE GOD

OF PEACE SHALL LIVE IN THE CITIES, AND THE INHABITANTS OF THEM SHALL BE COUNTED: AND IN THE SEVENTH CENSUS OF THE PEOPLE, THEIR EYES SHALL BE OPENED, AND THE GLORY OF THEIR INHERITANCE WILL SHINE OUT BEFORE THEM. NATIONS SHALL COME UP TO WORSHIP ON THE MOUNT THAT TESTIFIES OF THE PATIENCE AND LONG SUFFERING OF A SERVANT OF THE LORD."

Verse 11. And in the last days new announcements of the Gospel shall come forth out of Jerusalem, and the hearts of the people shall be filled with joy, and they shall look and spring of water shall be opened, and there shall be no more disease.

Verse 12. In those days there shall be wars and rumors of wars; and a king shall rise up, and his sword shall be for the healing of the nations, and peace he makes shall last, and the glory of his kingdom will be a wonder among princes.

Verse 13. And it came to pass that certain of the Druids came to Paul privately and showed by their rites and ceremonies (to prove) they were descended from the Jews which escaped from bondage in the land of Egypt, and the apostle believed these things, and he gave them the kiss of peace.

Verse 14. And Paul lived in his housing for three months proving the faith and preaching Christ continually.

Verse 15. And after these things Paul and his brethren left Raphinus, and sailed to Atium in Gaul.

Verse 16. And Paul preached in the Roman garrisons and among the people, encouraging all men to repent and confess their sins.

Verse 17. And there came to him certain of the Belgae to ask him about the new doctrine, and of the man Jesus; and Paul opened his heart unto them, and told them all things that had happened to him, how Christ Jesus came into the world to save sinners; and they departed wondering among themselves about the things they had heard.

Verse 18. And after he preached and toiled much Paul and his fellow workers went to Helvetia, and came to Mount Pontius Pilate, where he who condemned the Lord Jesus threw himself down headlong, and so miserably perished.

Verse 19. And immediately a torrent gushed from the mountain and washed his body (which had been) broken in pieces, into a lake.

Verse 20. And Paul stretched forth his hands upon the water, and prayed unto the Lord, saying, 0 Lord God, give a sign unto all nations that here Pontius Pilate, which condemned your only-begotten Son, plunged down headlong in to the pit.

Verse 21. And while Paul was still speaking, they looked there came a great earthquake, and the face of the waters was changed, and the lake took the form like unto the Son of Man hanging in an agony upon the Cross.

Verse 22. And a voice came out of heaven saying, Even Pilate has escaped the rage to come, for he washed his hands before the multitude at the shedding of the Lord Jesus' blood. (See Rev.21:8)

Verse 23. Because of this, when Paul and those with him saw the earthquake and heard the voice of the angel they glorified God and their spirits were greatly strengthened.

Verse 24. And they journeyed and came to Mount Julius where two pillars stood, one on the right hand and one on the left hand, erected by Caesar Augustus.

Verse 25. And Paul was filled with the Holy Ghost and stood up between the two pillars, saying, Men and brethren, these stones which you see this day shall testify of my journey here and truly I say they shall remain until the outpouring of the spirit upon all nations, and the way will not be hindered throughout all generations.

Verse 26. And they went forth and came to Illyricum, intending to go by Macedonia into Asia, and grace was found in all the churches; and they prospered and had peace. Amen.

The Epistle of Barnabas

The Epistle of Barnabas was written in Greek and preserved in the 4th century Codex Sinaiticus where it appears at the end of the New Testament. It is traditionally ascribed to Barnabas who is mentioned in the Acts of the Apostles. A form of the Epistle is listed in canonical works in the 6th century Codex Claromontanus. It is not to be confused with the Gospel of Barnabas. Origen calls it as "a Catholic Epistle" and it among the "Sacred Scriptures."

It was written after the destruction of Jerusalem, since reference is made to that event, however we have no way of knowing but how long after the destruction. Our best guess is that the date of writing is not later than the middle of the second century, and that it cannot be placed earlier than thirty years before. The purpose of the epistle is stated in the first chapter as "to perfect the knowledge" of those to whom he wrote. Hilgenfeld holds that a Gentile Christian of the school of Alexandria wrote it at the close of the first century. It was written to defeat a growing Judaic form of Christianity. Until the recent discovery of the Codex Sinaiticus by Tischendorf, the first four and a half chapters were known only in an ancient

Latin version. The whole Greek text is now recovered.

The Epistle of Barnabas

1:1 I Bid you peaceful greetings, sons and daughters, in the name of the Lord that loved us.

1:2 Seeing that the rites and laws of God are great and rich unto you, I rejoice with an exceedingly great and overflowing joy at your blessed and glorious spirits; so innate is the grace of the spiritual gift that you have received.

1:3 Wherefore also I the more congratulate myself hoping to be saved, for that I truly see the Spirit poured out among you from the riches of the fountain of the Lord. So greatly did the much-desired sight of you astonish me about you.

1:4 Being thusly persuaded of this, and being aware that I said much to you, I know that the Lord journeyed with me on the way of righteousness, and am completely given to love you more than my own soul (because great faith and love dwells in you through the hope of the life which is His.)

1:5 Because of this I shall take care to communicate to you some small part of that which I received, it shall turn to my reward for having ministered to such spirits, I was eager to send you a trifle, that along with your faith you might have your knowledge also perfect.

1:6 Well then, there are three rites and laws of the Lord; *the hope of life, which is the beginning and end of our faith; and righteousness, which is the beginning and end of judgment; love shown in gladness and exultation, the testimony of works of righteousness.

1:7 For the Lord made known to us by His prophets things past and present, giving us likewise the firstfruits of the taste of things future. And seeing each of these things severally coming to pass, according as He spoke, we ought to offer a richer and higher offering to the fear of Him. But I will show forth a few things, not as though I were a teacher, but as one of yourselves, whereby you shall be gladdened in the present circumstances.

2:1 Seeing then that the days are evil, and that the Active One himself has the authority, we ought to give heed to ourselves and to seek out the rites and laws of the Lord.

2:2 The aids of our faith then are fear and patience, and our allies are long-suffering and self-restraint.

2:3 While these abide in a pure spirit in matters relating to the Lord, wisdom, understanding, science, knowledge rejoice with them.

2:4 For He hath made manifest to us by all the prophets that He wants neither sacrifices nor whole burnt offerings nor oblations, saying at one time;

2:5 What to Me is the multitude of your sacrifices, said the Lord I am full of whole burnt-offerings, and the fat of lambs and the blood of bulls and of goats desire not, not though you should come to be seen of Me. or who required these things at your hands? You shall continue no more to tread My court. If you bring fine flour, it is in vain; incense is an abomination to Me; your new moons and your Sabbaths I cannot away with.

2:6 These things therefore He annulled, that the new law of our Lord Jesus Christ, being free from the yoke of constraint, might have its oblation not made by human hands.

2:7 And He said again unto them; Did I command your fathers when they went forth from the land of Egypt to bring Me whole burnt offerings and sacrifices?

2:8 No! This was My command unto them, Let none of you bear a grudge of evil against his neighbor in his heart, and love you not a false oath.

2:9 So we ought to perceive, unless we are without understanding, the mind of the goodness of our Father; for He spoke to us, desiring us not to go astray like them but to seek how we may approach Him.

2:10 Thus then spoke He to us; The sacrifice unto God is a broken heart, the smell of a sweet savor unto the Lord is a heart that glorifies its Maker. We ought therefore, brethren, to learn accurately concerning our salvation, lest the Evil One having created an entrance of error in us should fling us away from our life.

3:1 He spoke again therefore to them concerning these things; Wherefore fast you for Me, said the Lord, so that your voice is heard this day crying aloud? This is not the fast which have chosen, said the Lord; not a man abasing his soul;

3:2 not though you should bend your neck as a hoop, and put on sackcloth and make your bed of ashes, not even so shall you call a fast that is acceptable.

3:3 But unto us He said; Behold, this is the fast which I have chosen, said the Lord; loosen every band of wickedness, untie the tightened cords of forcible contracts, send away the broken ones released and tear in pieces every unjust bond. Break your bread to the hungry, and if you see one naked clothe him; bring the shelterless into your house, and if you see a humble man, you shall not despise him, neither shall any one of your household and of yours own seed.

3:4 Then shall your light break forth in the morning, and your healing shall arise quickly, and righteousness shall go forth before your face, and the glory of God shall environ you.

3:5 Then shall you cry out and God shall hear you; while you art still speaking, He shall say 'Lo, I am here'; if you shall take away from you the yoke and the stretching forth of the finger and the word of murmuring, and shall give your bread to the hungry heartily, and shall pity the abased soul.

3:6 To this end therefore, my brethren, He that is long-suffering, foreseeing that the people whom He had prepared in His well-beloved would believe in simplicity, manifested to us beforehand concerning all things, that we might not as novices shipwreck ourselves upon their law.

4:1 It behooves us therefore to investigate deeply concerning the present, and to search out the things which have power to save us. Let us therefore flee altogether from all the works of lawlessness, lest the works of lawlessness overpower us; and let us loathe the error of the present time, that we may be loved for that which is to come.

4:2 Let us give no relaxation to our soul that it should have liberty to consort with sinners and wicked men, or sadly we be made like unto them.

4:3 The last offence is at hand, concerning which the scripture spoke, as Enoch said. For to this end the Master has cut the seasons and the days short, that His beloved might hasten and come to His inheritance.

4:4 And the prophet also spoke on this wise; Ten reigns shall reign upon the earth, and after them shall arise another king, who shall bring low three of the kings under one.

4:5 In like manner Daniel spoke concerning the same; And I saw the forth beast to be wicked and strong and more intractable than all the beasts of the earth, and how there arose from him ten horns, and from these a little horn and excrescence, and how that it abased under one three of the great horns.

4:6 You ought therefore to understand. Moreover I ask you this one thing besides, as being one of yourselves and loving you all in particular more than my own soul, to give heed to yourselves now, and not to liken yourselves to certain persons who pile up sin upon sin, saying that our covenant remains to them also.

4:7 Ours it is; but they lost it in this way for ever, when Moses had just received it. For the scripture said; And Moses was in the mountain fasting forty days and forty nights, and he received the covenant from the Lord, even tablets of stone written with the finger of the hand of the Lord.

4:8 But they lost it by turning unto idols. For thus said the Lord; Moses, Moses, come down quickly; for your people whom you brought out of the land of Egypt has done unlawfully. And Moses understood, and threw the two tables from his hands; and their covenant was broken in pieces, that the covenant of the beloved Jesus might be sealed unto our hearts in the hope, which springs from faith in Him.

4:9 But though I would fain write many things, not as a teacher, but as becomes one who loves you not to fall short of that which we possess, I was anxious to write to you, being your devoted slave. Wherefore let us take heed in these last days. For the whole time of our faith shall profit us nothing, unless we now, in the season of lawlessness and in the offenses that shall be, as becomes sons of God, offer resistance, that the Black One may not effect an entrance.

4:10 Let us flee from all forms of vanity. Let us entirely hate the works of the evil way. Do not entering in secretly stand apart by yourselves, as if you were already justified, but assemble yourselves together and consult concerning the common welfare.

4:11 For the scripture said; Woe unto them that are wise for themselves, and understanding in their own sight. Let us become spiritual, let us become a temple perfect unto God. As far as in us lies, let us exercise ourselves in the fear of God, [and] let us strive to keep His commandments so that we may rejoice in His rites and laws.

4:12 The Lord judges the world without respect of persons; each man shall receive according to his deeds. If he be good, his righteousness shall go before him in the way; if he be evil, the recompense of his evil-doing is before him; lest perchance,

4:13 if we relax as men that are called, we should slumber over our sins, and the prince of evil receive power against us and thrust us out from the kingdom of the Lord.

4:14 Moreover, understand this also, my brothers. When you see that after so many signs and wonders wrought in Israel, even then they were abandoned, let us give heed, or sadly we be found, as the scripture said, many are called but few are chosen.

5:1 For to this end the Lord endured to deliver His flesh unto corruption, that by the remission of sins we might be cleansed, which cleansing is through the blood of His sprinkling.

5:2 For the scripture concerning Him contains some things relating to Israel, and some things relating to us. And it spoke thus; He was wounded for your transgressions, and He has been bruised for our sins; by His stripes we were healed. As a sheep He was led to slaughter, as a lamb is dumb (speechless) before his shearer.

5:3 We ought therefore to be very thankful unto the Lord, for that He both revealed unto us the past, and made us wise in the present, and as regards the future we are not without understanding.

5:4 Now the scripture said; Not unjustly is the net spread for the birds. He means this that a man shall justly perish, who having the knowledge of the way of righteousness forces himself into the way of darkness.

5:5 There is yet this also, my brethren; if the Lord endured to suffer for our souls, though He was Lord of the whole world, unto whom God said from the foundation of the world, Let us make man after our image and likeness, how then did He endure to suffer at the hand of men?

5:6 You must understand. The prophets, receiving grace from Him, prophesied concerning Him. But He Himself endured that He might destroy death and show forth the resurrection of the dead, for that He must need to be manifested in the flesh.

5:7 At the same time He might redeem the promise made to the fathers, and by preparing the new people for Himself might show, while He was on earth, that having brought about the resurrection He will Himself exercise judgment.

5:8 Yea and further, He preached teaching Israel and performing so many wonders and miracles, and He loved him exceedingly.

5:9 And when He chose His own apostles who were to proclaim His Gospel, who that He might show that He came not to call the righteous but sinners were sinners above every sin, then He manifested Himself to be the Son of God.

5:10 For if He had not come in the flesh neither would men have looked upon Him and been saved, forasmuch as when they look upon the sun that shall cease to be, which is the work of His own hands, they cannot face its rays.

5:11 Therefore the Son of God came in the flesh to this end, that He might sum up the complete tale of their sins against those who persecuted and slew His prophets.

5:12 To this end therefore He endured. For God said of the wounds of His flesh that they came from them; when they shall strike their own shepherd, then shall the sheep of the flock be lost.

5:13 But He Himself desired so to suffer. For it was necessary for Him to suffer on a tree. For he that prophesied said concerning Him, Spare My soul form the sword; and, Pierce My flesh with nails, for the congregations of evil-doers have risen up against Me.

5:14 And again He said; Behold I have given My back to stripes, and My cheeks to beating, and My face did I set as a hard rock.

6:1 When then He gave the commandment, what said He? Who is he that disputes with Me? Let him oppose Me. Or who is he that goes to law / court with Me? Let him draw near unto the servant of the Lord,

6:2 Woe unto you, for you all shall wax old as a garment, and the moth shall consume you. And again the prophet said, seeing that as a hard stone He was ordained for crushing; Behold I will put into the fountains of Zion a stone very precious, elect, a chief corner-stone, honorable.

6:3 Then again what said He; And whosoever shall set his hope on Him, shall live forever. Is our hope then set upon a stone? Far be it. But it is because the Lord has set His flesh in strength. For He said; And He set Me as a hard rock.

6:4 And the prophet said again; The stone which the builders rejected, this became the head and the corner. And again He said; "This is the great and wonderful day, which the Lord made."

6:5 I write to you the more simply, that you may understand, I who am the refuse of your love.

6:6 What then said the prophet again? The assembly of evildoers gathered around Me, they surrounded Me as bees surround a comb; and; For My garment they cast a lot.

6:7 Forasmuch then as He was about to be manifested in the flesh and to suffer, His suffering was manifested beforehand. For the prophet said concerning Israel; Woe unto their soul, for they have counseled evil counsel against themselves saying, Let us bind the righteous one, for he is unprofitable for us.

6:8 What say the other prophet Moses unto them? Behold, these things said the Lord God; enter into the good land which the Lord swear unto Abraham, Isaac, and Jacob, and inherit it, a land flowing with milk and honey

6:9 But what said knowledge? Understand you. Set your hope on Him who is about to be manifested to you in the flesh, even Jesus. For man is earth suffering; for from the face of the earth came the creation of Adam.

6:10 What then did He say? "Into the good land, a land flowing with milk and honey." Blessed is our Lord, brethren, who established among us wisdom and understanding of His secret things. For the prophet spoke a parable concerning the Lord. Who shall comprehend, save he that is wise and prudent and that loves his Lord?

6:11 Forasmuch then as He renewed us in the remission of sins, He made us to be a new type, so that we should have the soul of children, as if He were recreating us.

6:12 For the scripture said concerning us, how He said to the Son; Let us make man after our image and after our likeness, and let them rule over the beasts of the earth and the fowls of the heaven and the fishes of the sea. And the Lord said when He saw the fair creation of us men; Increase and multiply and fill the earth. These words refer to the Son.

6:13 Again I will show you how the Lord spoke concerning us. He made a second creation at the last; and the Lord said; Behold I make the last things as the first. In reference to this then the prophet preached; Enter into a land flowing with milk and honey, and be lords over it.

6:14 Behold then we have been created anew, as He said again in another prophet; Behold, said the Lord, I will take out from these, that is to say, from those whom the Spirit of the Lord foresaw, their stony hearts, and will put into them hearts of flesh; for He Himself was to be manifested in the flesh and to dwell in us.

6:15 For a holy temple unto the Lord, my brethren, is the abode of our heart.

6:16 For the Lord said again; For wherein shall I appear unto the Lord my God and be glorified? I will make confession unto

You in the assembly of my brethren, and I will sing unto You in the midst of the assembly of the saints. We therefore are they whom He brought into the good land

6:17 What then is the milk and the honey Because the child is first kept alive by honey, and then by milk. So in like manner we also, being kept alive by our faith in the promise and by the word, shall live and be lords of the earth.

6:18 Now we have already said above; And let them increase and multiply and rule over the fishes. But who is he that is able [now] to rule over beasts and fishes and fowls of the heaven, for we ought to perceive that to rule implies power, so that one should give orders and have dominion.

6:19 If then this cometh not to pass now, assuredly He spoke to us for the hereafter, when we ourselves shall be made perfect so that we may become heirs of the covenant of the Lord.

7:1 Understand therefore, children of gladness, that the good Lord manifested all things to us beforehand, that we might know to whom we ought in all things to render thanksgiving and praise.

7:2 If then the Son of God, being Lord and future Judge of quick and dead, suffered that His wound might give us life, let us believe that the Son of God could not suffer except for our sakes.

7:3 But moreover when crucified He had vinegar and gall given Him to drink. Hear how on this matter the priests of the temple have revealed. Seeing that there is a commandment in scripture, Whatsoever shall not observe the fast shall surely die, the Lord commanded, because He was in His own person about to offer the vessel of His Spirit a sacrifice for our sins, that the type also which was given in Isaac who was offered upon the alter should be fulfilled.

7:4 What then said He in the prophet? And let them eat of the goat that is offered at the fast for all their sins. Attend carefully; And let all the priests alone eat the entrails unwashed with vinegar.

7:5 Wherefore? Since you are to give Me, who am to offer My flesh for the sins of My new people, gall with vinegar to drink, eat you alone, while the people fast and wail in sackcloth and ashes; that He might show that He must suffer at their hands.

7:6 Attend you to the commandments which He gave. Take two goats, fair and alike, and offer them, and let the priest take the one for a whole burnt offering for sins.

7:7 But the other one--what must they do with it? Accursed, said He, is the one. Give heed how the type of Jesus is revealed.

7:8 And do you all spit upon it and goad it, and place scarlet wool about its head, and so let it be cast into the wilderness. And when it is so done, he that takes the goat into the wilderness leads it, and takes off the wool, and puts it upon the branch which is called Rachia, the same whereof we are wont to eat the shoots when we find them in the country. Of this briar alone is the fruit thus sweet.

7:9 What then means this? Give heed. The one at the alter, and the other accursed. And moreover the accursed one crowned. For they shall see Him in that day wearing the long scarlet robe about His flesh, and shall say, Is not this He, Whom once we crucified and set at nothing and spat upon; verily this was He, Who then said that He was the Son of God.

7:10 For how is He like the goat? For this reason it says the goats shall be fair and alike, that, when they shall see Him coming then, they may be astonished at the likeness of the goat. Therefore behold the type of Jesus that was to suffer.

7:11 But what means it, that they place the wool in the midst of the thorns? It is a type of Jesus set forth for the Church, since whosoever should desire to take away the scarlet wool it behooved him to suffer many things owing to the terrible nature of the thorn, and through affliction to win the mastery over it. Thus, He said, they that desire to see Me, and to attain unto My kingdom, must lay hold on Me through tribulation and affliction.

8:1 But what think you mean the type, where the commandment is given to Israel that those men, whose sins are full grown, offer an heifer and slaughter and burn it, and then that the children take up the ashes, and cast them into vessels, and twist the scarlet wool on a tree (see here again is the type of the cross and the scarlet wool), and the hyssop, and that this done the children should sprinkle the people one by one, that they may be purified from their sins?

8:2 Understand how in all plainness it is spoken unto you; the calf is Jesus, the men that offer it, being sinners are they that offered Him for the slaughter. After this it is no more men (who offer); the glory is no more for sinners.

8:3 The children who sprinkle are they that preached unto us the forgiveness of sins and the purification of our heart, they to whom, being twelve in number for a testimony unto the tribes (for there are twelve tribes of Israel), He gave authority over the Gospel, that they should preach it.

8:4 But wherefore are the children that sprinkle three in number? It is for a testimony unto Abraham, Isaac and Jacob, because these are mighty before God.

8:5 Then there is the placing the wool on the tree. This means that the kingdom of Jesus is on the cross, and that they who set their hope on Him shall live forever.

8:6 And why is there the wool and the hyssop at the same time? Because in His kingdom there shall be evil and foul days, in which we shall be saved; for he who suffers pain in the flesh is healed through the foulness of the hyssop.

8:7 Now to us indeed it is manifest that these things so befell for this reason, but to them they were dark, because they heard not the voice of the Lord.

9:1 Furthermore He said concerning the ears, how that it is our heart, which He circumcised. The Lord said in the prophet; With the hearing of the ears they listened to Me. And again He said; They that are afar off shall hear with their ears, and shall perceive what I have done. And; Be you circumcised in your hearts, said the Lord.

9:2 And again He said; Hear, O Israel, for thus said the Lord your God. Who is he that desires to live forever, let him hear with his ears the voice of My servant. And again He said; Hear, O heaven, and give ear, O earth, for the Lord has spoken these things for a testimony. And again He said; Hear the words of the Lord, you rulers of this people. And again He said; Hear, O my children, the voice of one crying in the wilderness. Therefore He circumcised our ears, that hearing the word we might believe.

9:3 But moreover the circumcision, in which they have confidence, is abolished; for He has said that a circumcision not of the flesh should be practiced. But they transgressed, for an evil angel taught them cleverness.

9:4 He said unto them; Thus said the Lord your God (so I find the commandment); sow not upon thorns, be you circumcised in to your Lord. And what said He? Be you circumcised in the hardness of your heart; and then you will not harden your neck. Take this again; Behold, says the Lord, all the Gentiles are uncircumcised in their foreskin, but this people is uncircumcised in their hearts.

9:5 But you will say; In truth the people has been circumcised for a seal. Nay, but so likewise is every Syrian and Arabian and all the priests of the idols. Do all those then too belong to their covenant? Moreover the Egyptians also are included among the circumcised.

9:6 Learn therefore, children of love, concerning all things abundantly, that Abraham, who first appointed circumcision, looked forward in the spirit unto Jesus, when he circumcised having received the rites and laws of three letters.

9:7 For the scripture said; And Abraham circumcised of his household eighteen males and three hundred. What then was the knowledge given unto him? Understand you that He said the eighteen first, and then after an interval three hundred In the eighteen 'I' stands for ten, 'H' for eight. Here you have IHSOYS (Jesus). And because the cross in the 'T' was to have grace, He said also three hundred. So He reveals Jesus in the two letters, and in the remaining one the cross.

9:8 He who placed within us the innate gift of His covenant knows; no man has ever learned from me a more genuine word; but I know that you are worthy.

10:1 But forasmuch as Moses said; You shall not eat seine nor eagle nor falcon nor crow nor any fish which has no scale upon it, he received in his understanding three rites and laws.

10:2 Yea and further He said unto them in Deuteronomy; And I will lay as a covenant upon this people My rites and laws. So then it is not a commandment of God that they should not bite with their teeth, but Moses spoke it in spirit.

10:3 Accordingly he mentioned the swine with this intent. You shall not cleave, said he, to such men who are like unto swine; that is, when they are in luxury they forget the Lord, but when they are in want they recognize the Lord, just as the swine when it eats knows not his lord, but when it is hungry it cries out, and when it has received food again it is silent.

10:4 Neither shall you eat eagle nor falcon nor kite nor crow. You shall not, He said, cleave unto, or be likened to, such men who now not how to provide food for themselves by toil and sweat, but in their lawlessness seize what belongs to others, and as if they were walking in guilelessness watch and search about for some one to rob in their rapacity, just as these birds alone do not provide food for themselves, but sit idle and seek how they may eat the meat that belongs to others, being pestilent in their evil-doings.

10:5 And you shall not eat, said He, lamprey nor polypus (octopus, squid) nor cuttlefish . You shall not, He means, become like unto such men, who are desperately wicked, and are already condemned to death, just as these fishes alone are accursed and swim in the depths, not swimming on the surface like the rest, but dwell on the ground beneath the deep sea.

10:6 Moreover you shall not eat the hare. Why so? You shall not be found a corrupter of boys, nor shall you become like such persons; for the hare gains one passage in the body every year; for according to the number of years it lives it has just so many orifices.

10:7 Again, neither shall you eat the hyena; you shall not, said He, become an adulterer or a fornicator, neither shall you resemble such persons. Why so? Because this animal changes its nature year by year, and becomes at one time male and at another time a female.

10:8 Moreover He has hated the weasel also and with good reason. You shall not, said He, become such as those men of whom we hear as working iniquity with their mouth for uncleanness, neither shall you cleave unto impure women who work iniquity with their mouth. For this animal conceives with its mouth.

10:9 Concerning meats then Moses received three decrees to this effect and uttered them in a spiritual sense; but they accepted them according to the lust of the flesh, as though they referred to eating.

10:10 And David also received knowledge of the same three decrees, and said; Blessed is the man who has not gone in the council of the ungodly--even as the fishes go in darkness into the depths; and has not stood in the path of sinners--just as they who pretend to fear the Lord sin like swine; and has not sat on the seat of the destroyers--as the birds that are seated for prey. You have now the complete lesson concerning eating.

10:11 Again Moses said; "You shall everything that divides the hoof and chews the cud." What means he? He that received the food knows Him that gives him the food, and being refreshed appears to rejoice in him. Well said he, having regard to the commandment. What then means he? Cleave unto those that fear the Lord, with those who meditate in their heart on the distinction of the word which they have received, with those who tell of the rites and laws of the Lord and keep them, with those who know that meditation is a work of gladness and who chew the cud of the word of the Lord. But why that which divides the hoof? Because the righteous man both walk in this world, and at the same time looks for the holy world to come. You see how wise a lawgiver Moses was.

10:12 But whence should they perceive or understand these things? Howbeit we having justly perceived the commandments tell them as the Lord willed. To this end He circumcised our ears and hearts, that we might understand these things.

11:1 But let us enquire whether the Lord took care to signify before hand concerning the water and the cross. Now concerning the water it is written in reference to Israel, how that they would not receive the baptism which brings remission of sins, but would build for themselves.

11:2 For the prophet said; Be astonished, O heaven, and let the earth shudder the more at this, for this people has done two evil things; they abandoned Me the fountain of life, and they dug for themselves a pit of death.

11:3 Is My holy mountain of Sinai a desert rock? For you shall be as the fledglings of a bird, which flutter aloft when deprived of their nest.

11:4 And again the prophet said; I will go before you, and level mountains and crush gates of brass and break in pieces bolts of iron, and I will give you treasures dark, concealed, unseen, that they may know that I am the Lord God.

11:5 And; you shall dwell in a lofty cave of a strong rock. And; His water shall be sure; you shall see the King in glory, and your soul shall meditate on the fear of the Lord.

11:6 And again He said in another prophet; And He that doeth these things shall be as the tree that is planted by the parting streams of waters, which shall yield his fruit at his proper season, and his leaf shall not fall off, and all things whatsoever he doeth shall prosper.

11:7 Not so are the ungodly, not so, but are as the dust which the wind scattered from the face of the earth. Therefore ungodly men shall not stand in judgment, neither sinners in the council of the righteous; for the Lord knows the way of the righteous, and the way of the ungodly shall perish.

11:8 You perceive how He pointed out the water and the cross at the same time. For this is the meaning; Blessed are they that set their hope on the cross, and go down into the water; for He spoke of the reward at his proper season; then, said He, I will repay. But now what said He? His leaves shall not fall off; He means by this that every word, which shall come forth from you through your mouth in faith and love, shall be for the conversion and hope of many.

11:9 And again another prophet said; And the land of Jacob was praised above the whole earth. He means this; He glorified the vessel of His Spirit.

11:10 Next what said He? And there was a river streaming from the right hand, and beautiful trees rose up from it; and whosoever shall eat of them shall live forever.

11:11 This He said, because we go down into the water laden with sins and filth, and rise up from it bearing fruit in the heart, resting our fear and hope on Jesus in the spirit. And whosoever shall eat of these shall live forever; He means this; whosoever, said He, shall hear these things spoken and shall believe, shall live forever.

12:1 In like manner again He defined concerning the cross in another prophet, who said; And when shall these things be accomplished? Said the Lord. Whenever a tree shall be bended and stand upright, and when ever blood shall drop from a tree. Again you art taught concerning the cross, and Him that was to be crucified.

12:2 And He said again in Moses, when war was waged against Israel by men of another nation, and that He might remind them when the war was waged against them that for their sins they were delivered unto death; the Spirit said to the heart of Moses, that he should make a type of the cross and of Him that was to suffer, that unless, said He, they shall set their hope on Him, war shall be waged against them for ever. Moses therefore piled arms one upon another in the midst of the encounter, and standing on higher ground than any he stretched out his hands, and so Israel was again victorious. Then, whenever he lowered them, they were slain with the sword.

12:3 Wherefore was this? That they might learn that they cannot be saved, unless they should set their hope on Him. 12:4 And again in another prophet He said; The whole day long have I stretched out My hands to a disobedient people that did gainsay My righteous way.

12:5 Again Moses made a type of Jesus, how that He must suffer, and that He Himself whom they shall think to have destroyed shall make alive in an emblem when Israel was falling. For the Lord caused all manner of serpents to bite them, and they died (forasmuch as the transgression was wrought in Eve through the serpent), that He might convince them that by reason of their transgression they should be delivered over to the affliction of death.

12:6 Yea and further though Moses gave the commandment; You shall not have a molten or a carved image for your God, yet he himself made one that he might show them a type of

Jesus. So Moses made a brazen serpent, and set it up conspicuously, and summoned the people by proclamation.

12:7 When therefore they were assembled together they entreated Moses that he should offer up intercession for them that they might be healed. And Moses said unto them; When ever, said he, one of you shall be bitten, let him come to the serpent which is placed on the tree, and let him believe and hope that the serpent being himself dead can make alive; and forthwith he shall be saved. And so they did. Here again you hast in these things also the glory of Jesus, how that in Him and unto Him are all things.

12:8 What again said Moses unto Jesus (Joshua) the son of Nun, when he gives him this name, as being a prophet, that all the people might give ear to him alone, because the Father revealed all things concerning His Son Jesus?

12:9 Moses therefore said to Jesus the son of Nun, giving him this name, when he sent him as a spy on the land; Take a book in your hands, and write what the Lord said, how the Son of God shall cut up by the roots all the house of Amalek in the last days.

12:10 Behold again it is Jesus, not a son of man, but the Son of God, and He was revealed in the flesh in a figure. Since then men will say that Christ is the son of David, David himself prophesied being afraid and understanding the error of sinners; The Lord said unto my Lord, Sit you on My right hand until I set yours enemies for a footstool under Your feet.

12:11 And again so said Isaiah; The Lord said unto my Christ the Lord, of whose right hand I laid hold, that the nations should give ear before Him, and I will break down the strength of kings. See how David called Him Lord, and did not call Him Son?

13:1 Now let us see whether this people or the first people has the inheritance, and whether the covenant had reference to us or to them.

13:2 Hear then what the scripture said concerning the people; And Isaac prayed concerning Rebecca his wife, for she was barren. And she conceived. Then Rebecca went out to enquire of the Lord. And the Lord said unto her; Two nations are in your womb, and two peoples in your belly, and one people shall vanquish another people, and the greater shall serve the less.

13:3 You ought to understand who Isaac is, and who Rebecca is, and in whose case He has shown that the one people is greater than the other.

13:4 And in another prophecy Jacob spoke more plainly to Joseph his son, saying; Behold, the Lord has not bereft me of your face; bring me your sons, that I may bless them.

13:5 And he brought Ephraim and Manasseh, desiring that Manasseh should be blessed, because he was the elder; for Joseph led him by the right hand of his father Jacob. But Jacob saw in the spirit a type of the people that should come afterwards. And what said He? And Jacob crossed his hands, and placed his right hand on the head of Ephraim, the second and younger, and blessed him. And Joseph said unto Jacob, Transfer your right hand to the head of Manasseh, for he is my first born son. And Jacob said to Joseph, I know it, my son, I know it; but the greater shall serve the less. Yet this one also shall be blessed.

13:6 Mark in whose cases He ordained that this people should be first and heir of the covenant.

13:7 If then besides this He also recorded it through Abraham, we attain the completion of our knowledge. What then said he to Abraham when he alone believed, and was ascribed for righteousness? Behold I have made you, Abraham, a father of nations that believe in God in uncircumcision.

14:1 Yea verily, but as regards the covenant which He swear to the fathers to give it to the people let us see whether He has actually given it. He has given it, but they themselves were not found worthy to receive it by reason of their sins.

14:2 For the prophet said; And Moses was fasting in Mount Sinai forty days and forty nights, that he might receive the covenant of the Lord to give to the people. And [Moses] received from the Lord the two tables which were written by the finger of the hand of the Lord in the spirit. And Moses took them, and brought them down to give them to the people.

14:3 And the Lord said unto Moses; Moses, Moses, come down quickly; for your people, whom you led forth from the land of Egypt, has done wickedly. And Moses perceived that they had made for themselves again molten images, and he cast them out of his hands and the tables of the covenant of the Lord were broken in pieces.

14:4 Moses received them, but they themselves were not found worthy. But how did we receive them? Mark this. Moses received them being a servant, but the Lord himself gave them to us to be the people of His inheritance, having endured patiently for our sakes.

14:5 But He was made manifest, in order that at the same time they might be perfected in their sins, and we might receive the covenant through Him who inherited it, even the Lord Jesus, who was prepared beforehand hereunto, that appearing in person He might redeem out of darkness our hearts which had already been paid over unto death and delivered up to the iniquity of error, and thus establish the covenant in us through the word.

14:6 For it is written how the Father charges Him to deliver us from darkness, and to prepare a holy people for Himself.

14:7 Therefore said the prophet; I the Lord your God called you in righteousness, and I will lay hold of your hand and will strengthen you, and I have given you to be a covenant of the race, a light to the Gentiles, to open the eyes of the blind, and to bring forth them that are bound from their fetters, and them that sit in darkness from their prison house. We perceive then whence we were ransomed.

14:8 Again the prophet said; Behold I have set You to be a light unto the Gentiles, that you should be for salvation unto the ends of the earth; thus said the Lord that ransomed you, even God.

14:9 Again the prophet said; The Spirit of the Lord is upon Me, wherefore He anointed Me to preach good tidings to the humble; He has sent Me to heal them that are broken-hearted, to preach release to the captives and recovery of sight to the blind, to proclaim the acceptable year of the Lord and the day of recompense, to comfort all that mourn.

15:1 Moreover concerning the Sabbath likewise it is written in the Ten Words, in which He spoke to Moses face to face on Mount Sinai; And you shall hallow the Sabbath of the Lord with pure hands and with a pure heart.

15:2 And in another place He said; If my sons observe the Sabbath then I will bestow My mercy upon them.

15:3 Of the Sabbath He spoke in the beginning of the creation; And God made the works of His hands in six days, and He ended on the seventh day, and rested on it, and He hallowed it.

15:4 Give heed, children, what this means; He ended in six days. He means this, that in six thousand years the Lord shall bring all things to an end; for the day with Him signified a thousand years; and this He himself bears me witness, saying; Behold, the day of the Lord shall be as a thousand years. Therefore, children, in six days, that is in six thousand years, everything shall come to an end.

15:5 And He rested on the seventh day. this He means; when His Son shall come, and shall abolish the time of the Lawless One, and shall judge the ungodly, and shall change the sun and the moon and the stars, then shall he truly rest on the seventh day.

15:6 Yea and furthermore He said; you shall hallow it with pure hands and with a pure heart. If therefore a man is able now to hallow the day which God hallowed, though he be pure in heart, we have gone utterly astray.

15:7 But if after all then and not till then shall we truly rest and hallow it, when we shall ourselves be able to do so after being justified and receiving the promise, when iniquity is no more and all things have been made new by the Lord, we shall be able to hallow it then, because we ourselves shall have been hallowed first.

15:8 Finally He said to them; Your new moons and your Sabbaths I cannot away with. You see what is His meaning ; it is not your present Sabbaths that are acceptable [unto Me], but the Sabbath which I have made, in the which, when I have set all things at rest, I will make the beginning of the eighth day which is the beginning of another world.

15:9 Wherefore also we keep the eighth day for rejoicing, in the which also Jesus rose from the dead, and having been manifested ascended into the heavens.

16:1 Moreover I will tell you likewise concerning the temple, how these wretched men being led astray set their hope on the building, and not on their God that made them, as being a house of God.

16:2 For like the Gentiles almost they consecrated Him in the temple. But what said the Lord abolishing the temple? Learn you. Who has measured the heaven with a span, or has measured the earth with his hand? Have not I, said the Lord? The heaven is My throne and the earth the footstool of My feet. What manner of house will you build for Me? Or what shall be my resting place? You perceive that their hope is vain.

16:3 Furthermore He said again; Behold they that pulled down this temple themselves shall build it.

16:4 So it cometh to pass; for because they went to war it was pulled down by their enemies. Now also the very servants of their enemies shall build it up.

16:5 Again, it was revealed how the city and the temple and the people of Israel should be betrayed. For the scripture said;

And it shall be in the last days, that the Lord shall deliver up the sheep of the pasture and the fold and the tower thereof to destruction. And it came to pass as the Lord spoke.

16:6 But let us enquire whether there be any temple of God. There is; in the place where he himself undertakes to make and finish it. For it is written, "And it shall come to pass, when the week is being accomplished, the temple of God shall be built gloriously in the name of the Lord."

16:7 I find then that there is a temple, How then shall it be built in the name of the Lord? Understand you. Before we believed on God, the abode of our heart was corrupt and weak. It was a temple truly built by hands; for it was full of idolatry and was a house of demons, because we did whatsoever was contrary to God.

16:8 But it shall be built in the name of the Lord. Give heed then that the temple of the Lord may be built gloriously.

16:9 How? Understand you. By receiving the remission of our sins and hoping on the Name we became new, created afresh from the beginning. Wherefore God dwells truly in our habitation within us. How? The word of his faith, the calling of his promise, the wisdom of the rites and laws, the commandments of the teaching, He Himself prophesying in us,

He Himself dwelling in us, opening for us who had been in bondage unto death the door of the temple, which is the mouth, and giving us repentance leads us to the incorruptible temple.

16:10 For he that desires to be saved looks not to the man, but to Him that dwells and spoke in him, being amazed at this that he has never at any time heard these words from the mouth of the speaker, nor himself ever desired to hear them. This is the spiritual temple built up to the Lord.

17:1 So far as it was possible with all simplicity to declare it unto you, my soul hopes that I have not omitted anything [of the matters pertaining unto salvation and so failed in my desire].

17:2 For if I should write to you concerning things immediate or future, you would not understand them, because they are put in parables. So much then for this.

18:1 But let us pass on to another lesson and teaching. There are two ways of teaching and of power, the one of light and the other of darkness; and there is a great difference between the two ways. For on the one are stationed the light giving angels of God, on the other the angels of Satan.

18:2 And the one is the Lord from all eternity and unto all eternity, whereas the other is Lord of the season of iniquity that now is.

19:1 This then is the way of light, if anyone desiring to travel on the way to his appointed place would be zealous in his works. The knowledge then which is given to us whereby we may walk therein as follows.

19:2 you shall love Him that made you, you shall fear Him that created you, you shall glorify Him that redeemed you from death; you shall be simple in heart and rich in spirit; you shall not cleave to those who walk the way of death; you shall hate everything that is not pleasing to God; you shall hate all hypocrisy; you shall never forsake the commandments of the Lord.

19:3 you shall not exalt yourself, but shall be lowly minded in all things. You shall not assume glory to yourself. You shall not entertain a wicked design against your neighbor; you shall not admit boldness into your soul.

19:4 you shall not commit fornication, you shall not commit adultery, you shall not corrupt boys. The word of God shall not come forth from you where any are unclean. You shall not make a difference in a person to reprove him for a transgression. You shall be meek, you shall be quiet, you shall be fearing the words which you hast heard. You shall not bear a grudge against your brother.

19:5 you shall not doubt whether a thing shall be or not be. You shall not take the name of the Lord in vain. You shall love your neighbor more than yours own soul. You shall not murder a child by abortion, nor again shall you kill it when it is born. You shall not withhold your hand from your son or daughter, but from their youth you shall teach them the fear of God.

19:6 you shall not be found coveting your neighbor's goods; you shall not be found greedy of gain. Neither shall you cleave with your soul to the lofty, but shall walk with the humble and righteous. The accidents that befall you shall you receive as good, knowing that nothing is done without God. You shall not be double minded nor double tongued.

19:7 you shall be subject unto your masters as to a type of God in shame and fear. You shall not command in bitterness your bondservant or yours handmaid who set their hope on the same God, or sadly, they should cease to fear the God who is over both of you; for He came not to call with respect of persons, but to call those whom the Spirit has prepared.

19:8 you shall make your neighbor partake in all things, and shall not say that anything is yours own. For if you are fellow partakers in that which is imperishable, how much rather shall you be in the things which are perishable. You shall not be hasty with yours own tongue, for the mouth is the snare of death. So far as you art able, you shall be pure for your soul's sake.

19:9 Be not you found holding out your hands to receive, and drawing them in to give. You shall love as the apple of yours eye every one that spoke unto you the word of the Lord.

19:10 you shall remember the day of judgment night and day, and you shall seek out day by day the persons of the saints, either laboring by word and going to exhort them and meditating how you may save souls by your word, or you shall work with your hands for a ransom for your sins.

19:11 you shall not hesitate to give, neither shall you murmur when giving, but you shall know who is the good paymaster of your reward. You shall keep those things which you hast received, neither adding to them nor taking away from them. You shall utterly hate the Evil One. You shall judge righteously.

19:12 you shall not make a schism, but you shall pacify them that contend by bringing them together. You shall confess your sins. You shall not betake yourself to prayer with an evil conscience. This is the way of light.

20:1 But the way of the Black One is crooked and full of a curse. For it is a way of eternal death with punishment wherein are the things that destroy men's souls--idolatry, boldness, exhalation of power, hypocrisy, doubleness of heart (fickle - unstable), adultery, murder, plundering, pride, transgression, treachery, malice, stubbornness, witchcraft, magic, covetousness, absence of the fear of God;

20:2 persecutors of good men, hating the truth, loving lies, not perceiving the reward of righteousness, not cleaving to the good nor to the righteous judgment, paying no heed to the widow and the orphan, wakeful not for the fear of God but for that which is evil; men from whom gentleness and forbearance stand aloof and far off; loving vain things, pursuing a recompense, not pitying the poor man, not toiling for him that is oppressed with toil, ready to slander, not recognizing Him that made them murderers of children, corrupters of the creatures of God, turning away from him that is in want, oppressing him that is afflicted, advocates of the wealthy, unjust judges of the poor, sinful in all things.

21:1 It is good therefore to learn the rites and laws of the Lord, as many as have been written above, and to walk in them. For he that doeth these things shall be glorified in the kingdom of God; whereas he that chooses their opposites shall perish together with his works. For this cause is the resurrection, for this the recompense.

21:2 I entreat those of you who are in a higher station, if you will receive any counsel of good advice from me, keep amongst you those to whom you may do good. Fail not.

21:3 The day is at hand, in which everything shall be destroyed together with the Evil One. The Lord is at hand and his reward.

21:4 Again and again I entreat you; be good lawgivers one to another; continue faithful councilors to yourselves; take away from you all hypocrisy.

21:5 And may God, who is Lord of the whole world, give you wisdom, judgment, learning, knowledge of His rites and laws, patience.

21:6 And be you taught of God, seeking diligently what the Lord requires of you, and act that you may be found in the day of judgment.

21:7 But if you have any remembrance of good, call me to

mind when you practice these things these things, that both my desire and my watchfulness may lead to some good result. I entreat you asking it as a favor.

21:8 So long as the good vessel (of the body) is with you, be lacking in none of these things, but search them out constantly, and fulfill every commandment; for they deserve it.

21:9 For this reason I was the more eager to write to you so far as I was able, that I might give you joy. Fare you well, children of love and peace. The Lord of glory and of every grace be with your spirit.

THE GOSPEL OF NICODEMUS, OR ACTS OF PILATE

Based on "The Apocryphal New Testament" M.R. James-Translation and Notes Oxford: Clarendon Press, 1924

The book is divided into two sections (1) the story of the Passion; (2) the Descent into hell. The oldest sections seem to be written first in Greek. The text contains multiple parts, which vary in style and are of different authors. The oldest section containing the Report of Pilate to the Emperor Claudius was composed in the late 2nd century, but most of the text was written later. The Acts of Pilate does not purport to have been written by Pilate, but instead claims to have been derived from the official acts preserved in the praetorium at Jerusalem. The book was first attributed to Nicodemus and thus the text gained its name in the Middle Ages. It had a considerable effect on medieval Christianity. The Catholic Church still propagates some of the information contained herein. The number of languages and editions found attests the widespread transmission and popularity.

The first part of the book, containing the story of the Passion and Resurrection, is not earlier than the fourth century. Its object in the main is to furnish irrefragable testimony to the resurrection. Attempts have been made to show that it is of early date-that it is, for instance, the writing which Justin Martyr meant when in his Apology he referred his heathen readers to the 'Acts' of Christ's trial preserved among the archives of Rome. The truth of that matter is that he simply assumed that such records must exist. False 'acts' of the trial were written in the Pagan interest under Maximin, and introduced into schools early in the fourth century. It is imagined by some that our book was a counterblast to these.

The account of the Descent into Hell (Part II) is an addition to the text. It does not appear in any Oriental version, and the Greek copies are rare. It is in Latin and thus in every European language.

The central idea, the delivery of the righteous fathers from Hades is ancient. Second-century writers are full of it. The embellishments, the dialogues of Satan with Hades, which are so dramatic, come in later, perhaps with the development of pulpit oratory among Christians. We find them in fourth-century sermons of Eusebius of Emesa.

This second part is attributed to Leucius. When his name came to be attached to the Descent into Hell we do not yet know: nor do we know when the Descent was first appended to the Acts of Pilate. Writing style and structure points to the fifth century.

MEMORIALS OF OUR LORD JESUS CHRIST DONE IN THE TIME OF PONTIUS PILATE

Prologue (Not found in some manuscripts.)

I Ananias, the Protector, of praetorian rank, learned in the law, did from the divine scriptures recognize our Lord Jesus Christ and came near to him by faith and was accounted worthy of holy baptism: and I sought out the memorials that were made at that season in the time of our master Jesus Christ, which the Jews deposited with Pontius Pilate, and found the memorials in Hebrew (letters), and by the good pleasure of God I translated them into Greek (letters) for the informing of all them that call upon the name of our Lord Jesus Christ: in the reign of our Lord Flavius Theodosius, in the seventeenth year, and the eighteenth year of Theodosius, when Valentinian was proclaimed Augustus, A. D. 425.

All you therefore that read this and translate (or copy) it into other books, remember me and pray for me that God will be gracious unto me and be merciful unto my sins which I have sinned against him.

Peace be to them that read and that hear these things and to their servants. Amen.

In the fifteenth (Other Ms have nineteenth) year of the governance of Tiberius Caesar, emperor of the Romans, and of Herod, king of Galilee, in the nineteenth year of his rule, on the eighth of the Calends of April, which is the 25th of March, in the consulate of Rufus and Rubellio, in the fourth year of the two hundred and second Olympiad, Joseph who is Caiaphas being high priest of the Jews: (Note – the new year once began is April.) These be the things which after the cross and passion of the Lord Nicodemus recorded and delivered unto the high priest and the rest of the Jews: and the same Nicodemus set them forth in Hebrew (letters).

Chapter 1

1 For the chief priests and scribes assembled in council, even Annas and Caiaphas and Somne and Dothain and Gamaliel, Judas, Levi and Nepthalim, Alexander and Jairus and the rest of the Jews, and came unto Pilate accusing Jesus for many deeds, saying: We know this man, that he is the son of Joseph the carpenter, begotten of Mary, and he said that he is the Son of God and a king; more-over he doth pollute the Sabbaths and he would destroy the law of our fathers.

Pilate said: And what things are they that he doeth, and would destroy the law?

The Jews say: We have a law that we should not heal any man on the Sabbath: but this man of his evil deeds has healed the lame and the bent, the withered and the blind and the paralytic, the dumb and them that were possessed, on the Sabbath day!

Pilate said unto them: By what evil deeds?

They say unto him: He is a sorcerer, and by Beelzebub the prince of the devils he casts out devils, and they are all subject unto him.

Pilate said unto them: This is not to cast out devils by an unclean spirit, but by the god Asclepius.

2 The Jews say unto Pilate: We beseech your majesty that he appear before your judgment-seat and be heard. And Pilate called them unto him and said: Tell me, how can I that am a governor examine a king? They say unto him: We say not that he is a king, but he said it of himself.

And Pilate called the messenger and said unto him: Let Jesus be brought hither, but with gentleness. And the messenger went forth, and when he perceived Jesus he worshipped him and took the kerchief that was on his hand and spread it upon the earth and said unto him: Lord, walk hereon and enter in, for the governor called you. And when the Jews saw what the messenger had done, they cried out against Pilate saying: Wherefore didst you not summon him by an herald to enter in, but by a messenger? The messenger when he saw him worshipped him and spread out his kerchief upon the ground and has made him walk upon it like a king!

3 Then Pilate called for the messenger and said unto him: Wherefore hast you done this, and hast spread your kerchief upon the ground and made Jesus to walk upon it? The messenger said unto him: Lord governor, when you sent me to Jerusalem unto Alexander, I saw Jesus sitting upon an ass, and the children of the Hebrews held branches in their hands and cried out, and others spread their garments beneath him, saying: Save now, you that art in the highest: blessed is he that cometh in the name of the Lord.

4 The Jews cried out and said unto the messenger: The children of the Hebrews cried out in Hebrew: how then hast you it in the Greek? The messenger said to them: I did ask one of the Jews and said: What is it that they cry out in Hebrew? Then he interpreted it unto me.

Pilate said unto them: And how cried they in Hebrew? The Jews say unto him: Hosanna membrome barouchamma adonai. Pilate said unto them: And the Hosanna and the rest, how is it interpreted? The Jews say unto him: Save now, you that art in the highest: blessed is he that cometh in the name of the Lord. Pilate said unto them: If you yourselves bear witness of the words which were said of the children, wherein has the messenger sinned? And they held their peace.

The governor said unto the messenger: Go forth and bring him in after what manner you will. And the messenger went forth and did after the former manner and said unto Jesus: Lord, enter in: the governor called you.

5 Now when Jesus entered in, and the ensigns were holding the standards, the images (images were from chest up) of the standards bowed and did reverence to Jesus. And when the Jews saw the carriage of the standards, how they bowed themselves and did reverence unto Jesus, they cried out above measure against the ensigns. But Pilate said unto the Jews: Marvel you not that the images bowed themselves and did reverence unto Jesus. The Jews say unto Pilate: We saw how the ensigns made them to bow and did reverence to him. And the governor called for the ensigns and said unto them: Wherefore

did you so? They say unto Pilate: We are Greeks and servers of temples, and how could we do him reverence? Indeed, whilst we held the images they bowed of themselves and did reverence unto him.

6 Then said Pilate unto the rulers of the synagogue and the elders of the people: Choose you out able and strong men and let them hold the standards, and let us see if they bow of themselves. And the elders of the Jews took twelve men strong and able and made them to hold the standards by sixes, and they were set before the judgment-seat of the governor; and Pilate said to the messenger: Take him out of the judgment place in the praetorium and bring him in again after what manner you will. And Jesus went out of the judgment hall, he and the messenger. And Pilate called unto him them that before held the image and said unto them: I have sworn by the safety of Caesar that if the standards bow not when Jesus entered in, I will cut off your heads.

And the governor commanded Jesus to enter in the second time. And the messenger did after the former manner and besought Jesus much that he would walk upon his kerchief; and he walked upon it and entered in. And when he had entered, the standards bowed themselves again and did reverence unto Jesus.

Chapter 2

1 Now when Pilate saw it he was afraid, and sought to rise up from the judgment-seat. And while he yet thought to rise up, his wife sent unto him, saying: Have you nothing to do with this just man, for I have suffered many things because of him by night. And Pilate called unto him all the Jews, and said unto them: You know that my wife fears God and favors rather the customs of the Jews, with you? They say unto him: Yea, we know it. Pilate said unto them: Lo, my wife has sent unto me, saying: Have you nothing to do with this just man: for I have suffered many things because of him by night. But the Jews answered and said unto Pilate: Said we not unto you that he is a sorcerer? Behold, he has sent a vision of a dream unto your wife.

2 And Pilate called Jesus unto him and said to him: What is it that these witness against you? Speak you nothing? But Jesus said: If they had not had power they would have spoken nothing; for every man has power over his own mouth, to speak good or evil: they shall see to it.

3 The elders of the Jews answered and said unto Jesus: What shall we see? Firstly, that you were born of fornication; secondly, that your birth in Bethlehem was the cause of the

slaying of children; thirdly, that your father Joseph and your mother Mary fled into Egypt because they had no confidence before the people.

4 Then said certain of them that stood by, devout men of the Jews: We say not that he came of fornication; but we know that Joseph was betrothed unto Mary, and he was not born of fornication. Pilate said unto those Jews which said that he came of fornication: This your saying is not true for there were espousals, as these also say which are of your nation. Annas and Caiaphas say unto Pilate: The whole multitude of us cried out that he was born of fornication, and we are not believed: but these are proselytes and disciples of his. And Pilate called Annas and Caiaphas unto him and said to them: What be proselytes? They say unto him: They were born children of Greeks, and now are they become Jews. Then said they which said l that he was not born of fornication, even Lazarus, Asterius, Antonius, Jacob, Amnes, Zenas, Samuel, Isaac, Phinees, Crispus, Agrippa and Judas: We were not born proselytes are not Greeks, but we are children of Jews and we speak the truth; for verily we were present at the espousals of Joseph and Mary.

5 And Pilate called unto him those twelve men which said that he was not born of fornication, and said unto them: I adjure

you by the safety of Caesar, are these things true which you have said, that he was not born of fornication? They say unto Pilate: We have a law that we swear not, because it is sin: But let them swear by the safety of Caesar that it is not as we have said, and we will be guilty of death. Pilate said to Annas and Caiaphas: Answer you nothing to these things? Annas and Caiaphas say unto Pilate: These twelve men are believed which say that he was not born of fornication, but the whole multitude of us cry out that he was born of fornication, and is a sorcerer, and said that he is the Son of God and a king, and we are not believed.

6 And Pilate commanded the whole multitude to go out, saving the twelve men which said that he was not born of fornication and he commanded Jesus to be set apart: and Pilate said unto them: For what cause do they desire to put him to death? They say unto Pilate: They have jealousy, because he healed on the Sabbath day. Pilate said: For a good work do they desire to put him to death? They say unto him: Yea.

Chapter 3

1 And Pilate was filled with indignation and went forth without the judgment hall and said unto them: I call the Sun to witness that I find no fault in this man. The Jews answered and

said to the governor: If this man were not a malefactor we would not have delivered him unto you. And Pilate said: Take you him and judge him according to your law. The Jews said unto Pilate: It is not lawful for us to put any man to death. Pilate said: Has God forbidden you to slay, and allowed me?

2 And Pilate went in again into the judgment hall and called Jesus apart and said unto him: Are you the King of the Jews? Jesus answered and said to Pilate: Say you this thing of yourself, or did others tell it you of me? Pilate answered Jesus: Am I also a Jew? Your own nation and the chief priests have delivered you unto me: what hast you done? Jesus answered: My kingdom is not of this world; for if my kingdom were of this world, my servants would have striven that I should not be delivered to the Jews: but now is my kingdom not from hence. Pilate said unto him: Are you a king, then? Jesus answered him: you say that I am a king; for this cause was I born and am come, that every one that is of the truth should hear my voice. Pilate said unto him: What is truth? Jesus said unto him: Truth is of heaven. Pilate said: Is there not truth upon earth? Jesus said unto Pilate: you see how that they that speak the truth are judged of them that have authority upon earth.

Chapter 4

1 And Pilate left Jesus in the judgment hall and went forth to the Jews and said unto them: I find no fault in him. The Jews say unto him: This man said: I am able to destroy this temple and in three days to build it up. Pilate said: What temple? The Jews say: That which Solomon built in forty and six years but which this man said he will destroy and build it in three days. Pilate said unto them: I am guiltless of the blood of this just man: see you to it. The Jews say: His blood be upon us and on our children.

2 And Pilate called the elders and the priests and Levites unto him and said to them secretly: Do not so: for there is nothing worthy of death whereof you have accused him, for your accusation is concerning healing and profaning of the Sabbath. The elders and the priests and Levites say: If a man blasphemes against Caesar, is he worthy of death or no? Pilate said: He is worthy of death. The Jews say unto Pilate: If a man be worthy of death if he blaspheme against Caesar, this man has blasphemed against God.

3 Then the governor commanded all the Jews to go out from

the judgment hall, and he called Jesus to him and said unto him: What shall I do with you? Jesus said unto Pilate: Do as it has been given you. Pilate said: How has it been given? Jesus said: Moses and the prophets did foretell concerning my death and rising again. Now the Jews inquired by stealth and heard, and they say unto Pilate: What need you to hear further of this blasphemy? Pilate said unto the Jews: If this word be of blasphemy, take you him for his blasphemy, and bring him into your synagogue and judge him according to your law. The Jews say unto Pilate: It is contained in our law, that if a man sin against a man, he is worthy to receive forty stripes save one: but he that blasphemed against God, that he should be stoned with stoning.

4 Pilate said unto them: Take you him and avenge yourselves of him in what manner you will. The Jews say unto Pilate: We will that he be crucified. Pilate said: He deserved not to be crucified.

5 Now as the governor looked round about upon the multitude of the Jews which stood by, he beheld many of the Jews weeping, and said: Not all the multitude desire that he should be put to death. The elder of the Jews said: To this end have the whole multitude of us come Hither, that he should be put to death. Pilate said to the Jews: Wherefore should he die? The Jews said: Because he called himself the Son of God, and a king.

Chapter 5

1 But a certain man, Nicodemus, a Jew, came and stood before the governor and said: I beseech you, good (pious) lord, bid me speak a few words. Pilate said: Say on. Nicodemus said: I said unto the elders and the priests and Levites and unto all the multitude of the Jews in the synagogue: Wherefore contend you with this man? This man doeth many and wonderful signs, which no man has done, neither will do: let him alone and contrive not any evil against him: if the signs which he doeth are of God, they will stand, but if they be of men, they will come to nothing. For verily Moses, when he was sent of God into Egypt did many signs, which God commanded him to do before Pharaoh, king of Egypt; and there were there certain men servants of Pharaoh, Jannes and Jambres, and they also did signs not a few, of them which Moses did, and the Egyptians held them as gods, even Jannes and Jambres: and whereas the signs which they did were not of God, they perished and those also that believed on them. And now let this man go, for he is not worthy of death.

2 The Jews say unto Nicodemus: you didst become his disciple and you speak on his behalf. Nicodemus said unto them: Is the governor also become his disciple, that he spoke on his behalf?

Did not Caesar appoint him unto this dignity? And the Jews were raging and gnashing their teeth against Nicodemus. Pilate said unto them: Wherefore gnash you your teeth against him, you have heard the truth? The Jews say unto Nicodemus: May you receive his truth and his portion. Nicodemus said: Amen, Amen: may I receive it as you have said.

Chapter 6

1 Now one of the Jews came forward and besought the governor that he might speak a word. The governor said: If you will say aught, speak on. And the Jew said: Thirty and eight years lay I on a bed in suffering of pains, and at the coming of Jesus many that were possessed and laid with divers diseases were healed by him, and certain (faithful) young men took pity on me and carried me with my bed and brought me unto him; and when Jesus saw me he had compassion, and spoke a word unto me: Take up your bed and walk. And I took up my bed and walked. The Jews say unto Pilate: Ask of him what day it was whereon he was healed? He that was healed said: On the Sabbath. The Jews say: Did we not inform you so, that upon the Sabbath he healed and cast out devils?

2 And another Jew came forward and said: I was born blind: I heard words but I saw no man's face: and as Jesus passed by I cried with a loud voice: Have mercy on me, O son of David.

And he took pity on me and put his hands upon mine eyes and I received sight immediately. And another Jew came forward and said: I was bowed and he made me straight with a word. And another said: I was a leper, and he healed me with a word.

Chapter 7

And a certain woman named Bernice crying out from afar off said: I had an issue of blood and touched the hem of his garment, and the flowing of my blood was stayed which I had twelve years. The Jews say: We have a law that a woman shall not come to give testimony.

Chapter 8

And certain others, even a multitude both of men and women cried out, saying: This man is a prophet and the devils are subject unto him. Pilate said to them which said: The devils are subject unto him: Wherefore were not your teachers also subject unto him? They say unto Pilate: We know not. Others also said: He raised up Lazarus which was dead out of his tomb after four days. And the governor was afraid and said unto all the multitude of the Jews: Wherefore will you shed innocent blood?

Chapter 9

1 And he called unto him Nicodemus and those twelve men which said that he was not born of fornication, and said unto them: What shall I do, for there rose sedition among the people? They say unto him: We know not, let them see to it. Again Pilate called for all the multitude of the Jews and said: You know that you have a custom that at the feast of unleavened bread I should release unto you a prisoner. Now I have a prisoner under condemnation in the prison, a murderer, Barabbas by name, and this Jesus also which stands before you, in whom I find no fault: Whom will you that I release unto you? But they cried out: Barabbas. Pilate said: What shall I do then with Jesus who is called Christ? The Jews say: Let him be crucified. But certain of the Jews answered: you are not a friend of Caesar's if you let this man go; for he called himself the Son of God and a king: you will therefore have him for king, and not Caesar.

2 And Pilate was wroth and said unto the Jews: Your nation is always seditious and you rebel against your benefactors. The Jews say: Against what benefactors? Pilate said: According as I have heard, your God brought you out of Egypt out of hard bondage, and led you safe through the sea as by dry land, and in the wilderness he nourished you with manna and gave you

quails, and gave you water to drink out of a rock, and gave unto you a law. And in all these things you provoked your God to anger, and sought out a molten calf, and angered your God and he sought to slay you: and Moses made supplication for you and you were not put to death. And now you do accuse me that I hate the king (emperor).

3 And he rose up from the judgment-seat and sought to go forth. And the Jews cried out, saying: We know our king, even Caesar and not Jesus. For indeed the wise men brought gifts from the east unto him as unto a king, and when Herod heard from the wise men that a king was born, he sought to slay him, and when his father Joseph knew that, he took him and his mother and they fled into Egypt. And when Herod heard it he destroyed the children of the Hebrews that were born in Bethlehem.

4 And when Pilate heard these words he was afraid. And Pilate silenced the multitude, because they cried still, and said unto them: So, then, this is he whom Herod sought? The Jews say: Yea, this is he. And Pilate took water and washed his hands before the sun, saying: I am innocent of the blood of this just man: see you to it. Again the Jews cried out: His blood be upon us and upon our children.

5 Then Pilate commanded the veil to be drawn before the judgment-seat whereon he sat, and said unto Jesus: Your nation has convicted you (accused you) as being a king: therefore have I decreed that you should first be scourged according to the law of the pious emperors, and thereafter hanged upon the cross in the garden wherein you were taken: and let Dysmas and Gestas the two malefactors be crucified with you.

Chapter 10

1 And Jesus went forth of the judgment hall and the two malefactors with him. And when they were come to the place they stripped him of his garments and girt him with a linen cloth and put a crown of thorns about his head: likewise also they hanged up the two malefactors. But Jesus said: Father forgive them, for they know not what they do. And the soldiers divided his garments among them.

And the people stood looking upon him, and the chief priests and the rulers with them derided him, saying: He saved others let him save himself: if he be the son of God [let him come down from the cross]. And the soldiers also mocked him, coming and offering him vinegar with gall; and they said: If you be the King of the Jews, save yourself.

And Pilate after the sentence commanded his accusation to be written for a title in letters of Greek and Latin and Hebrew according to the saying of the Jews: that he was the King of the Jews.

2 And one of the malefactors that were hanged [by name Gestas] spoke unto him, saying: If you be the Christ, save yourself, and us. But Dysmas answering rebuked him, saying: Dost you not at all fear God, seeing you are in the same condemnation? And we indeed justly, for we receive the due reward of our deeds; but this man has done nothing amiss. And he said unto Jesus: Remember me, Lord, in your kingdom. And Jesus said unto him: Verily, verily, I say unto you, that today you shall be (are) with me in paradise.

Chapter 11

1 And it was about the sixth hour, and there was darkness over the land until the ninth hour, for the sun was darkened: and the veil of the temple was rent asunder in the midst. And Jesus called with a loud voice and said: Father, baddach ephkid rouel, which is interpreted: Into your hands I commend my spirit. And having thus said he gave up the ghost. And when

the centurion saw what was done, he glorified God, saying: This man was righteous. And all the multitudes that had come to the sight, when they beheld what was done smote their breasts and returned.

2 But the centurion reported unto the governor the things that had come to pass: and when the governor and his wife heard, they were sore vexed, and neither ate nor drank that day. And Pilate sent for the Jews and said unto them: Did you see that which came to pass? But they said: There was an eclipse of the sun after the accustomed sort.

3 And his acquaintance had stood afar off, and the women which came with him from Galilee, beholding these things. But a certain man named Joseph, being a counselor, of the city of Arimathaea, who also himself looked for the kingdom of God this man went to Pilate and begged the body of Jesus. And he took it down and wrapped it in a clean linen cloth and laid it in a hewn sepulcher wherein was never man yet laid.

Chapter 12

1 Now when the Jews heard that Joseph had begged the body of Jesus, they sought for him and for the twelve men which

said that Jesus was not born of fornication, and for Nicodemus and many others which had come forth before Pilate and declared his good works. But all they hid themselves, and Nicodemus only was seen of them, for he was a ruler of the Jews. And Nicodemus said unto them: How came you into the synagogue? The Jews say unto him: How didst you come into the synagogue? For you are confederate with him, and his portion shall be with you in the life to come. Nicodemus said: Amen, Amen. Likewise Joseph also came forth and said unto them: Why is it that you are vexed against me, for that I begged the body of Jesus? Behold I have laid it in my new tomb, having wrapped it in clean linen, and I rolled a stone over the door of the cave. And you have not dealt well with the just one, for you repented not when you had crucified him, but you also pierced him with a spear.

But the Jews took hold on Joseph and commanded him to be put in safeguard until the first day of the week: and they said unto him: Know you that the time allowed us not to do anything against you, because the Sabbath dawned: but knew that you shall not obtain burial, but we will give your flesh unto the fowls of the heaven. Joseph said unto them: This is the word of Goliath the boastful which reproached the living God and the holy David. For God said by the prophet: Vengeance is mine, and I will recompense, said the Lord. And now, lo, one that was uncircumcised, but circumcised in heart, took water and washed his hands before the sun, saying: I am Innocent of the blood of this just person: see you to it. And you answered Pilate and said: His blood be upon us and upon our children. And now I fear lest the rage of the Lord come upon you and upon your children, as you have said. But when the Jews heard these words they waxed bitter in soul, and caught hold on Joseph and took him and shut him up in an house wherein was no window, and guards were set at the door: and they sealed the door of the place where Joseph was shut up.

2 And upon the Sabbath day the rulers of the synagogue and the priests and the Levites made an ordinance that all men should appear in the synagogue on the first day of the week. And all the multitude rose up early and took council in the synagogue by what death they should kill him. And when the council was set they commanded him to be brought with great dishonor. And when they had opened the door they found him not. And all the people were beside themselves and amazed, because they found the seals closed, and Caiaphas had the key. And they dared not any more lay hands upon them that had spoken in the behalf of Jesus before Pilate.

Chapter 13

1 And while they yet sat in the synagogue and marveled because of Joseph, there came certain of the guard which the Jews had asked of Pilate to keep the sepulcher of Jesus lest peradventure his disciples should come and steal him away. And they spoke and declared unto the rulers of the synagogue and the priests and the Levites that which had come to pass: how that there was a great earthquake, and we saw an angel descend from heaven, and he rolled away the stone from the mouth of the cave, and sat upon it. And he did shine like snow and like lightning, and we were sore afraid and lay as dead men. And we heard the voice of the angel speaking with the women which waited at the sepulcher, saying: Fear you not: for I know that you seek Jesus which was crucified. He is not here: he is risen, as he said. Come, see the place where the Lord lay, and go quickly and say unto his disciples that he is risen from the dead, and is in Galilee.

2 The Jews say: With what women spoke he? They of the guard say: We know not who they were. The Jews say: At what hour was it? They of the guard say: At midnight. The Jews say: And wherefore did you not take the women? They of the guard say: We were become as dead me through fear, and we looked not

to see the light of the day; how then could we take them? The Jews say: As the Lord lives, we believe you not. They of the guard say unto the Jews: So many signs saw you in that man, and you believed not, how then should you believe us? Verily you swore rightly 'as the Lord lives', for he lives indeed. Again they of the guard say: We have heard that you shut up him that begged the body of Jesus, and that you scaled the door; and when you had opened it you found him not. Give you therefore Joseph and we will give you Jesus. The Jews say: Joseph is departed unto his own city. They of the guard say unto the Jews: Jesus also is risen, as we have heard of the angel, and he is in Galilee.

3 And when the Jews heard these words they were sore afraid, saying: Take heed lest this report be heard and all men incline unto Jesus. And the Jews took counsel and laid down much money and gave it to the soldiers, saying: Say you: While we slept his disciples came by night and stole him away. And if this come to the governor's hearing we will persuade him and secure you. And they took the money and did as they were instructed. [And this their saying was published abroad among all men. lat.]

Joseph B. Lumpkin

Chapter 14

1 Now a certain priest named Phinees and Addas a teacher and Aggaeus a Levite came down from Galilee unto Jerusalem and told the rulers of the synagogue and the priests and the Levites, saying: We saw Jesus and his disciples sitting upon the mountain which is called Mamilch, and he said unto his disciples: Go into all the world and preach unto every creature (the whole creation): he that believes and is baptized shall be saved, but he that did not believed shall be condemned. [And these signs shall follow upon them that believe: in my name they shall cast out devils, they shall speak with new tongues, they shall take up serpents, and if they drink any deadly thing it shall not hurt them: they shall lay hands upon the sick and they shall recover.] And while Jesus yet spoke unto his disciples we saw him taken up into heaven.

2 The elders and the priests and Levites say: Give glory to the God of Israel and make confession unto him: did you indeed (or that you did) hear and see those things which you have told us? They that told them say: As the Lord God of our fathers Abraham, Isaac, and Jacob live, we did hear these things and we saw him taken up into heaven. The elders and the priests and the Levites say unto them: Came you for this end, that you

might tell us, or came you to pay your vows unto God? And they say: To pay our vows unto God. The elders and the chief priests and the Levites say unto them: If you came to pay your vows unto God, to what purpose is this idle tale which you have babbled before all the people? Phinees the priest and Addas the teacher and Aggaeus the Levite say unto the rulers of the synagogue and priests and Levites: If these words which you have spoken and seen be sin, lo, we are before you: do unto us as seemed good in your eyes. And they took the book of the law and adjured them that they should no more tell any man these words: and they gave them to eat and to drink, and put them out of the city: moreover they gave them money, and three men to go with them, and they set them on their way as far as Galilee, and they departed in peace.

3 Now when these men were departed into Galilee, the chief priests and the rulers of the synagogue and the elders gathered together in the synagogue, and shut the gate, and lamented with a great lamentation, saying: What is this sign which is come to pass in Israel? But Amlas and Caiaphas said: Wherefore are you troubled? Why weep you? Know you not that his disciples gave much gold unto them that kept the sepulcher and taught them to say that an angel came down and rolled away the stone from the door of the sepulcher? But the priests and the elders said: Be it so, that his disciples did steal

away his body; but how is his soul entered into his body, and how abided he in Galilee? But they could not answer these things, and hardly in the end said: It is not lawful for us to believe the uncircumcised. Ought we to believe the soldiers, that an angel came down from heaven and rolled away the stone from the door of the sepulcher? But in truth his disciples gave . . . (missing text) sepulcher. Know you not that it is not lawful for Jews to believe any word of the uncircumcised, knowing that they who received much good from us have spoken according as we taught them.]

Chapter 15

And Nicodemus rose up and stood before the council, saying: You say well. Know you not, O people of the Lord, the men that came down out of Galilee, that they fear God and are men of substance, hating covetousness (a lie, Lat.), men of peace? And they have told you with an oath, saying: We saw Jesus upon the mount Mamilch with his disciples and that he taught them all things that you heard of them, and, say they, we saw him taken up into heaven. And no man asked them in what manner he was taken up. For like as the book of the holy scriptures has taught us that Elias also was taken up into heaven, and Eliseus cried out with a loud voice, and Elias cast his hairy cloak upon Eliseus, and Eliseus cast the cloak upon Jordan and passed over and went unto Jericho. And the sons of the prophets met him and said: Eliseus, where is your lord Elias? and he said that he was taken up into heaven. And they said unto Eliseus: Has not a spirit caught him up and cast him upon one of the mountains? But let us take our servants with us and seek after him. And they persuaded Eliseus and he went with them, and they sought him three days and found him not: and they knew that he had been taken up. And now hearken unto me, and let us send into all the coasts (al. mountains) of Israel and see whether the Christ were not taken up by a spirit and cast upon one of the mountains. And this saying pleased them all: and they sent into all the coasts (mountains, Lat.) and sought Jesus and found him not. But they found Joseph in Arimathaea, and no man durst lay hands upon him.

2 And they told the elders and the priests and the Levites, saying: We went about throughout all the coasts of Israel, and we found not Jesus; but Joseph we found in Arimathaea. And when they heard of Joseph they rejoiced and gave glory to the God of Israel. And the rulers of the synagogue and the priests and the Levites took counsel how they should meet with Joseph, and they took a volume of paper and wrote unto Joseph these words:

Peace be unto you. We know that we have sinned against God and against you, and we have prayed unto the God of Israel that you should vouchsafe to come unto your fathers and unto your children for we are all troubled, because when we opened the door we found you not: and we know that we devised an evil counsel against you, but the Lord helped you. And the Lord himself made of no effect and scattered our counsel against you, O father Joseph, you that are honorable among all the people.

3 And they chose out of all Israel seven men that were friends of Joseph, whom Joseph also himself accounted his friends, and the rulers of the synagogue and the priests and the Levites said unto them: See: if he receive our epistle and read it, know that he will come with you unto us: but if he read it not, know that he is vexed with us, and salute you him in peace and return unto us. And they blessed the men and let them go.

And the men came unto Joseph and did him reverence, and said unto him: Peace be unto you. And he said: Peace be unto you and unto all the people of Israel. And they gave him the book of the epistle, and Joseph received it and read it and embraced (or kissed) the epistle and blessed God and said: Blessed be the Lord God, which has redeemed Israel from shedding innocent blood; and blessed be the Lord, which sent his angel and sheltered me under his wings. (And he kissed them) and set a table before them, and they did eat and drink and lay there.

4 And they rose up early and prayed: and Joseph saddled his she-ass and went with the men, and they came unto the holy city, even Jerusalem. And all the people came to meet Joseph and cried: Peace be to yours entering-in. And he said unto all the people: Peace be unto you, and all the people kissed him. And the people prayed with Joseph, and they were astonished at the sight of him.

And Nicodemus received him into his house and made a great feast, and called Annas and Caiaphas and the elders and the priests and the Levites unto his house. And they made merry eating and drinking with Joseph. And when they had sung a hymn (or blessed God) every man went unto his house. But Joseph abode in the house of Nicodemus.

5 And on the morrow, which was the preparation, the rulers of the synagogue and the priests and the Levites rose up early and came to the house of Nicodemus, and Nicodemus met them and said: Peace be unto you. And they said: Peace be unto you and to Joseph and unto all your house and to all the house of Joseph. And he brought them into his house. And the whole

council was set, and Joseph sat between Annas and Caiaphas and no man durst speak unto him a word. And Joseph said: Why is it that you have called me? And they beckoned unto Nicodemus that he should speak unto Joseph. And Nicodemus opened his mouth and said unto Joseph: Father, you know that the reverend doctors and the priests and the Levites seek to learn a matter of you. And Joseph said: Inquire you. And Annas and Caiaphas took the book of the law and adjured Joseph saying: Give glory to the God of Israel and make confession unto him: [for Achar, when he was adjured of the prophet Jesus (Joshua), swore not himself but declared unto him all things and hid not a word from him: you therefore also hide not from us so much as a word. And Joseph: I will not hide one word from you.] And they said unto him: We were greatly vexed because you did beg the body of Jesus and wrapped it in a clean linen cloth and did lay him in a tomb. And for this cause we put you in safeguard in an house wherein was no window, and we put keys and seals upon the doors, and guards did keep the place wherein you were shut up. And on the first day of the week we opened it and found you not, and we were sore troubled, and amazement fell upon all the people of the Lord until yesterday. Now, therefore, declare unto us what befell you.

6 And Joseph said: On the preparation day about the tenth hour you did shut me up, and I continued there the whole Sabbath. And at midnight as I stood and prayed the house wherein you shut me up was taken up by the four corners, and I saw as it were a flashing of light in mine eyes, and being filled with fear I fell to the earth. And one took me by the hand and removed me from the place whereon I had fallen; and moisture of water was shed on me from my head unto my feet, and a scent of ointment came about my nostrils. And he wiped my face and kissed me and said unto me: Fear not, Joseph: open yours eyes and see who it is that spoke with you. And I looked up and saw Jesus and I trembled, and supposed that it was a spirit: and I said the commandments: and he said them with me. And [as] you are not ignorant that a spirit, if it meet any man and hear the commandments, straightway fled. And when I perceived that he said them with me, I said unto him: Rabbi Elias? And he said unto me: I am not Elias. And I said unto him: Who are you, Lord? And he said unto me: I am Jesus, whose body you did beg of Pilate, and did clothe me in clean linen and cover my face with a napkin, and lay me in your new cave and roll a great stone upon the door of the cave. And I said to him that spoke with me: Show me the place where I laid you. And he brought me and showed me the place where I laid him, and the linen cloth lay therein, and the napkin that was upon his face. And I knew that it was Jesus. And he took me by the hand and

set me in the midst of mine house, the doors being shut, and laid me upon my bed and said unto me: Peace be unto you. And he kissed me and said unto me: Until forty days be ended go not out of yours house: for behold I go unto my brethren into Galilee.

Chapter 16

1 And when the rulers of the synagogue and the priests and the Levites heard these words of Joseph became as dead men and fell to the ground, and they fasted until the ninth hour. And Nicodemus with Joseph comforted Annas and Caiaphas and the priests and the Levites, saying: Rise up and stand on your feet and taste bread and strengthen your souls, for tomorrow is the Sabbath of the Lord. And they rose up and prayed unto God and did eat and drink, and departed every man to his house.

2 And on the Sabbath our teachers and the priests and Levites sat and questioned one another and said: What is this rage that is come upon us? For we know his father and his mother. Levi the teacher said: I know that his parents feared God and kept not back their vows and paid tithes three times a year. And when Jesus was born, his parents brought him up unto this place and gave sacrifices and burnt-offerings to God. And

[when] the great teacher Symeon took him into his arms and said: Now let you your servant, Lord, depart in peace for mine eyes have seen your salvation which you hast prepared before the face of all peoples, a light to lighten the Gentiles and the glory of your people Israel. And Symeon blessed them and said unto Mary his mother: I give you good tidings concerning this child. And Mary said: Good, my lord? And Symeon said to her: Good. Behold, he is set for the fall and rising again of many in Israel, and for a sign spoken against: and a sword shall pierce through yours own heart also, that the thoughts of many hearts may be revealed.

3 They say unto Levi the teacher: How know you these things? Levi said unto them: Know you not that from him I did learn the law? The council said unto him: We would see your father. And they sent after his father, and asked of him, and he said to them: Why believed you not my son? The blessed and righteous Symeon, he did teach him the law. The council said: Rabbi Levi, is the word true which you hast spoken? And he said: It is true.

Then the rulers of the synagogue and the priests and the Levites said among themselves: Come, let us send into Galilee unto the three men which came and told us of his teaching and his taking-up, and let them tell us how they saw him taken up.

And this word pleased them all, and they sent the three men which before had gone with them into Galilee and said to them: Say unto Rabbi Addas and Rabbi Phinees and Rabbi Aggaeus: peace be to you and to all that are with you. Inasmuch as great questioning has arisen in the council, we have sent unto you to call you unto this holy place of Jerusalem.

4 And the men went into Galilee and found them sitting and meditating upon the law, and saluted them in peace. And the men that were in Galilee said unto them that were come to them: Peace be upon all Israel. And they said: Peace be unto you. Again they said unto them: Wherefore are you come? And they that were sent said: The council called you unto the holy city Jerusalem. And when the men heard that they were bidden by the council, they prayed to God and sat down to meat with the men and did eat and drink, and rose up and came in peace unto Jerusalem.

5 And on the morrow the council was set in the synagogue, and they examined them, saying: Did you in very deed see Jesus sitting upon the mount Mamilch, as he taught his eleven disciples, and saw you him taken up? And the men answered them and said: Even as we saw him taken up, even so did we tell it unto you.

6 Annas said: Set them apart from one another, and let us see if their word agreed. And they set them apart one from another, and they call Addas first and say unto him: How did you see Jesus taken up? Addas said: While he yet sat upon the Mount Mamilch and taught his disciples, we saw a cloud that overshadowed him and his disciples: and the cloud carried him up into heaven, and his disciples lay (al. prayed, lying) on their faces upon the earth. And they called Phinees the priest, and questioned him also, saying: How did you see Jesus taken up? And he spoke in like manner. And again they asked Aggaeus, and he also spoke in like manner. And the council said: It is contained in the law of Moses: At the mouth of two or three shall every word be established.

Abuthem the teacher said: It is written in the law: Enoch walked with God and is not, because God took him. Jaeirus the teacher said: Also we have heard of the death of the holy Moses and have not seen him; for it is written in the law of the Lord: And Moses died at the mouth of the Lord, and no man knew of his sepulcher unto this day. And Rabbi Levi said: Wherefore was it that Rabbi Symeon said when he saw Jesus: Behold, this child is set for the fall and rising again of many in Israel and for a sign spoken against? And Rabbi Isaac said: It is written in the law: Behold I send my messenger before your face, which shall go before you to keep you in every good way, for my name is

Joseph B. Lumpkin

named thereon.

7 Then said Annas and Caiaphas: You have well said those things which are written in the law of Moses, that no man saw the death of Enoch, and no man has named the death of Moses. But Jesus spoke before Pilate, and we know that we saw him receive shaking, striking, and spitting upon his face, and that the soldiers put on him a crown of thorns and that he was scourged and received condemnation from Pilate, and that he was crucified at the place of a skull and two thieves with him, and that they gave him vinegar to drink with gall, and that Longinus the soldier pierced his side with a spear, and that Joseph our honorable father begged his body, and that, as he said, he rose again, and that (lit. as) the three teachers say: We saw him taken up into heaven, and that Rabbi Levi spoke and testified to the things which were spoken by Rabbi Symeon, and that he said: Behold this child is set for the fall and rising again of many in Israel and for a sign spoken against.

And all the teachers said unto all the people of the Lord: If this has come to pass from the Lord, and it is marvelous in our eyes, you shall surely know, O house of Jacob, that it is written: Cursed is every one that hangs upon a tree. And another scripture teaches: The gods which made not the heaven and the earth shall perish.

And the priests and the Levites said one to another: If his memorial endure until the Sommos which is called the Jubilee, know you that he will prevail for ever and raise up for himself a new people.

Then the rulers of the synagogue and the priests and the Levites admonished all Israel, saying: Cursed is that man who shall worship that which man's hand has made, and cursed is the man who shall worship creatures beside the Creator. And all the people said: Amen, Amen.

And all the people sang a hymn unto the Lord and said: Blessed be the Lord who has given rest unto the people of Israel according to all that he spoke. There has not one word fallen to the ground of all his good saying which he spoke unto his servant Moses. The Lord our God be with us as he was with our fathers: let him not forsake us. And let him not destroy us from turning our heart unto him, from walking in all his ways and keeping his statutes and his judgments which he commanded our fathers. And the Lord shall be King over all the earth in that day. And there shall be one Lord and his name one, even the Lord our King: he shall save us.

There is none like unto you, O Lord. Great are you, O Lord, and great is your name.

Heal us, O Lord, by your power, and we shall be healed: save us, Lord, and we shall be saved: for we are your portion and yours inheritance.

And the Lord will not forsake his people for his great name's sake, for the Lord has begun to make us to be his people.

And when they had all sung this hymn they departed every man to his house, glorifying God. [For his is the glory, world without end. Amen.]

ACTS OF PILATE

PART II. THE DESCENT INTO HELL

This writing, or the nucleus of it, the story of the Descent into Hell was not originally part of the Acts of Pilate. It is an older document. When it was first attached to the Acts of Pilate is uncertain. Part I ends with words of the rulers of the synagogue, "All nations shall serve him, and kings shall come from afar worshipping and magnifying him."

Chapter 17

1 And Joseph arose and said unto Annas and Caiaphas: Truly and of right do you marvel because you have heard that Jesus has been seen alive after death, and that he has ascended into heaven. Nevertheless it is more marvelous that he rose not alone from the dead, but did raise up alive many other dead out of their sepulchers, and they have been seen of many in Jerusalem. And now hearken unto me; for we all know the blessed Simeon, the high priest which received the child Jesus in his hands in the temple. And this Simeon had two sons,

brothers in blood and we all were at their falling asleep and at their burial. Go therefore and look upon their sepulchers: for they are open, because they have risen, and behold they are in the city of Arimathaea dwelling together in prayer. And indeed men hear them crying out, yet they speak with no man, but are silent as dead men. But come, let us go unto them and with all honor and gentleness bring them unto us, and if we adjure them, perchance they will tell us concerning the mystery of their rising again.

2 When they heard these things, they all rejoiced. And Annas and Caiaphas, Nicodemus and Joseph and Gamaliel went and found them not in their sepulcher, but they went unto the city of Arimathaea, and found them there, kneeling on their knees and giving themselves unto prayer. And they kissed them, and with all reverence and in the fear of God they brought them to Jerusalem into the synagogue. And they shut the doors and took the law of the Lord and put it into their hands, and adjured them by the God Adonai and the God of Israel which spoke unto our fathers by the prophets, saying: Believe you that it is Jesus which raised you from the dead? Tell us how you have arisen from the dead.

3 And when Karinus and Leucius heard this adjuration, they

trembled in their body and groaned, being troubled in heart. And looking up together unto heaven they made the seal of the cross with their fingers upon their tongues, and forthwith they spoke both of them, saying: Give us each a volume of paper, and let us write that which we have seen and heard. And they gave them unto them, and each of them sat down and wrote, saying:

Chapter 18

1 O Lord Jesus Christ, the life and resurrection of the dead (al. resurrection of the dead and the life of the living), suffer us to speak of the mysteries of your majesty which you did perform after your death upon the cross, inasmuch as we have been adjured by your Name. For you did command us your servants to tell no man the secrets of your divine majesty which you performed in hell.

Now when we were set together with all our fathers in the deep, in obscurity of darkness, on a sudden there came a golden heat of the sun and a purple and royal light shining upon us. And immediately the father of the whole race of men, together with all the patriarchs and prophets, rejoiced, saying: This light is the beginning (author) of everlasting light which did promise to send unto us his co-eternal light. And Esaias cried out and said: This is the light of the Father, even the Son of God, according as I prophesied when I lived upon the earth: The land of Zabulon and the land of Nephthalim beyond Jordan, of Galilee of the Gentiles, the people that walked in darkness have seen a great light, and they that dwell in the land of the shadow of death, upon them did the light shine. And now has it come and shone upon us that sit in death.

2 And as we all rejoiced in the light which shined upon us, there came unto us our father Simeon, and he rejoicing said unto us: Glorify you the Lord Jesus Christ, the Son of God; for I received him in my hands in the temple when he was born a child, and being moved of the Holy Ghost I made confession and said unto him: Now have mine eyes seen your salvation which you hast prepared before the face of all people, a light to lighten the Gentiles, and to be the glory of your people Israel. And when they heard these things, the whole multitude of the saints rejoiced yet more.

3 And after that there came one as it were a dweller in the wilderness, and he was asked by all, "Who are you?" And he answered them and said: I am John, the voice and the prophet of the most High, which came before the face of his advent to prepare his ways, to give knowledge of salvation unto his

people, for the remission of their sins. And when I saw him coming unto me, being moved of the Holy Ghost, I said: Behold the Lamb of God, behold him that takes away the sins of the world. And I baptized him in the river of Jordan, and saw the Holy Ghost descending upon him in the likeness of a dove, and heard a voice out of heaven saying: This is my beloved Son, in whom I am well pleased. And now have I come before his face, and come down to declare unto you that he is at hand to visit us, even the day spring, the Son of God, coming from on high unto us that sit in darkness and in the shadow of death.

Chapter 19

1 And when father Adam that was first created heard this, even that Jesus was baptized in Jordan, he cried out to Seth his son, saying: Declare unto your sons the patriarchs and the prophets all that you did hear from Michael the archangel, when I sent you unto the gates of paradise that you might entreat God to send you his angel to give you the oil of the tree of mercy to anoint my body when I was sick. Then Seth drew near unto the holy patriarchs and prophets, and said: When I, Seth, was praying at the gates of paradise, behold Michael the angel of the Lord appeared unto me, saying: I am sent unto you from the Lord: it is I that am set over the body of man. And I say unto you, Seth, vex not yourself with tears, praying and

entreating for the oil of the tree of mercy, that you may anoint your father Adam for the pain of his body: for you will not be able to receive it save in the last days and times, save when five thousand and five hundred (5,952) years are accomplished: then shall the most beloved Son of God come upon the earth to raise up the body of Adam and the bodies of the dead, and he shall come and be baptized in Jordan. And when he is come forth of the water of Jordan, then shall he anoint with the oil of mercy all that believe on him, and that oil of mercy shall be unto all generations of them that shall be born of water and of the Holy Ghost, unto life eternal. Then shall the most beloved Son of God, even Christ Jesus, come down upon the earth and shall bring in our father Adam into paradise unto the tree of mercy.

And when they heard all these things of Seth, all the patriarchs and prophets rejoiced with a great rejoicing.

Chapter 20

1 And while all the saints were rejoicing, behold Satan the prince and chief of death said unto Hell: Make yourself ready to receive Jesus who boasted himself that he is the Son of God, whereas he is a man that fears death, and say: My soul is

sorrowful even unto death. And he has been much mine enemy, doing me great hurt, and many that I had made blind, lame, dumb, leprous, and possessed he has healed with a word: and some whom I have brought unto you dead, them has he taken away from you.

2 Hell answered and said unto Satan the prince: Who is he that is so mighty, if he be a man that feared death? For all the mighty ones of the earth are held in subjection by my power, even they whom you hast brought me subdued by your power. If, then, you are mighty, what manner of man is this Jesus who, though he fear death, resisted your power? If he be so mighty in his manhood, verily I say unto you he is almighty in his godhead, and no man can withstand his power. And when he said that he feared death, he would ensnare you, and woe shall be unto you for everlasting ages. But Satan the prince of Tartarus said: Why doubt you and fear to receive this Jesus, which is yours adversary and mine? For I tempted him, and have stirred up my ancient people, the Jews, with envy and anger against him. I have sharpened a spear to thrust him through, gall and vinegar have I mingled to give him to drink, and I have prepared a cross to crucify him and nails to pierce him: and his death is nigh at hand, that I may bring him unto you to be subject unto you and me.

3 Hell answered and said: you hast told me that it is he that has taken away dead men from me. For there be many which while they lived on the earth have taken dead men from me, yet not by their own power but by prayer to God, and their almighty God has taken them from me. Who is this Jesus which by his own word without prayer has drawn dead men from me? Perchance it is he which by the word of his command did restore to life Lazarus which was four days dead and stank and was corrupt, whom I held here dead. Satan the prince of death answered and said: It is that same Jesus. When Hell heard that he said unto him: I adjure you by your strength and mine own that you bring him not unto me. For at that time I, when I heard the command of his word, did quake and was overwhelmed with fear, and all my ministries with me were troubled. Neither could we keep Lazarus, but he like an eagle shaking himself leaped forth with all agility and swiftness, and departed from us, and the earth also which held the dead body of Lazarus straightway gave him up alive. Wherefore now I know that that man which was able to do these things is a God strong in command and mighty in manhood, and that he is the savior of mankind. And if you bring him unto me he will set free all that are here shut up in the hard prison and bound in the chains of their sins that cannot be broken, and will bring them unto the life of his god head for ever.

Chapter 21

1 And as Satan the prince, and Hell, spoke this together, suddenly there came a voice as of thunder and a spiritual cry: Remove, O princes, your gates, and be you lift up, you everlasting doors, and the King of glory shall come in. When Hell heard that he said unto Satan the prince: Depart from me and go out of mine abode: if you be a mighty man of war, fight you against the King of glory. But what hast you to do with him? And Hell cast Satan forth out of his dwelling. Then said Hell unto his wicked ministers: Shut you the hard gates of brass and put on them the bars of iron and withstand stoutly, lest we that hold captivity be taken captive.

2 But when all the multitude of the saints heard it, they spoke with a voice of rebuking unto Hell: Open your gates so that the King of glory may come in. And David cried out, saying: Did I not when I was alive upon earth, foretell unto you: Let them give thanks unto the Lord, even his mercies and his wonders unto the children of men; who has broken the gates of brass and smitten the bars of iron in sunder? He has taken them out of the way of their iniquity. And thereafter in like manner Esaias said: Did not I when I was alive upon earth foretell unto you: The dead shall arise, and they that are in the tombs shall rise again, and they that are in the earth shall rejoice, for the

dew which cometh of the Lord is their healing? And again I said: O death, where is your sting? O Hell, where is your victory?

3 When they heard that of Esaias, all the saints said unto Hell: Open your gates: now shall you be overcome and weak and without strength. And there came a great voice as of thunder, saying: Remove, O princes, your gates, and be you lift up you doors of hell, and the King of glory shall come in. And when Hell saw that they so cried out twice, he said, as if he knew it not: Who is the King of glory? And David answered Hell and said: The words of this cry do I know, for by his spirit I prophesied the same; and now I say unto you that which I said before: The Lord strong and mighty, the Lord mighty in battle, he is the King of glory. And: The Lord looked down from heaven that he might hear the groaning of them that are in fetters and deliver the children of them that have been slain. And now, O you most foul and stinking Hell, open your gates so that the King of glory may come in. And as David spoke thus unto Hell, the Lord of majesty appeared in the form of a man and lightened the eternal darkness and brake the bonds that could not be loosed: and the aid of his everlasting might visited us that sat in the deep darkness of our transgressions and in the shadow of death of our sins.

Chapter 22

1 When Hell and death and their wicked ministers saw that, they were stricken with fear, they and their cruel officers, at the sight of the brightness of so great light in their own realm, seeing Christ of a sudden in their abode, and they cried out, saying: We are overcome by you. Who are you that are sent by the Lord for our confusion? Who are you that without all damage of corruption, and with the signs (?) of your majesty unblemished, dost in rage condemn our power? Who are you that are so great and so small, both humble and exalted, both soldier and commander, a marvelous warrior in the shape of a bondsman, and a King of glory dead and living, whom the cross bare slain upon it? You that did lie dead in the sepulcher has come down unto us living and at your death all creation quaked and all the stars were shaken and you hast become free among the dead and dost rout our legions. Who are you that sets free the prisoners that are held bound by original sin and restores them into their former liberty? Who are you that sheds your divine and bright light upon them that were blinded with the darkness of their sins? After the same manner all the legions of devils were stricken with like fear and cried out all together in the terror of their confusion, saying: Where are you, Jesus, a man so mighty and bright in majesty, so excellent without spot and clean from sin? For that world of earth which

has been always subject unto us until now, and did pay tribute to our profit, has never sent unto us a dead man like you, nor ever dispatched such a gift unto Hell. Who then are you that so fearlessly enters our borders, and not only fears not our torments, but besides plans (consents) to bear away all men out of our bonds? Could it be that you are that Jesus, of whom Satan our prince said that by your death of the cross you should receive the dominion of the whole world.

2 Then did the King of glory in his majesty trample upon death, and laid hold on Satan the prince and delivered him unto the power of Hell, and drew Adam to him unto his own brightness.

Chapter 23

Then Hell, receiving Satan the prince, with sore reproach said unto him: O prince of perdition and chief of destruction, Beelzebub, the scorn of the angels and spitting of the righteous why would you do this? You would crucify the King of glory and at his decease did promise us great spoils of his death: like a fool you knew not what you did. For behold now, this Jesus puts to flight by the brightness of his majesty all the darkness of death, and has broken the strong depths of the prisons, and let out the prisoners and loosed them that were bound. And all that were sighing in our torments do rejoice against us, and at their prayers our dominions are vanquished and our realms conquered, and now no nation of men feared us any more. And beside this, the dead which were never wont to be proud triumph over us, and the captives which never could be joyful do threaten us. O prince Satan, father of all the wicked and ungodly and renegades wherefore would you do this? They that from the beginning until now have despaired of life and salvation now none of their depraved roaring is heard, neither does any groan from them sound in our ears, nor is there any sign of tears upon the face of any of them. O prince Satan, holder of the keys of hell, those who are your riches which you had gained by the tree of transgression and the losing of paradise, you hast lost by the tree of the cross, and all your gladness has perished. When you did hang up Christ Jesus the King of glory you performed against yourself and against me. Henceforth you shall know what eternal torments and infinite pains you are to suffer in my keeping forever. O prince Satan, author of death and head of all pride, you ought first to have sought out matter of evil in this Jesus: Wherefore did you adventure without cause to crucify him unjustly against whom you found no blame, and to bring into our realm the innocent and righteous one, and to lose the guilty and the ungodly and unrighteous of the whole world? And when Hell had spoken thus unto Satan the prince, then said the King of glory unto Hell: Satan the prince shall be in your power unto all ages in the place of Adam and his children, even those that are my righteous ones.

Chapter 24

1 And the Lord stretching forth his hand, said: Come unto me, all you my saints which bear mine image and my likeness. You that by the tree and the devil and death were condemned, behold now the devil and death condemned by the tree. And right away all the saints were gathered in one under the hand of the Lord. And the Lord holding the right hand of Adam, said unto him: Peace be unto you with all your children that are my righteous ones. But Adam, casting himself at the knees of the Lord entreated him with tears and pleading, and said with a loud voice: I will magnify you, O Lord, for you have set me up and not made my foes to triumph over me: O Lord my God I cried unto you and you have healed me; Lord, you have brought my soul out of hell, you have delivered me from them that go down to the pit. Sing praises unto the Lord all you saints of his, and give thanks unto him for the remembrance of his holiness. For there is rage in his indignation and life is in his good pleasure. In like manner all the saints of God kneeled and

cast themselves at the feet of the Lord, saying with one accord: you are come, O redeemer of the world: that which you did foretell by the law and by your prophets, that have you accomplished in deed. You have redeemed the living by your cross, and by the death of the cross you have come down unto us, that you might save us out of hell and death through your majesty. O Lord, like as you have set the name of your glory in the heavens and set up your cross for a token of redemption upon the earth, so, Lord, set you up the sign of the victory of your cross in hell, that death may have no more dominion.

2 And the Lord stretched forth his hand and made the sign of the cross over Adam and over all his saints, and he took the right hand of Adam and went up out of hell, and all the saints followed him. Then did holy David cry aloud and say: Sing unto the Lord a new song, for he has done marvelous things. His right hand has wrought salvation for him and his holy arm. The Lord has made known his saving health, before the face of all nations has he revealed his righteousness. And the whole multitude of the saints answered, saying: Such honor have all his saints. Amen, Alleluia.

3 And thereafter Habacuc the prophet cried out and said: you went forth for the salvation of your people to set free your chosen. And all the saints answered, saying: Blessed is he that

comes in the name of the Lord. God is the Lord and has showed us light. Amen, Alleluia. Likewise after that the prophet Micheas also cried, saying: What God is like you, O Lord, taking away iniquity and removing sins? And now you withhold your rage for a testimony that you are merciful of free will, and you dost turn away and have mercy on us, you forgive all our iniquities and have sunk all our sins in the depths of the sea, as you swear unto our fathers in the days of old. And all the saints answered, saying: This is our God forever and ever, he shall be our guide, world without end. Amen, Alleluia. And so spoke all the prophets, making mention of holy words out of their praises, and all the saints followed the Lord, crying Amen, Alleluia.

Chapter 25

But the Lord holding the hand of Adam delivered him unto Michael the archangel, and all the saints followed Michael the archangel, and he brought them all into the glory and beauty (grace) of paradise. And there met with them two men, ancients of days, and when they were asked of the saints: Who are you that have not yet been dead in hell with us and are set in paradise in the body? Then one of them answering, said: I am Enoch which was translated hither by the word of the Lord, and this that is with me is Elias the Thesbite which was taken up in a chariot of fire: and up to this day we have not tasted death, but we are received unto the coming of Antichrist to fight against him with signs and wonders of God, and to be slain of him in Jerusalem, and after three days and a half to be taken up again alive on the clouds.

Chapter 26

And as Enoch and Elias spoke thus with the saints, behold there came another man of vile habit, bearing upon his shoulders the sign of the cross; whom when they beheld, all the saints said unto him: Who are you? For yours appearance is as of a robber; and wherefore is it that you bear a sign upon your shoulders? And he answered them and said: You have rightly said: for I was a robber, doing all manner of evil upon the earth. And the Jews crucified me with Jesus, and I beheld the wonders in the creation which came to pass through the cross of Jesus when he was crucified, and I believed that he was the maker of all creatures and the almighty king, and I besought him, saying: Remember me, Lord, when you come into your kingdom. And forthwith he received my prayer, and said unto me: Verily I say unto you, this day shall you be with me in paradise: and he gave me the sign of the cross, saying: Bear this and go unto paradise, and if the angel that keeps paradise suffer you not to enter in, show him the sign of the cross; and you shall say unto him: Jesus Christ the Son of God who now is crucified has sent me. And when I had so done, I spoke all these things unto the angel that keeps paradise; and when he heard this of me, forthwith he opened the door and brought me in and set me at the right hand of paradise, saying: Lo now, tarry a little, and Adam the father of all mankind will enter in with all his children that are holy and righteous, after the triumph and glory of the ascending up of Christ the Lord that is crucified. When they heard all these words of the robber, all the holy patriarchs and prophets said with one voice: Blessed be the Lord Almighty, the Father of eternal good things, the Father of mercies, you that have given such grace unto your sinners and have brought them again into the beauty of paradise and into your good pastures: for this is the most holy life of the spirit. Amen, Amen.

Chapter 27

These are the divine and holy mysteries which we saw and heard, even I, Karinus, and Leucius: but we were not suffered to relate further the rest of the mysteries of God, according as Michael the archangel strictly charged us, saying: You shall go with your brethren unto Jerusalem and remain in prayer, crying out and glorifying the resurrection of the Lord Jesus Christ, who has raised you from the dead together with him: and you shall not be speaking with any man, but sit as dumb men, until the hour come when the Lord himself requires you to declare the mysteries of his god head. But unto us Michael the archangel gave commandment that we should go over Jordan unto a place rich and fertile, where are many which rose again together with us for a testimony of the resurrection of Christ the Lord. For three days only were allowed unto us who rose from the dead, to keep the Passover of the Lord in Jerusalem with our kindred (parents) that are living for a testimony of the resurrection of Christ the Lord: and we were baptized in the holy river of Jordan and received white robes, every one of us. And after the three days, when we had kept the Passover of the Lord, all they were caught up in the clouds which had risen again with us, and were taken over Jordan and were no more seen of any man. But unto us it was said that we should remain in the city of Arimathaea and continue in prayer.

These be all things which the Lord bade us declare unto you: give praise and thanksgiving (confession) unto him, and repent that he may have mercy upon you. Peace be unto you from the same Lord Jesus Christ which is the Savior of us all. Amen.

And when they had finished writing all things in the several volumes of paper they arose; and Karinus gave that which he had written into the hands of Annas and Caiaphas and Gamaliel; likewise Leucius gave that which he had written into the hands of Nicodemus and Joseph. And suddenly they were transfigured and became white exceedingly and were no more seen. But their writings were found to be the same (lit. equal), neither more nor less by one letter.

And when all the synagogue of the Jews heard all these marvelous sayings of Karinus and Leucius, they said one to another: Of a truth all these things were wrought by the Lord, and blessed be the Lord, world without end, Amen. And they went out all of them in great trouble of mind, smiting their breasts with fear and trembling, and departed every man unto his own home.

And all these things which were spoken by the Jews in their synagogue, did Joseph and Nicodemus forthwith declare unto the governor. And Pilate himself wrote all the things that were done and said concerning Jesus by the Jews, and laid up all the words in the public books of his judgment hall (praetorium).

Chapter 28

This chapter is not found in the majority of copies.

After these things Pilate entered into the temple of the Jews and gathered together all the chief of the priests, and the teachers and scribes and doctors of the law, and went in with them into the holy place of the temple and commanded all the doors to be shut, and said unto them: We have heard that you have in this temple a certain great Bible; wherefore I ask you that it be presented before us. And when that great Bible adorned with gold and precious jewels was brought by four ministers, Pilate said to them all: I adjure you by the God of your fathers which commanded you to build this temple in the place of his sanctuary, that you hide not the truth from me. You know all the things that are written in this Bible; but tell me now if you have found in the scriptures that this Jesus whom you have crucified is the Son of God which should come for the salvation of mankind, and in what year of the times he must come. Declare unto me whether you crucified him in ignorance or knowingly.

And Annas and Caiaphas when they were thus adjured commanded all the rest that were will them to go out of the temple; and they themselves shut all the doors of the temple and of the sanctuary, and said unto Pilate: you have adjured us,

O excellent judge, by the building of this temple to make manifest unto you the truth and reason (or a true account). After that we had crucified Jesus, knowing not that he was the Son of God, but supposing that by some chance he did his wondrous works, we made a great assembly (synagogue) in this temple; and as we conferred one with another concerning the signs of the mighty works which Jesus had done, we found many witnesses of our own nation who said that they had seen Jesus alive after his passion, and that he was passed into the height of the heaven. Moreover, we saw two witnesses whom Jesus raised from the dead, who declared unto us many marvelous things which Jesus did among the dead, which things we have in writing in our hands. Now our custom is that every year before our assembly we open this holy Bible and inquire the testimony of God. And we have found in the first book of the Seventy how that Michael the angel spoke unto the third son of Adam the first man concerning the five thousand and five hundred years, wherein should come the most beloved Son of God, even Christ: and furthermore we have thought that peradventure this same was the God of Israel which said unto Moses: Make you an ark of the covenant in length two cubits and a half, and in breadth one cubit and a half, and in height one cubit and a half. For by those five cubits and a half we have understood and known the fashion of the ark of the old covenant, for that in five thousand and a half thousand years Jesus Christ should come in the ark of his body: and we have found that he is the God of Israel, even the Son of God. For after his passion, we the chief of the priests, because we marveled at the signs which came to pass on his account did open the Bible, and searched out all the generations unto the generation of Joseph, and Mary the mother of Christ, taking her to be the seed of David: and we found that from the day when God made the heaven and the earth and the first man, from that time unto the Flood are 2,212 years: and from the Flood unto the building of the tower 531 years: and from the building of the tower unto Abraham 606 years: and from Abraham unto the coming of the children of Israel out of Egypt 470 years: and from the going of the children of Israel out of Egypt unto the building of the temple 511 years: and from the building of the temple unto the destruction of the same temple 464 years: so far found we in the Bible of Esdras: and inquiring from the burning of the temple unto the coming of Christ and his birth we found it to be 636 years, which together were five thousand and five hundred years like as we found it written in the Bible that Michael the archangel declared before unto Seth the third son of Adam, that after five thousand and a half thousand years Christ the Son of God will come. Hitherto have we told no man, lest there should be a schism in our synagogues; and now, O excellent judge, you have adjured us by this holy Bible of the testimonies of God, and we do declare it unto you: and we also have adjured you by your life and health that you declare not these words unto any man in Jerusalem.

Chapter 29

And Pilate, when he heard these words of Annas and Caiaphas, laid them all up amongst the acts of the Lord and Savior in the public books of his judgment hall, and wrote a letter unto Claudius the king of the city of Rome, saying:

Pontius Pilate unto Claudius, greeting.

There befell of late a matter which I myself brought to light (or made trial of): for the Jews through envy have punished themselves and their posterity with fearful judgments of their own fault; for whereas their fathers had promises (al. had announced unto them) that their God would send them out of heaven his holy one who should of right be called their king, and did promise that he would send him upon earth by a virgin; he, then (or this God of the Hebrews, then), came when I was governor of Judaea, and they beheld him enlightening the blind, cleansing lepers, healing the palsied, driving devils out of men, raising the dead, rebuking the winds, walking upon the waves of the sea dry-shod, and doing many other wonders, and all the people of the Jews calling him the Son of God: the chief priests therefore, moved with envy against him, took him and delivered him unto me and brought against him one false accusation after another, saying that he was a sorcerer and did things contrary to their law.

But I, believing that these things were so, having scourged him, delivered him unto their will: and they crucified him, and when he was buried they set guards upon him. But while my soldiers watched him he rose again on the third day: yet so much was the malice of the Jews kindled that they gave money to the soldiers, saying: Say you that his disciples stole away his body. But they, though they took the money, were not able to keep silence concerning that which had come to pass, for they also have testified that they saw him arisen and that they received money from the Jews. And these things have I reported for this cause, lest some other should lie unto you (lat. lest any lie otherwise) and you should deem right to believe the false tales of the Jews.

Joseph B. Lumpkin

THE LOST GOSPEL ACCORDING TO PETER

1886 by the French archaeologist Urbain Bouriant, was on a mission excavating in the valley of the Upper Nile. On the bank of the river, in the town of Akhmim, which was also called Panopolis in ancient times. The intellectual life of a former day was marked by the remnants of monasteries ruins. Within these ruins was the grave of a monk, and within the grave came upon a parchment codex buried in the tomb of a monk at Akhmim in Upper Egypt. Six years later a translation of this was published in the Memoirs of the French Archaological Mission at Cairo.

On the basis of the cursive script this copy dates to the 8th or 9th century CE. Scholars realized for the first time that a discovery of great importance had been made. A portion of **The Gospel According to Peter** had been restored.

According to Eusebius, the 4th century church historian, it was being used by the Syrian Christians around the year 200 CE, and Serapion, bishop of Antioch, raised doubts about its orthodoxy, while declaring that most of it reflected the "right teachings of the Savior" (Eccl. Hist. 6.12..2-6).

In 190 A.D. Origen, a historian, refered to it in 253 A.D.; Eusebius, Bishop of Caesarea in 300 A.D. and Theodoret in 455 in writings and said that the Nazarenes used it and Justin Martyr includes the *Memoirs of Peter* in his "Apostolic Memoirs." Scholars of long ago knew of it but to us it was lost – until now.

This account of the trail and crucifixion is readable and open. The events between the burial and resurrection of our Lord, is detailed, adding to our small amount of knowledge found in the canonical tradition.

Some of the information is at variance with the four traditional gospels. Some facts seem to add depth. In certain phrases there is seen a Gnostic tradition, such as the cry from our Lord at his near the time of his death of, "My power, My Power, why have you left me?" Other information is simply interesting, such as the name of the centurion who kept watch at the tomb being Petronius.

Other slightly Gnostic notes occur such as the prominence assigned to Mary Magdalene. Also, the Resurrection and Ascension are here recorded not as separate events but as occurring on the same day.

According to ancient sources we must conclude that ***The Gospel of Peter*** once held a place of honor and importance, comparable to that of the Four Gospels. The fragment begins as Pilate washes his hands.

Gospel of Peter

1. But of the Jews none washed his hands, neither Herod nor any one of his judges. And when they had refused to wash them, Pilate rose up. And then Herod the king commanded that the Lord be taken saying to them, "What things I commanded you to do unto him, do."

2 And there was standing there Joseph the friend of Pilate and of the Lord; and, knowing that they were about to crucify him, he came to Pilate and asked the body of the Lord for burial. And Pilate sent to Herod and asked his body. And Herod said, Brother Pilate, even if no one has asked for him, we purposed to bury him, especially as the Sabbath drew on: for it is written in the law, that the sun set not upon one that has been put to death.

3 And he delivered him to the people on the day before the unleavened bread, their feast. And they took the Lord and pushed him as they ran, and said, Let us drag away the Son of God, having obtained power over him. And they clothed him with purple, and set him on the seat of judgment, saying, Judge righteously, 0 king of Israel. And one of them brought a crown of thorns and put it on the head of the Lord. And others stood and spat in his eyes, and others smote his cheeks: others pricked him with a reed; and some scourged him, saying, With this honor let us honor the Son of God.

4 And they brought two malefactors, and they crucified the Lord between them. But he held his peace, as though having no pain. And when they had raised the cross, they wrote the title: This is the king of Israel. And having set his garments before him they parted them among them, and cast lots for them. And one of those malefactors reproached them, saying, We for the evils that we have done have suffered thus, but this man, who has become the Savior of men, what wrong has he done to you? And they, being angered at him, commanded that his legs should not be broken, that he might die in torment.

5 And it was noon, and darkness came over all Judaea: and they were troubled and distressed, lest the sun had set, whilst he was yet alive: for it is written for them, that the sun set not

on him that has been put to death. And one of them said, Give him to drink gall with vinegar. And they mixed and gave him to drink, and fulfilled all things, and accomplished their sins against their own head. And many went about with lamps, supposing that it was night, and fell down. And the Lord cried out, saying, "My power, my power, you have forsaken me."

And when he had said it he was taken up. And in that hour the veil of the temple of Jerusalem was rent in twain.

6 And then they drew out the nails from the hands of the Lord, and laid him upon the earth, and the whole earth quaked, and great fear arose. Then the sun shone, and it was found the ninth hour: and the Jews rejoiced, and gave his body to Joseph that he might bury it, since he had seen what good things he had done. And he took the Lord, and washed him, and rolled him in a linen cloth, and brought him to his own tomb, which was called the Garden of Joseph.

7 Then the Jews and the elders and the priests, perceiving what evil they had done to themselves, began to lament and to say, Woe for our sins: the judgment has drawn nigh, and the end of Jerusalem. And I with my companions was grieved; and being wounded in mind we hid ourselves: for we were being sought for by them as malefactors, and as wishing to set fire to the

temple. And upon all these things we fasted and sat mourning and weeping night and day until the Sabbath.

8 But the scribes and Pharisees and elders being gathered together one with another, when they heard that all the people murmured and beat their breasts saying, If by his death these most mighty signs have come to pass, see how righteous he is, - the elders were afraid and came to Pilate beseeching him and saying, Give us soldiers, that we may guard his sepulcher for three days, lest his disciples come and steal him away, and the people suppose that he is risen from the dead and do us evil. And Pilate gave them Petronius the centurion with soldiers to guard the tomb. And with them came elders and scribes to the sepulcher, and having rolled a great stone together with the centurion and the soldiers, they all together who were there set it at the door of the sepulcher; and they affixed seven seals, and they pitched a tent there and guarded it. And early in the morning as the Sabbath was drawing on, there came a multitude from Jerusalem and the region round about, that they might see the sepulcher that was sealed.

9 And in the night in which the Lord's day was drawing on, as the soldiers kept guard two by two in a watch, there was a great voice in the heaven; and they saw the heavens opened, and two men descend from thence with great light and

approach the tomb. And that stone which was put at the door rolled of itself and made way in part; and the tomb was opened, and both the young men entered in.

10 When therefore those soldiers saw it, they awakened the centurion and the elders; for they too were hard by keeping guard. And as they declared what things they had seen, again they see three men come forth from the tomb, and two of them supporting one, and a cross following them: and of the two the head reached unto the heaven, but the head of him who was lead by them was higher than the heavens. And they heard a voice from the heavens, saying, you have preached to them that sleep. And a response was heard from the cross, "Yea."

11 They therefore considered one with another whether to go away and show these things to Pilate. And while they yet thought thereon, the heavens again are seen to open, and a certain man to descend and enter into the sepulcher. When the centurion and they that were with him saw these things, they hurried in the night to Pilate, leaving the tomb which they were watching, and declared all things which they had seen, being greatly distressed and saying, Truly he was the Son of God. Pilate answered and said, I am pure from the blood of the Son of God: but it was you who determined this. Then they all drew

near and besought him and entreated him to command the centurion and the soldiers to say nothing of the things which they had seen: For it is better, say they, for us to be guilty of the greatest sin before God, and not to fall into the hands of the people of the Jews and to be stoned. Pilate therefore commanded the centurion and the soldiers to say nothing.

12 And at dawn upon the Lord's day Mary Magdalene, a disciple of the Lord, fearing because of the Jews, since they were burning with rage, had not done at the Lord's sepulcher the things which women are wont to do for those that die and for those that are beloved by them -- she took her friends with her and came to the sepulcher where he was laid. And they feared lest the Jews should see them, and they said, "Although on that day on which he was crucified we could not weep and lament, yet now let us do these things at his sepulcher. But who shall roll away for us the stone that was laid at the door of the sepulcher, that we may enter in and sit by him and do the things that are due? For the stone was large, and we feared that some one see us. And if we cannot, yet if we but set at the door the things which we bring as a memorial of him, we will weep and lament, until we come unto our home."

13 And, they went and found the tomb opened, and coming near they looked in there; and they see there a certain young

man sitting in the midst of the tomb, beautiful and clothed in a robe exceeding bright; who said to them, "Wherefore are you come? Whom seek you? Him that was crucified?"

He is risen and gone. But if you believe not, look in and see the place where he lay, that he is not here because he is risen and gone thither, where he was sent. Then the women feared and fled.

14 Now it was the last day of the unleavened bread, and many were going forth, returning to their homes, as the feast was ended. But we, the twelve disciples of the Lord, wept and were grieved: and each one, being grieved for that which was come to pass, departed to his home. But I Simon Peter and Andrew my brother took our nets and went to the sea; and there was with us Levi the son of Alphaeus, whom the Lord . . . .

At this point the fragment ends.

Epistle to the Laodiceans

This epistle, along with those to the Colossians, Ephesians, Philippians, and Philemon were likely written during Paul's Roman captivity, about A.D. 61- 63.

Several texts bearing this title have been known to have existed, but none are believed to have been written by Paul.

One explanation to its existence comes from the time of Marcion. The early Christian Marcion believed that Paul was the only apostle who truly understood Jesus's message. Based on his assumption he constructed a canon consisting of only one single combined Gospel and some of the Pauline epistles all of which were edited to remove passages that he did not agree with. According to the Muratorian fragment, Marcion's canon contained a forgery entitled Epistle to the Laodiceans which was written to conform to his own point of view

The epistle appears in more than 100 manuscripts of the Bible. It is in the Latin Vulgate, including the oldest codex of Fuldensis estimated to date to 546 A.D. It is also in manuscripts of early Albigensian, Bohemian, English, and Flemish versions.

Many Bibles used to contain a small Epistle from Paul to the Laodiceans. It is referenced in Colossians 4 vers 16. It reads, "After this letter has been read to you, see that it is also read in the church of the Laodiceans and that you in turn read the letter from Laodicea." Colosse and Laodicea are less than fifteen miles apart.

It continued to be mentioned by various writers from the fourth century onwards, including Gregory the Great. The epistle occurs in more English Bibles than in others.

About 1165 CE John of Salisbury, writing about the canon to Henry count of Champagne (Epist. 209), acknowledges that 'it is the common, indeed almost universal.

The Epistle to the Laodiceans is included in all 18 German Bibles printed prior to Luther's translation, beginning with the first German Bible, issued by Johann Mental at Strassburg in 1488. In these the Pauline Epistles, with the Epistle to the Hebrews, immediately follow the Gospels, with Laodiceans standing between Galatians and Ephesians.

There are ancient copies of the letter in Latin but there is no evidence of a Greek text. This adds to controversy about the authenticity of the text. Owing to this, in the Council of Florence (1439-43) that the See of Rome delivered for the first time a categorical opinion on the Scriptural canon. In the list of 27 books of the New Testament there are 14 Pauline Epistles, that to the Hebrews being last, with the book of Acts coming immediately before the Revelation of John. The Epistle to the Laodiceans is absent.

THE EPISTLE OF PAUL THE APOSTLE TO THE LAODICEANS

1. Paul an Apostle, not of men, neither by man, but by Jesus Christ, to the brethren which are at Laodicea.

2. Grace be to you, and peace, from God the Father and our Lord Jesus Christ.

3. I thank Christ in every prayer of mine that you may continue and persevere in good works, looking for that which is promised in the Day of Judgment.

4. Do not be troubled by the vain speeches of anyone who perverts the truth, that they may draw you aside from the truth of the Gospel which I have preached.

5. And now may God grant that my converts may attain to a perfect knowledge of the truth of the Gospel, be beneficent, and doing good works which accompany salvation.

6. And now my bonds, which I suffer in Christ, are manifest, in which I rejoice and am glad.

7. For I know that this shall turn to my salvation forever, which shall be through your prayer and the supply of the Holy Spirit.

8. Whether I live or die, to me to live shall be a life to Christ, to die will be joy.

9. And our Lord will grant us his mercy, that you may have the same love, and be like-minded.

10. Wherefore, my beloved, as you have heard of the coming of the Lord, so think and act reverently, and it shall be to you life eternal.

11. For it is God who is working in you;

12. And do all things without sin.

13. And what is best, my beloved; rejoice in the Lord Jesus Christ, and avoid all filthy lucre.

14. Let all your requests by made known to God, and be steady in the doctrine of Christ.

15. And whatever things are sound and true, and of good report, and chaste, and just, and lovely, these things do.

16. Those things which you have heard and received, think on these things, and peace shall be with you.

17. All the saints salute you.

18. The grace of our Lord Jesus Christ be with your spirit. Amen.

19. Cause this Epistle to be read to the Colossians, and the Epistle of the Colossians to be read among you.

This ends the Epistle.

Joseph B. Lumpkin

ABOUT THE AUTHOR

Joseph Lumpkin has written for various newspapers and is the author of a number of books on the subjects of religion and philosophy including the best selling book, The Lost Book Of Enoch: A Comprehensive Transliteration, published by Fifth Estate Publishers.

Joseph holds his Doctorate in the field of Ministry. He lives a very full life near Birmingham, Alabama with his wife, Lynn, and his son, Breandan.

www.ingramcontent.com/pod-product-compliance
Lightning Source LLC
Chambersburg PA
CBHW050248170426
43202CB00011B/1596